Making Sense of Sports

Sports are not necessarily a pastime or pure recreation. They are an integral part of contemporary culture and have connections with industry, commerce and politics. This new expanded edition of *Making Sense of Sports* includes all you need to know on the history and theories of sports and on more controversial issues:

- how black sports performers are made;

- why women are devalued by sports;

- drug use and attempts to contain it;

- commercialism and sports;

- why sports and television are inseparable;

- violence and the legal battleground;

Making Sense of Sports is a comprehensive introdu[ction to] the study of sports which combines perspectives fr[om a] spectrum of natural and social sciences to produce a scholarly yet provocative analysis of one of the most important elements of today's culture.

Ellis Cashmore is Professor of Sociology at Staffordshire University, England.

Routledge titles by Ellis Cashmore

. . . and there was television

Dictionary of Race and Ethnic Relations

Out of Order? Policing Black People

Black Sportsmen

Other titles

United Kingdom?: Class, Race and Gender Since the War

The Logic of Racism

Having To – The World of One-parent Families

No Future: Youth and Society

Rastaman: The Rastafarian Movement in England

Introduction to Race Relations
(*with Barry Troyna*)

Black Youth in Crisis
(*with Barry Troyna*)

Approaching Social Theory
(*with Bob Mullan*)

LONDON AND NEW YORK

Making Sense of Sports

SECOND EDITION

- Ellis Cashmore

First published in 1990
by Routledge
11 New Fetter Lane, London EC4P 4EE

Simultaneously published in the USA and
Canada
by Routledge
29 West 35th Street, New York, NY 10001

*Routledge is an International Thomson
Publishing company*

Reprinted 1994

Second edition 1996

© 1990, 1996 Ellis Cashmore

Typeset in Times and Futura by Keystroke,
Jacaranda Lodge, Wolverhampton
Printed and bound in Great Britain by
T. J. Press (Padstow) Ltd, Padstow,
Cornwall

*British Library Cataloguing in Publication
Data*
A catalogue record for this book is
available from the British Library

*Library of Congress Cataloging in
Publication Data*
Cashmore, E.
    Making sense of sport / Ellis Cashmore.
    — 2nd ed.
        p.   cm.
    Includes bibliographical references and
index.
    ISBN 0–415–13306–8 (alk. paper). —
    ISBN 0–415–13307–6 (pbk.) : alk. paper)
    1. Sports—Social aspects. I. Title.
GV706.5.C38   1996   95–25971
306.4′83—dc20   CIP

ISBN 0–415–13306–8 (hbk)
ISBN 0–415–13307–6 (pbk)

Contents

Acknowledgements

Thanks to friends and colleagues whose counsel I have sought in writing this book. They include David Jary, Chris Rojek and David Newton of Staffordshire University; George Paton, Ossie Jones and John Overend of Aston University; Mickey Wells and Amy Shepper of University of Tampa and Ray Guins of University of Leeds. Thanks also to Sarah Ereira for steadfastly working on the index.

Note to the
second edition

This new expanded edition of *Making Sense of Sports* has a completely revised and expanded text, new graphics and features and updated guides to further reading, all designed to keep pace with changing times. There are now thirteen chapters, as against the nine of the first edition, with fresh arguments on drugs, television, violence, women and the future of sports.

The first edition of the book has been used as a text for classes in the USA and Britain, and this second edition has been modified to take account of comments and criticisms of faculty and students. Many students majoring in social science/studies found Chapter 3, which covers the structure and functions of the human body, a detour from their main interests. The author has chosen to keep it, albeit with modifications, his argument being that a genuine comprehension of sports is not possible without an understanding of the physical and mental apparatus that makes movement and performance possible.

Chapter one

Introduction

Why . . . ?

Question: Who would pay to sit for over three hours watching individuals propel a small pigskin ball toward an imaginary area called a strike zone, while another individual defends the zone with an implement fashioned out of a 3-foot long piece of ash? *Answer:* Billions.

Sports are wondrously puzzling things. Spellbinding audiences with activities that have no apparent rhyme, less still reason, they remind us that one of the oldest preoccupations in the world is that of challenge. Attempting to surmount obstacles – natural or artificial – has provided people with endless episodes of triumph or folly and, sometimes, disaster. Where the challenges don't exist, we just invent them. Sports are perfect inventions because they have challenge, confrontation, and the climactic finality of a result. Someone – or something – always wins, loses, or draws.

There's something satisfying, yet oddly discomfiting about this. The idea that someone might play the occasional game of pool as a mild stimulant, just to get the competitive juices flowing, is understandable enough. But explaining why people will travel great distances, spend small fortunes, and sometimes die in the process not of competing but watching others compete is confounding. Ask sports' fans why they're

prepared to do it and the answer will be because they enjoy it. That's *their* version; but nothing is quite what it seems. The world as it appears masks more than it reveals.

In this book, we'll slide behind the mask to assess the mechanisms and processes that make sports irresistible. To understand sport as a phenomenon, its seeming irrationality and total lack of purpose, we need to view it prismatically: sport as a kind of splintered structure of perspectives, each disclosing a different aspect of the same thing. So *Making Sense of Sports* combines contributions from behavioral and physical sciences, such as anthropology, biology, history and sociology. This in no way denies that people watch football and other sports because they enjoy them. It simply means that this version gives us only one angle on why people are drawn to sports. There are others, two of which I will cover in the remainder of this introduction.

The culture of which we are part has become so organized that the results of almost any action is calculable. With this effort to make the product of our actions calculable, or predictable, is a corresponding attempt to make it as safe as possible. Two perfectly reasonable enterprises, you might think. But, perhaps we want to assert the unpredictability of life. We might actually need some element of risk. Sports can be viewed as a way of maintaining these as features of contemporary culture.

Life is too predictable

"The why of a fan" is the title of an article published way back in 1929 in which A. A. Brill argued that "life organised too well becomes monotonous; too much peace and security breed boredom; and old instincts, bred into the very cells of the body . . . still move the masses of normal men" (1929: 431). Brill wrote in terms of the "restrictions of modern life" depriving people of their "activity and scope, the triumphs and *réclame*" which were achievable through physical prowess under "more primitive conditions." In explaining the fans' attraction to sport, Brill exposed what he took to be a dark truth about human nature: "an animal formed for battle and conquest, for blows and strokes and swiftness, for triumph and applause" (1929: 434).

As the necessity for physical struggle was removed and modern organized society brought stability and security, so the nasty and brutish qualities were made redundant – but not irrelevant. They were of great use in sport. Here was a group of activities that required physical prowess. Not everyone had the star power to be able to exhibit their attributes; but they could at least identify with those who did. In the process, they would recover something of their natural state; they would "achieve exaltation, vicarious but real" and be "a better individual, better citizen."

Improbable as Brill's argument might have been as a total theory of sport, it offered a timeless insight about the drabness and formality of much in the world and the security it holds for most of us. Security is something we seek, yet do not want. Probing this paradox of security has led novelists to some ingenious alternatives, such as running one's life as if a Vegas crap game, in Rinehart's *The Dice Man*, or discovering Pirsig's *Zen and the Art of Motorcycle Maintenance*; both cult novels of the 1970s and both in their own ways tracts against the uniformity of bureaucracy.

Bureaucracy

From the Latin *burrus*, meaning dark red, the color of the baize that covered Roman office desks, which later referred to the desks themselves, and *krato*, the Greek for strength (combined by the French to *bureaucratie*), this nowadays refers to a highly organized system of administration in which individualism and imagination is minimized and official rules, regulations, and practices are of paramount importance.

Bureaucracies proliferate in every major area of society. The ever-widening latticework of bureaucratic administrations has produced what the social theorist Max Weber called "calculability," meaning that the workings of bureaucracy are, as far as possible, protected against the personal emotions and whims of those who administer its policies. As a result, the performance of a bureaucracy is highly predictable. Once the applicable regulations and procedures are known, it's possible to calculate exactly how a bureaucracy is going to deal with a matter and what are the chances of a certain type of outcome. So, bureaucracy stabilizes a society, orders it, regulates it, and renders it entirely predictable. All this makes for a rational and smooth-running society. It also affects the mentalities of people who live in such a society.

Calculability is an organizing principle in the overall personality. Spontaneity and randomness may be pleasant diversions but, in large doses, they can prove severely disruptive and threaten an individual's sense of security. Still, there is a residual attraction in the unplanned, surprise happening; a pleasant intrigue as to what its consequences might be. Were this to invade our working, or public lives, it would lead to serious disorientation. So, in the main, we confine the fascination for the unpredictable to our private lives. Office workers can approach their daily tasks with a strangulating regard for rationality and precision. Once out of the office, they might retreat to the tumult of a home resembling a Hal Hartley movie – everywhere cluttered with formless confusion. Workers might have one set of rules for the office, but another for the home.

The separation of life into public and private spheres is itself a product of contemporary industrial society. It has the advantage of allowing the individual to compensate in one sphere for the tensions or frustrations that build up in the other. Office workers may quietly boil in rage at the meaningless or sheer prolixity of their employment. They might keep a lid on themselves at work but wreak havoc at home. Most of us experience bureaucracies, if only indirectly, and, equally, most of us have been irritated or angered by them. But we don't usually scream or assault others. We find outlets for these emotions elsewhere.

Sports can be seen as one attempt to compensate for bureaucracy and the discontents it brings. Kicking or throwing balls, riding horses in a circle, or inflicting pointless damage on others may be irrational pursuits. But that is their beauty; whether watched or performed, they guide the participant well clear of the formal limits of bureaucracies and into an area where the outcomes of situations are wholly unpredictable and, therefore, in total contrast to those of bureaucracies.

For all its institutionalization and officialdom, sport has retained its fascinating nucleus: indeterminacy. Wrap it in red tape and smother it with a bureaucracy to rival that of the Kremlin, but you can never quite fix the outcome of a contest (unless by foul means, of course; in which case it ceases to be sport). The doubtfulness of sports, the way in which they resist predictability and the order they usually bring, make sports constant challenges to predictability. A result can never be ascertained in advance, even when odds overwhelmingly favor one party over another. It's one area where fairy-tale endings occasionally do come true: the underdog has a chance, however remote.

Perhaps this tells us something about the resilience of sports, their continuing popularity, and even their future. In a world where certainty has become a virtual norm, *uncertainty* is a prized commodity, especially if it is packaged in a visually moving and colorful display that excites the senses. Sports offer this uncertainty. It could be argued that they do so artificially, pitting contestants against each other in mock rivalry and in circumstances not of their own making. Then again, it could also be argued that, in this respect, sports reflect much of life anyway.

Sports have accumulated their own bureaucracy in recent years, especially as contemporary states have intruded progressively into areas once thought to be relatively autonomous. Yet, indeterminacy can never be removed, or "sport" simply stops being sport and becomes mere spectacle or drama. Sports have the same kind of job specialization, production, deadlines, and monotonous training regimes of industrial work. Computer-ization in both spheres has enhanced the similarity. Much of sports is routine and reasonably predictable. But not all: the uncertainty that hangs over the actual competitive matchup can be reduced but never eliminated; nor, therefore, can the inspirational freedom, self-controlled skill, independent vision, and innovative originality that emerge in the competitive encounter. No amount of bureaucratization can flush these out of sports.

Bureaucracy predominates in most countries where there is organized sport and the shift from goods-producing to service-producing economies promises no significant reduction in formal organization and standardization. Sports themselves have been and will continue to be affected in much the same way as all other institutions, such as religion, education, and science, have been subject to bureaucratic imperatives. At the same time, they will continue to prosper as, in some senses, an antithesis to bureaucracy; a virtual opposition in its reliance on an essential doubt over outcomes.

Life is too safe

The outcome of sport is never known, so the actual pattern of behavior leading to it is fraught with uncertainty too. In some sports, danger lurks. As well as becoming bureaucratized, society has also become safer. The civilizing process has brought with it a reduction, though not elimination, of violence and physical danger. Of course, there are road deaths, unconquerable dis-eases, homicides, fatal accidents and so on. But, in replacing barbarism with civilization, we have controlled our lives in such a way as to maintain order, safety and control, specifically control over risk. This may seem desirable: after all, who would want to run the gauntlet when they leave home in the morning, or sleep with a weapon under their pillow, or live in fear of speeding cars?

Yet life might have become a little too safe and sports – at least some sports – may provide a way of reintroducing the element of risk back into our lives. The more we find ways of controlling or even wiping out risk, the more we find ingenious ways of flirting with danger. Odd as it sounds, there is a supporting structure to this. Let me approach it like this: many cars today are equipped with anti-lock braking systems (ABS) which enable the driver to continue braking or steer around any obstacle or accident while keeping the car stable. In a car without ABS, hard braking, especially on a slippery road, can cause all four wheels to lock up and any attempt at steering except into the skid to try to remedy it, is not advised; once locked, the braking effect is lost and the vehicle slides. Cars of the future will improve on ABS with electronic stability programs (ESP), which will virtually do away with the dangers posed by slippery surfaces.

A significant contribution to road safety, one might assume. Maybe not: ABS might save the lives of bad drivers, but, by encouraging everyone to go faster and perhaps drive more recklessly, the system can cause the deaths of other road users, such as backseat passengers, pedestrians and bikers. The same principle can be applied to compulsory air bags and seat belts (try the test yourself: get on a freeway, accelerate to 70 mph, then undo your seat belt; you'll feel unsafe and slow down almost immediately). Life can be made safer; yet there is no guarantee we will not compensate for the reduction in risks by seeking new forms of danger. A number of American states have taken stock of this and repealed laws that required motorcyclists to wear helmets

---

Security

From the Latin *curas*, for care, this refers to the condition of being reliable and certain, untroubled by danger or apprehension and safe against attack. Its presence in contemporary society serves to minimize our exposure to danger by limiting the hazards of chance. The tolerance of risk is reduced in proportion to the amount of organization and order available.

Author of the book *Risk*, John Adams believes we have inside us a "risk thermostat" which we can set to our own tastes, according to our particular culture: "Some like it hot – a Hell's Angel or a Grand Prix racing driver for example; others like it cool . . . But no one wants absolute zero" (1995: 15). We all want to restore some danger to our lives; contemporary society has rendered it too safe. So, most people wouldn't go to a restaurant declared unsafe by state sanitary inspectors, but some of those same people might go white water rafting, or on survivalist expeditions; they might ski off-piste, scuba, or bungee jump. A game of chess or snooker may offer no hint of danger; skiing, surfing, all air, combat and motor sports certainly do. Even sitting in a crowd watching these sports carries a vicarious sense of danger. And, of course, if the crowd happens to be at a game of soccer, then the danger may not be vicarious as we will see in Chapter 11. As sports resist the organizing onslaught of bureaucracy, they also resist security. The risk in some sports may be infinitesimal; but its presence is what counts and, where it doesn't exist, we will invent it.

Conventional wisdoms of the "I climbed Everest because it was there" variety begin to look like terrible simplifications when we start to think about the other possible sources of our preoccupation with sports. We don't do anything just because it's there. And that includes diving into water or hurdling over barriers. There are reasons and many of them will be uncovered in the pages ahead.

Sport's relation with other areas of life are dual-sided. On the one hand, it expresses a liberation from bureaucracy; on the other it progressively integrates elements of bureaucracy into its own structure. It reintroduces the magical ingredient risk into a culture that has become virtually obsessed with security, yet, at the same time, reflects such an obsession in its own procedures. Sport is like the exploits of the actor Patrick McGoohan in the old, but endlessly re-run TV series *The Prisoner*: try as you might to escape the suffocating aspects of society, you run up against more of them in your efforts to flee.

Sports have obviously undergone transmutations, but we can still discern in them the kind of escape attempt that inspired early industrial workers in the nineteenth century to enrich their lives by organizing games. In these attempts we find the first gropings to what we now recognize as legitimate sports. The early pursuits were as lacking in purpose as today's sports. They were not – and *are* not – intended to represent a "real" activity, except in the most tenuous sense (as I explain in Chapter 4). They weren't reducible to anything at all: they were simply activities enjoyed for their own sake. This may no longer be true for a professional who plays for money, or a gambler, or an assortment of others who watch with a pecuniary motive uppermost. But, for the overwhelming majority of fans and amateur players, sports still have this quality: we view and do for nothing more functional than avoiding what we do during the rest of our working week.

In this respect, we might be seen to be striding toward what Umberto Eco (1986) and Jean Baudrillard (1983) called "hyperreality." Sport, at least in its latest incarnation, has nothing to do with anything at all, certainly not work. It doesn't resemble anything, it doesn't represent anything and it doesn't actually do anything, save for providing a momentary release from other, less pleasurable facets of life. We savor sport as an end in itself.

Baudrillard believes that hyperreality has permeated and transformed culture. We organize our lives around gestures, displays, even fantasies that have no underlying reference points. We visit theme parks, like Disney World and surround ourselves with artificial phenomena that have no reality outside themselves. In accepting or encouraging this, we have become receptive to a logic of pure performance: what we see is what we get – nothing more. At various stages in history, sports have held practical value, military, industrial, commercial; some sports, like football, were about locality, pride and identity with place.

Now, as modernity passes into postmodernity, there is a process of detachment. Our interest in sport is an escape, but to nowhere and nothing.

This makes it no less powerful or compelling. Far from it, sport is *more* arresting now: it is watched by more people, turns over more money and probably bears more responsibility for hope and heartache than ever before. We will soon discover the particular reasons for this.

Chapter two

Naturals
The role of evolution

No limits

"A Natural!" We hear the term a lot in sports. Whether it's muttered by a perceptive football scout about a schoolboy player, or a tennis coach discerning qualities in the play of an aspiring junior, the meaning is clear: there are some individuals who have properties that suit them ideally for a successful career; properties, in fact, that are wondrous and peculiar, which no amount of training can duplicate in lesser beings. Bernard Malamud's novel, *The Natural*, was a story of one such sports performer, Roy Hobbes, an invincible baseball player.

Actually, we are all "naturals"; we are all naturally endowed with some capacity for sporting activity. Some, more than others, may possess great mechanical efficiency and skill in performing certain tasks and may even refine these to the point where their expertise appears so effortless as to be the product of a gift. But, on analysis, their mastery is more likely to be the result of painstaking learning than a special inborn ability. All human beings have some natural ability; sport expresses this in exaggerated and often extravagant forms. It provides opportunities to wring from our natural mental and physical equipment behavior that deviates, frequently quite drastically, from our normal responses. The deviation

has, it seems, no limits: runners, rowers, and swimmers cover distances even faster; gymnasts perform with greater technical perfection; golfers play more accurately.

Those who can't squeeze from their bodies such efforts are often drawn to watch and admire others innovate, sometimes for only seconds. A 100-meter race in London in August 1992 drew television audiences from around the world to watch the two central antagonists, Carl Lewis and Linford Christie, sprint for exactly 10 seconds (Lewis's losing time). The two rivals reputedly shared $500,000 (£313,000). A Barry Bonds–John Smoltz pitching matchup is over in less time than it takes to read a tabloid newspaper, yet American fans clamor to see it; as British fans will to see Ryan Giggs, whose actual contact with a football is perhaps 15 seconds during the 90 actual minutes of a Manchester United game. A Christian Styren dive, spectacular as it may be, takes less than 1.5 seconds. No matter what the sport, spectators will go to great lengths and pay money to witness a human performance that may well be over in moments. (A supreme example is Mike Tyson vs Peter McNeeley: Tyson won by KO in 89 seconds of the first round; ringside seat price – $1,500; cost – $16.85 per second!)

The ways in which we watch sporting events, the reasons we watch them, and those whom we watch are shaped by culture, not nature. In other words, we *learn* to appreciate performances, just as competitors learn basic techniques and styles on which they later innovate. The sports fan is like an art critic who acquires a knowledge of what to look for, how to evaluate, the meaning of specific moves. The performer needs not only knowledge, but a physical mastery, a skill. This involves lengthy and, sometimes, complex processes in which he or she is made to call into service devices, ingenuities, and powers that might have gone completely undiscovered had the performer not been encouraged, influenced or even forced in some way to develop them. During this time, a sports competitor undergoes physical and mental changes and learns to control his or her bodily movements, in many cases synchronizing body movements with inanimate objects, like rackets and balls. In this way, a sport is learned.

But, it's also completely natural, for without the basic anatomical and behavioral equipment, one couldn't perform even the simplest operations, let alone the more complicated maneuvers needed for a sporting performance. There are limiting "givens" in the physical make-up of humans, just as there are in those of other animals. Humans have succeeded in overcoming all manner of limitations set by nature, basically by creating and employing technologies (though it should be noted that they are not alone in this achievement; many other species use technologies, though not on the scale of humans).

Technology has assisted sporting performance and has been integrated

---

Culture

From the Latin *cultivara* (*terra*) meaning land suitable for growth, this is often used in contrast to *nature*, and refers to the learnt traditions that are socially acquired and appear among mammals – especially primates. Human culture means the lifestyle of a group of people, including their patterned repetitive ways of thinking behaving and even feeling. These ways are picked up through learning experiences rather than through natural inheritance The classical anthropologist, Edward B. Tylor, in his book *Primitive Culture* (first published in 1871 by J. Murray), proposed a definition of culture that included "knowledge, belief, art, morals and habits acquired by man as a member of society." This is a very inclusive definition and others prefer to restrict the use of "cultural" to refer to *rules* for thought and behavior and regard the ways in which the rules are put into practice in society.

---

into most spheres of sporting activity. Yet what is technology but an extension of natural human capabilities? Not that we're born with poles to help us vault, or surfboards to ride, or rifles to fire: these are artifacts – manufactured, accumulated and transmitted; their use is communicated from person to person, from one generation to the next. Essential to these processes is a set of physical equipment: a brain large and complex enough to imagine a product, movable limbs and prehensile hands and feet to create and utilize it, and an acute sense of sight to envisage the product and gauge distance. These properties are not unique to humans, but the way in which they are combined in the human species is very particular and is resembled only in other higher primates, namely monkeys and apes. The question is: what is it about the special combination in humans that enables them to develop the potentialities of their animal nature to levels far removed from other species?

Sports, as I will argue in detail later, have only been possible because of such advanced developments; other animals engage in activities that look like sports, but aren't. Pursuing this logic, not only sports, but religion, industry, warfare, education and so on – all conventionally regarded as social institutions – are grounded in our animal origins and biologically determined behavior. Thus, the entire discipline of physical (or biological) anthropology is dedicated to the task of assessing the relative contributions to social life made by heredity and environment.

Sociology may, in a very different way, examine the same things, but finds the former approach too reductionist in its attempt to break down, or reduce, phenomena into their constituent parts to understand them. In a sociological perspective, the human effort to challenge, manipulate or transcend physical and biological facts of life gives rise to distinct patterns of thought and behavior which cannot necessarily be explained by reference to biological factors alone, but needs some analysis of the interactions between humans and between them and their natural environment. From these interactions, events and processes emerge that defy explanation in purely biological terms.

Determinism

This is a doctrine that states that internal or external forces impinge on the human will, propelling us to think and act in specific ways. To be biologically determined would mean to be under the influence of factors that we inherit rather than learn. It follows that action is never spontaneous but always caused by factors beyond the individual's capacity to influence. Ideas about "free will" are misguided according to this doctrine.

Between the two disciplinary perspectives, there is a whole range of diverse attempts to describe and analyse human behavior, each with its own version of causes and theories about the origins of elements of human life. In the course of this book, I will consider several of them and assess what contribution they may make to our understanding of just one element – sports.

Seven keys

Stripped to their bare elements, human beings are mobile, multi-celled organisms that derive their motive force from eating other organisms. In taxonomic terms, humans are Animalia, as distinct from members of the plant kingdom, bacteria, single-celled organisms, and fungi. So, we have a great many characteristics in common with other animals, especially those with whom we share common ancestors, our closest evolutionary relatives being other primates, a taxon that includes monkeys, apes, lemurs, tarsiers, and others. There are seven key characteristics of primates that set them apart from the rest of the living world and afford them special advantages for survival. Humans have extra-special advantages, but, for the moment, we will focus on similarities. The seven features are: an ability to grip and control; relatively great strength of limb; stereoscopic eyes positioned at the front of the head; small numbers of offspring; a high degree of interdependence and a corresponding tendency toward living in groups; a use of reliable, efficient communication systems; and a large brain relative to body size. Now, let us deal with each of these key characteristics in more detail.

Reductionism

A method for analyzing phenomena based on the philosophy that matter is best understood once divided into its component parts. So, human societies can be approached in terms of individual beings, who in turn may be reduced to genes, which in turn may be reduced further and so on. In other words, complex phenomena can only be fully understood by isolating their parts. Critics argue that the "sum of the parts" is frequently not the same as the "whole" and that there are *emergent* qualities produced when all the elements come together, which are distinct and need to be analyzed as a whole. ("How can one understand something like fashion by reducing it to its component parts?" they might ask, adding that it becomes meaningful only when everything comes together.) This approach is known as *holism*.

All primates have prehensile hands and feet: they can catch, grip, and hold, thanks to relatively long, flexible digits. The ability to grip and control is enhanced by opposable thumbs or big toes which make it possible to lock around objects rigidly and so control an object's movement, as a golfer carefully guides the arc of a club's swing. From an evolutionary point of view, the origins of prehensility are not difficult to trace: distinguishing primates from other mammals was their tree-dwelling capacity. Prehensile hands and feet were useful for climbing up and down and to and from trees in forests, and additionally for plucking fruits and berries and overturning stones to pick up insects to eat.

The ability to grip is complemented by a strong versatile set of forelimbs. Suspending full body weight and swinging needs extremely powerful, long arms and legs. The very specialized functions of arms and legs for primates are reflected not only in the size and heavy muscle of the limbs, but in their range of movement: they can flex (bend), extend, and rotate. Combined with the dexterity of the hands and feet this assists fast, multi-directional travel sometimes over great distances. Gymnasts offer examples of how this ability has not been completely lost despite the human's transition from the trees to the ground.

Taxon
From the Greek *tasso*, meaning fix, this refers to a group in a classification system, usually referring to a genus, species, or subspecies. The science of classifying is called *taxonomy*. The term *Homo sapiens*, meaning literally "wise man", is taken from the work of the Swedish botanist Linnaeus who, in 1735, published a vast taxonomic system for classifying all living beings.

Related to this mobility is the position of the eyes, which are typically to the front rather than the sides of the head. Two eyes enable stereoscopic vision, which permits reasonably accurate estimates of distances. The sense of vision is highly developed in primates, as opposed to, say, dogs which see the world in monochrome, but have sensitive snouts and use their acute sense of smell as their chief source of information about their environments. It's no accident that no sport is based on smelling or sniffing ability, whereas a great many are organized around the ability to gauge distance and co-ordinate hand movements accordingly, archery and shooting being obvious examples. (It seems feasible to imagine that if humans were sensitive to smell we might have devised a sport in which an acute sense of smell was employed in conjunction with other capacities; a modified form of orienteering perhaps.)

With other primates, humans share a tendency to give birth to one or two infants at a time; larger births are known, of course, but they are deviations from the norm. Mammals that have large litters lose some offspring at, or shortly after, birth. Primates have a smaller number of births, usually after a relatively long pregnancy, and accentuate the role of the mother in caring for and protecting the infant in an environment uncomplicated by the kind of competition that comes from large litters.

One very important consequence of having small families with intense mother–infant contact is that primates learn interdependence. They rely on each other far more than many other species which are abandoned at a young age and learn to adapt and survive individually, or else perish. Primates, by contrast, never learn the skills associated with lone survival. Having a protective mother, the infant has no need of such skills. What an infant does acquire is an ability to co-operate and communicate with others. And this helps explain why primates spend their lives in groups, caring for and co-operating with others. Individual survival for humans as well as other primates is a matter of communicating effectively in groups. Hence all primates are gregarious: they grow and mature socially and not in isolation. Very few sports do not reflect this; most are organized in terms of a club structure with high degrees of interdependence and mutual co-operation needed. Even fabled long-distance runners need coaches to plan their training and other competitors to make their racing meaningful.

A lifetime spent in the company of others on whom one has to depend for survival necessitates a high degree of communication. The process of inculcating communication skills begins with the passing of auditory, visual, and tactile (touch) signals from mother to infant. It continues through life; in fact, group life is contingent on the successful storage and transmission of large volumes of information. At its simplest level, the warning conveys perhaps the single most important communication for survival. The human cry of "Fire!" imparts much the same effect as a screech of a panicking baboon. In both cases the first communicator supposes the recipients have some facility for recalling the image of impending danger.

It seems that the necessity of communicating and the ability to do so quickly and efficiently has a connection with the large size of the brain of the primate compared to other mammals. Human beings have the largest brains and are clearly the most adept at communicating. They are, as a direct result, most developed socially. A growth in the size of the human brain can be traced back to two periods. The first, between 1.6 and 2 million years ago, witnessed a rapid expansion in cranial capacity, a change which accompanied the origin of what we now call *Homo erectus* (probably in Africa) and the use of new types of primitive tools. Bipedalism emerged as a result of a transference from the trees to the ground; the change in habitat necessitated a behavioral adaptation in posture and, eventually, an anatomical change of great significance, particularly in relation to arms and hands which were no longer employed to suspend the body and could be used for many other purposes.

Anthropological evidence suggests that the size of the typical skull then remained stable for about 1.3 million years, before a second, sudden increase in brain size. The appearance of *Homo sapiens* about 0.2 or 0.3 million years ago was followed by a burst of cultural change in the spheres of manufacture, settlement, and subsistence. This is important as there is much contention about the precise relationship between the growth of what is now the human brain and changes in habitat and activity. What is absolutely certain is that there is some form of close relationship, though the direction and way in which it worked is still in dispute.

The idea of a spontaneous expansion is not supportable. More plausible is a scenario in which the actual size of the brain after the advent of *Homo erectus* stayed the same, but the number of brain cells and neural pathways between them continued to increase. This made it possible for *Homo erectus* to become a more effective bipedal hunter and gatherer, operating at the time of day when other predatory creatures (and, therefore, competitors) were

NATURE AND CULTURE

Prehensility, the ability to grip, combined with the possibility of supinating (turning palm upwards) and pronating and the options of flexing, extending or hyperextending, enables humans to manipulate the environment intricately and create cultures. In this sense, sports are products of culture as well as nature.

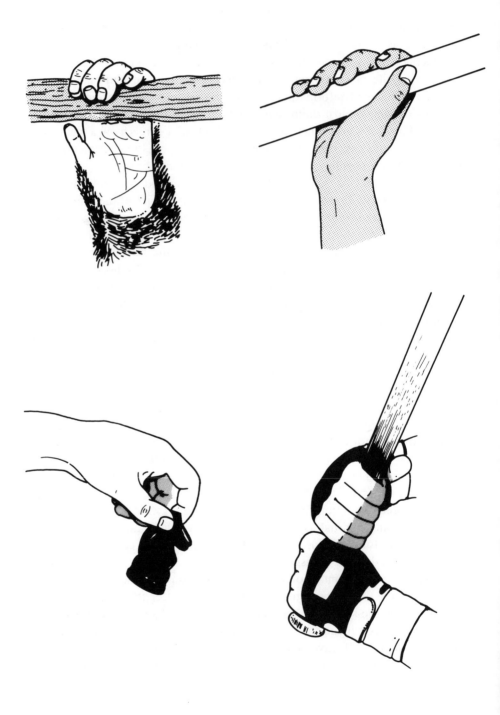

sheltering from the intensely hot midday sun. Growing extra brain cells, in this interpretation, was a defense mechanism against the harmful effects of the sun's rays on the brain; that is, the humans grew bigger brains, leaving many of the cells redundant, as mere "fail safe" devices in the tropical heat. This might well have established a neural potential for more sophisticated communication and imaginative thought, which, in turn, stimulated a phase of modifying physical environments rather than adapting to them. The phase marks the beginning of sport as we will see later in Chapter 3. One often hears of triathletes who swim, cycle, and run for 7 hours or more, sometimes in hot atmospheres, described as "mad." Ironically, they may be demonstrating the extraordinary adaptive brilliance of the human brain in acquiring an ability to function effectively all day in extreme climates. The adaptation dates back to *Homo erectus*'s pursuit of game animals.

The human edge: language

The exact causes of the human brain's exponential growth may prompt argument. Beyond this is the fact that this organ is responsible for what many insist is a qualitative difference between *Homo sapiens* and the rest of the Animalia. The enlarged neural capacity introduced the possibility of ever-more elaborate forms of communication. The physiology of the human ear and vocal tract meant that audial messages could be sent with a high probability that they would be received with reasonable efficiency. These elements, combined with the enhanced capacity for imaginative thinking, laid the foundations for human language and, by implication, new systems of word-associated thought.

Language assists the accumulation of information to be stored in the brain and confirms the awareness that other humans have similar stores of information. At the blandest level, we might ask how a game of hockey would be possible unless the players were cognizant of the rules and aware that all other players had the same knowledge. Any sport has the same prerequisite. Without language or, at least, some derivative communication system, abstract rules would not be possible; nor, therefore, would sport.

Humans are not alone in being able to pass on knowledge from one generation to another and so perpetuate cultures, but they have the special ability to add to, or recreate, cultures whereas other primates merely inherit and receive. A verbal language as opposed to sign-based systems of communication makes this possible. Culture, we should note, refers to anything acquired and transmitted by learning and not by physical inheritance. While other animals most certainly maintain recognizable cultures, even higher apes are quite limited in their capacity to communicate and, as a result, do not pass on a vast amount of experience to new generations. The transmission has to be direct and immediate (for example, modelling and imitation); apes lack the linguistic capability to standardize, encode, classify, and concentrate meanings and experience.

By contrast, humans can transmit sometimes quite abstract meanings through several generations without any significant loss of informational accuracy. Ancient Greeks (from c. 3000 BC) left a largess of information about themselves in the form of inscriptions, mostly on walls or clay tablets. A comprehension of these inscriptions tells us that the Greeks pursued athletics in a recognizable, rule-governed form more than any other ancient culture. Language which articulates this information is such that we can actually use it to project into the future. A future tense permits the communication of imaginative schemes and the transmission of such activities as sport. The unique elements of human language that provide for this type of knowledge of ancient cultures almost certainly arise from our genetic adaptations related to social co-operation and interdependence and changing patterns of subsistence. We have the neural equipment for picking up language; that much is clear. Less clear is the reason for the bewildering diversity of human cultures. Our biological equipment scarcely changes at all over time and space; languages, customs, religions, laws, etc. vary greatly from society to society and from one time period to another.

The suggestion is that, once acquired, the developed language, and the new styles of thought it ushers in, launches its users into all manner of trajectories. Humans plan and create complex organizations and institutions of a quite different quality and order than those found among other animals. Obviously these elaborate phenomena are ultimately dependent on biological factors; but their accomplishment can't be exclusively traced to biological equipment and inheritance. The often extraordinary transformations in human performance engendered by an inspirational coach, for example, remind us that we should approach biology as a license not a limit.

My prehensility and neural circuitry make it possible for me to write this book, but there are countless other non-physical influences on my ability and disposition to write – and on your willingness to read. The very concept of a book to be produced and used reflects an extremely sophisticated and unique level of communication. Books are needed for records, and records have been vital to the evolution of sport. Any balanced comprehension of sports clearly needs a range of scientific approaches: one "-ology" isn't enough. We must refer to hereditary nature; equally, though, we must examine environmental life experience, how organisms react to physical conditions surrounding them. Between the gene and the environment there are all sorts of intervening factors and processes that must be studied if we are to reach an understanding.

Inspirers

Individuals, usually coaches, who are able to combine technical knowledge with motivational qualities such that performers respond to their commands in ways that belie conventional definitions of their abilities. Among the most inspirational coaches are:

Vince Lombardi, who led the Green Bay Packers from a ailing outfit to two Super Bowl victories in the 1960s and was known to be a strict disciplinarian. His martinetish style was described by one of his players: "Lombardi is very fair – he treats us all like dogs." Contrary to popular myth, Lombardi did not utter the oft-quoted maxim about winning not being everything, but the only thing. His message actually had a very different import: winning, he insisted, "is not everything, but *trying* to win is."

Brian Clough, who won a total of 12 major titles for English soccer clubs between 1969 and 1993, when he retired, his most notable success being with Nottingham Forest which was twice European champion. In terms of wins only the second most successful head coach (Bob Paisley being number one), Clough achieved his success with limited resources and at unfashionable clubs. He allowed no stars at his clubs, all players being equal parts of one unit; only his status was bigger than that of the team. "His sheer presence transformed players," one of his ex-players wrote of him. An observer reflected on his coaching: "He would be god one day, the devil the next."

Franz Stampfl, an Austrian track coach who, in the 1950s, moved to England where he transformed training methods: his innovative interval training, in which repeated punishing attacks on a specific distance, replaced the old notion of trying to improve one's time for the whole distance. He demonstrated that ferocious pace and not mere stamina was the key to middle-distance success. In the process, his charges became accustomed to physical pain. Stampfl's principal success was Roger Bannister's historic 3:59.8 mile, the first under 4 minutes, but he also guided Chris Chataway, Chris Brasher and a squad that dominated middle-distance running in the mid-1950s.

Emmanuel Steward, who presided over the Kronk boxing gym in Philadelphia, where training was designed to weed out the weak through a gruelling ordeal of near-inhuman floor and bag exercises and give-no-quarter sparring. Multiple world champion Thomas Hearns was one of his products, but his supervision of Evander Holyfield, before his tactical win over much-heavier Riddick Bowe, indicated Steward's mastery of strategy as well as conditioning techniques. Commenting on a beaten boxer who had shown little resilience, Steward said: "He wouldn't be allowed to shadow box at our gym."

The biological characteristics which distinguish humans from other animals – bipedalism, prehensility, large and more complicated brains, and language – are necessary conditions for culture building. Necessary, but by no means sufficient. Yet in recognizing this, we must at least begin our analysis of sports with a scenario: creative human beings striving to satisfy at least the minimal requirements for subsistence while subjected to the physical constraints imposed by their own biology and the material world around them. Their primary needs are to produce food, shelter, tools, and to reproduce human populations. Unless they can complete these tasks, they will have no opportunity to believe in religions and ethics, create political and economic systems, engage in war, or perform any of the other activities associated with culture.

These activities, almost by definition, depend to some extent on genetically predetermined capacities. It follows that an aesthetic, expressive, and intellectual cultural activity such as sport must be a response to physical constraints and conditions. In the next two chapters, I will approach sport as such a response. Beginning with a breakdown of the physical constraints and conditions, I will address the issue of how sporting performance is physically possible. From "how" I move to "why," specifically asking the reasons for humans' attraction to sporting endeavors. An answer to this first requires us to look at human efforts to survive and subsist in their material environment and how these efforts have effects on their total life experiences.

FURTHER READING ▬▬▬▬▬▬▬▬▬▬▬▬▬▬▬▬▬▬▬▬▬▬

Culture, People, Nature, 6th edn, by Marvin Harris (HarperCollins, 1993) is an introduction to general anthropology and a model of clarity. Harris favors a materialist approach which complements the one taken in this book. His view is that the shaping of thought and behavior is the outcome of adaptations to ecological conditions. Taking a Darwinian starting point, Harris argues: "As a result of natural selection, organisms may be said to become adapted to the needs and opportunities present in their environments." And further: "All individuals are the products of the interaction of their genes and their environment." More extreme versions of materialism would insist that thought and behavior can be understood by studying the constraints to which human existence is subjected; these constraints arise from the need to produce food, shelter, tools, and machines and to reproduce human populations within the limits set by biology and the environment.

Tools, Language and Cognition in Human Evolution edited by Kathleen Gibson and Tim Ingold (Cambridge University Press, 1993) has several pertinent chapters, including "The emergence of language," "The intelligent use of tools" and "Early stone industries and influences regarding language and cognition." The use of tools, in particular spears and bows used for hunting, is seen as one of "the hallmarks of anatomically modern humans."

Biology, 3rd edn, by Elidra Solomon, Linda Berg, Diana Martin and Claude Villee (Saunders College Press, 1993) is a 1,200-page volume covering all anatomical facets of the human body. It is divided into three parts: The organization of life; Engery in living systems; Continuity of life: genetics. Of particular importance to sports students is the chapter on human ability to create and employ technologies in the chapter "The evolution of primates."

Sociobiology: The New Synthesis by E. O. Wilson (Harvard University Press, 1975) is now into its third decade and still provoking arguments: it is a hugely ambitious attempt to explain differences and similarities in living forms by reference to the tendency to optimize reproductive success. A central principle states that natural selection favors characteristics that disperse an individual's genes by increasing the number of offspring of close relatives who carry many of the same genes. This is called inclusive fitness. Wilson's arguments have been criticized by many who oppose his emphasis on biological factors rather than social, or cultural ones.

ASSIGNMENT

"Between the gene and the environment there are all sorts of intervening factors and processes that must be studied" (see p. 18). List as exhaustively as possible the factors and processes that contribute to the creation of what we might regard as "natural" sports performers; in other words, the kinds of factors and processes that show that performers learn and develop as much as they inherit.

Chapter three

Built for action
Structure and functions
of the human body

All systems "go" – for 48.21 seconds

June 18, 1994: the body of 22-year-old Russian Aleksandr Popov breaks the water of a pool at Monaco, Monte Carlo. Moments later, Popov fully surfaces, having travelled a hundred meters through water faster than any other human. In 48.21 seconds, Popov has set in motion processes and mechanisms of immense complexity: for 61 strokes, his every muscle has contracted, stretched and twisted; his lungs have filled and emptied repeatedly; his heart has pumped about 6.6 gallons (30 liters) of blood into all areas of the body. All this has been made possible by the intricate organizing and synchronizing capacity of his brain, which has submitted his entire body to one purpose for the duration of the race, the performance.

Question anyone who has witnessed a sports event at first hand, or even on television, and they will be unlikely to disagree that the essence of sports lies in the actual sporting performance. The moment when competitive humans bring to an end their preparations and make visible their self-willed mastery of a particular set of skills is an engaging experience that easily surpasses reading reports, watching interviews, studying form, or any of the other ancillary activities associated with sports. The performance itself occupies center stage in sports. And while the stage itself – its structure,

23

scenery and props, and the audience – will occupy our attention in the pages to follow, we must provide some analysis of the performance before progressing. Actually, "performance" is too abstract for present purposes: we should properly focus our sights on the *performer*, whose actions take precedence over all other events, at least for the duration of the contest. When we watch sports, we watch bodies move: the peaks of even a chess game are when the players extend their arms to propel pieces across the board.

So, what makes bodies move? It's an obvious, fundamental question, but one which needs a precise answer and I will at least approach one by offering a portrait. Specifically, I will offer a physical portrait; one in which the structure of the human organism and the functions of its various components will be analyzed with a view to understanding how they all interact in the sporting performance. What constitutes a sporting performance? Let's return to our example.

Imagine Popov as a series of systems, interacting so as to produce motion. When the starter's gun fires, Popov's central nervous system receives the signal and very rapidly relays messages to his muscular system which is stimulated to move by electrical impulses. Muscular contractions move his limbs mechanically, this being made possible by the fact that the muscles are attached to the bones of Popov's skeleton, which is yielding, yet tough enough to withstand the stress of movement without fracturing. Fuel is needed for the performer to be able to repeat the motion and this comes via breathing, circulation, and digestion; once burned up, the waste matter of fuel has to be disposed of.

Viewed as a lump of matter, Popov's body is a bundle of about 60 billion living units called cells, each of which has the same basic structure, comprising membrane (which holds the unit together), ribosomes (which manufacture proteins), iysosomes (which destroy harmful substances and diseased parts of the cell), golgi complex (which stores endoplasmic substance), reticulum (which transports substances throughout a cell), cytoplasm (which is the liquid in which the other elements float), mitochondria (which are power-houses, where oxygen and food react to produce vital energy to keep the cell alive) and a nucleus (which contains the chromosomes carrying coded instructions for the workings of the cell).

Cells often cluster together to form other substances, such as tissue and muscle (which comprises 50 percent of cells, being a type of tissue) and these tissues can also work in groups to become organs (heart and lungs, for instance). When organs operate together to perform a particular function, like transporting blood around the body, we usually talk in terms of systems. For a swimmer like Popov to perform at his maximum, all his systems need to be working maximally and synchronously. For our purposes – which are heuristic in this instance – we will probe the body as if it were a series of systems acting interdependently. A logical first step is to ask how a swimmer, or indeed any living animal, is able to move at all and here we're drawn to an examination of the skeletal and muscular systems.

Heuristic

Usually refers to a device or strategy that serves to stimulate investigation. It doesn't attempt to describe reality, but assists in discovery, often by way of analogy or metaphor. Analyzing human behavior by using the metaphors of a vast drama or perhaps a competitive game would be examples of heuristic devices. From the Greek *heurisko*, meaning find.

Moving the skeleton

The skeleton isn't just a framework, an elaborate coat-hanger on which we drape skin and muscle. It's a rather elaborate, living structure that serves four important functions: protection, support, storage, and movement. Structurally, it has two aspects: the axial comprises the skull, backbone, ribs and sternum; the appendicular refers to appendages (legs and arms), the pelvic girdle (to which the legs are attached), and the pectoral girdle (to which the arms are connected). In total, there are over 200 bones.

The human brain is disproportionately large compared to those of other mammals and, together with the spinal cord, controls in large part the movements of the whole body. As a complex, yet delicate, piece of equipment, it needs maximum protection: *ergo* the skull (or cranium), a resilient helmet composed of plates of bone fused together to form a hard casing around the brain. The interstices between the bones are called sutures and allow growth in the size of the brain until around the age of 20, after which they weld together. The skull affords sufficient protection for the brain in most activities, although motor sports, hang gliding and other sports in which the risk of direct collision is high (e.g. football, cricket and cycling) utilize headgear for additional protection.

The other main part of the central nervous system, the spine, also needs the protection of bone; in this case a long, flexible column of vertebrae separated by discs of cartilage. In functional terms, the spine represents a remarkable adaptation, affording protection to a sensitive cable of nerves that runs from the brain to all areas of the body. The spine is articulate so as to permit the movement and flexibility so necessary to survival.

This flexibility is bought at a cost, for in certain parts of the back the spine has little or no support. Hence weightlifters strap broad belts around their waists so as to maintain rigidity in and give support to the vulnerable areas of their lower back when it is likely to be exposed to stress. Some other sensitive organs, like the lungs and heart are also given skeletal protection, but, unlike some vertebrates (armadillos and tortoises), humans have discarded external physical protection and rely more on the wit and ingenuity that derive from the large brain, and the fleetness of foot made possible by bipedalism to protect themselves.

The conventional notion of the skeleton as a means of support is true for the majority of bones. But this needs qualification. The bony material itself is not solid, but is a composite of collagen protein fibers and inorganic mineral crystals ordered in a meshwork of cylindrical layers. This honeycombed arrangement prevents brittleness and gives bone some degree of elasticity: should stress be applied, bone distributes it to prevent a concentration. Excessive stress will cause cracks or breaks, of course, but bone's yielding capacity, or "give," reduces the danger of breakage. These qualities make it ideal as a supporting apparatus because it combines tensile strength with the yield needed for a wide range of motions.

As a general principle, the heavier the load a bone must bear, the greater its diameter must be. Human thigh bones, or femur, are large, as are tibia and fibula connecting the knee to the foot; they are responsible for supporting the upper body weight. But, while the femur has some protection from the quadriceps, the tibia and fibula are exposed and may need artificial cushioning from direct knocks in sports like soccer and hockey.

The skeleton can support effectively only if it grows in correspondence with the rest of the body. And bone does grow; it receives food and oxygen from blood vessels. New layers of tissue encircle existing material and form new bone, thus increasing the diameter (growth in length ceases before the age of 20). Bone grows in response to force, as does muscle. Bend, twist, compress, load, or combine these and, over time, the bone will grow to meet its task and fulfill its function, within limits of course. It will react to certain pressures or movements by fracturing, breaking, or shearing. (When this happens, cells in the outer layer of the bone the periosteum – multiply and grow over the break, joining the two parts together.) At the other extreme, bone will lose mass if deprived of function.

Stored inside bone are the minerals calcium and potassium which are delivered to the cells by blood (and which give bone its hardness) and marrow, a soft jelly-like tissue that produces red and white blood cells.

The fourth major function of the skeleton – and the most important for our purposes – is that of providing mechanical levers for movement. Bones are connected to each other at joints which serve as axes for rotation. For instance, the forearm, the upperarm bone or the humerus, acts as a fulcrum, and the radius and ulna as a lever. The elbow joint, which is a hinge, makes possible a simple range of movement; flexion (bending) and extension (stretching). Other joints, like the biaxial (between forearm and wrist and at the knee), the pivot (at the wrist), and the ball-and-socket (at the shoulder and hip) are more complicated arrangements and permit multiple movements in different planes and directions. Were the joint a manufactured piece of equipment, the articular surfaces would grind together and need the addition of lubricants. The human body takes care of this by interposing a film of lubricating fluid between opposing bone surfaces (in which case, they are called synovial joints), or by sandwiching a tough pad of gristle between articulating bones (cartilaginous joints). An engineer would love this natural bearing which reduces friction.

Cartilage belongs to a class of connective tissues which, as the name suggests, joins or ties together the various parts of the body and makes movement smooth. Its capacity isn't limitless, however, and cartilage can wear out. Ligaments, which are flexible collagen bands that connect and support joints, are also liable to wear-and-tear, especially amongst sports performers, such as throwers or shot putters, who maximize the intensity or repetition of stresses on shoulder and elbow joints and are therefore prone to sprains (torn ligaments) and dislocations of joints.

Perhaps the most troublesome connective tissue for sports competitors is tendon, which is basically a collagen cable that joins muscle to bone and so transmits the pull, which makes the bone move. Tendons make it possible to use a muscle to move a bone at a distance. In the case of fingers, which are clearly vital in dexterous activities (e.g. table tennis, darts, and spin-bowling in cricket), we need muscular control of the fine movements without the invasive presence of muscles at the immediate site. Were the necessary muscles attached directly to the finger bones, the size of the digits would be so large that catching, holding, or even forming a fist would be a problem. Without the action permitted at distance by slender tendons, primate prehensility would be severely restricted. Special nerves in the tendon are designed to inhibit over-contraction, but tears do occur often when co-ordination is impaired by fatigue or poor skill. Tendon tears may be partial or complete and, although any muscle tendon is at risk, those subjected to violent or repetitive stresses, such as the Achilles tendon and shoulder tendons are most frequently involved.

The way the skeleton is framed and its levers fitted together gives the body the potential for a great variety of movement through all planes. But we still need to analyze the source of its motion. Plainly stated, muscle moves our bones; it does so with two actions, contraction and relaxation. Usually, the arrangement features tendons connecting bones to one or more muscles which are stimulated by nerves to contract, causing the tendons to tighten and the bone to move. (Some muscles appear to be attached directly to bone, obviating the need for tendons, but motion is accomplished by basically the same process.)

Muscle use is present in every sporting activity, right from sprinting where muscles are maximally in use, to playing chess where muscles function perhaps only to position eyeballs in their sockets or to move a finger by inches. The various types of muscle present in humans differ in structure and properties, but the striated muscle, which acts as the motor of the skeleton, is our chief concern. Striated muscle is under our control in the sense that we voluntarily induce its contraction and hence movement. Other types of muscles contract in the absence of nerve stimulation: cardiac (heart) muscle, for example, contracts independently of our will and has the property of "inherent rhythmicity" (we will return to this on pp. 34–5).

Skeletal muscle consists of fibers, which are long tubes that run parallel to each other and are encased in sheaths of the ubiquitous collagen. Each fiber is made up of strands called myofibrils, which are themselves composed of two types of interlocking filaments. Thick filaments are made of a protein called myosin and thin ones of actin, and they are grouped in a regular, repeated pattern, so that, under the microscope, they give a striated, or streaky, appearance. The lengths of myosin and actin filaments are divided into units called sarcomeres, the size of which is recognized as the distance between two "Z-lines" (the structures to which the actin filaments are attached).

Although the filaments can't change length, they can slide past each other to produce the all-important contraction. We will see later how messages from the central nervous system are taken to muscles by nerve impulses. When such an impulse reaches a muscle fiber with the instruction "Move!" energy is released in mitochondria and the filaments move closer together, shortening the muscle. As they pass, a chemical reaction occurs in which: (1) calcium is released from storage in the tubular bundles; (2) in the calcium's presence, myosin molecules from the thicker filaments form bonds with the actin filaments; (3) the myosin molecule is then thought to undergo a change in shape, yanking the actin filaments closer together; (4) the contraction of the muscle fiber ends when the calcium ions are pumped back into storage so as to prevent the formation of new chemical bonds.

The effect of the contraction is a pull on the bones to which the muscles are attached and, as the four phases take no more than a few thousandths of a second, we are capable of mechanical movements at very high speed. The flexion and extension of boxer Roy Jones's famous left hook was timed in terms of hundredths of a second. Such a punch, which had a concussing effect, required a great force of movement, so many fibers would have been required to contract together at speed. Nick Faldo's putt, by contrast, would involve fewer fibers.

Mitochondria

These are the power-stations of a cell where glucose and oxygen react together to create energy which converts the chemical adenosine diphosphate (ADP), which is like a flat battery, to charged-up adenosine triphosphate (ATP). This then supplies the rest of the cell with power. As its energy is used up, the ATP reverts back to ADP and returns to the mitochondria for recharging. ATP is most likely the supplier of energy for every activity in animals and plants. Energy, of course, is needed for muscular movements, but also for nerve conduction and other functions.

In both instances, opposing, or antagonistic pairs of muscles would be working to allow free movement. For the hook or the putt, biceps muscle would contract to bend the elbow, which its opposing member, the triceps, would relax. To straighten the arm in the action of a shot putter the triceps need to contract, while biceps relax. Muscles are equipped with special receptors that let the brain know the extent of contraction and the position in three-dimensional space without having to look constantly to check. We can close our eyes, but know the movement and position of our limbs.

The 206 bones of the adult skeletal system form a protective casing for the brain and the spinal cord, a sturdy internal framework to support the rest of the body, and a set of mechanical levers that can be moved by the action of muscles. All of these make the human body a serviceable locomotive machine for walking, running, and, to a lesser degree, swimming, climbing, and jumping. But, like other machines, the body depends on fuel supply for its power, a method for burning the fuel, and a system for transportng the waste products away. Again, the human body has evolved systems for answering all these needs.

Not by food alone: energy

As a living organism, the human being depends on energy. Plants get by with light and water; animals need food. In particular, humans need protein (built up of chemical units called amino acids), carbohydrates (comprising sugars which provide most of our energy), lipids (or fats for storage and insulation), vitamins (about 15 types to assist various chemical processes), minerals (like iron and zinc), and water (to replace liquids). These provide raw energy sources that drive the machinery of the body; that is, making the compounds that combine with oxygen to release energy, and ensure the growth and repair of tissues. (The combination with oxygen will be dealt with on pp. 32–6.)

Obtaining food is of such vital importance to survival that the entire plan of the human body is adapted to its particular mode of procuring food. Sports, as I will argue later, reflects our primitive food-procurement even to this day. For the moment, we need to understand not so much the way in which food is obtained, but how it is used. In their original forms, most of the above substances are unusable to human beings. So we have evolved mechanisms for rendering them usable as energy sources. Processing food is the function of the digestive system, which consists of a long, coiled tube, called the digestive tract, and three types of accessory glands.

Typically, food is introduced to the body through the mouth where it is chewed, pulped, and mixed with saliva in a process of ingestion. After being formed into lumps, it is swallowed and drops into the pharynx (throat) and, then, to the epiglottis, which is a small valve that closes off the windpipe. Water falls under the force of gravity, but food is ushered along by a wave of muscular contractions called peristalsis. Fibers in the wall of the oesophagus tube (gullet) push the food downwards to the stomach (which explains why cosmonauts can still eat in the absence of gravity).

From here, the food passes into the stomach, a sausage-shaped organ which can expand to about a two-pints capacity. At this stage, a churning process starts in which the food is mixed with mucus, hydrochloric acid, and enzymes (chemical substances that speed up processes – in this instance, the breaking up of protein). The effect of this is to liquefy the food, so that after between three and four hours the churned-up mass (called chyme), which now resembles a cream soup, gets transferred, via peristaltic waves, to the stomach's exit point and then to the duodenum which is the first chamber of the small intestine. Contrary to popular belief, it is here rather than the stomach, where most of the chemical digestion gets done: bile from the liver and enzymes from the pancreas are released. (An exception is alcohol, which is readily absorbed in the stomach and doesn't pass through.)

A note here about the role of the brain in regulating the discharge of naturally secreted juices that aid digestion: seeing, smelling, tasting, or even thinking about food can stimulate the brain to send messages to the glands in the mouth and stomach to release a hormone called gastrin that is quickly absorbed into the blood and then to glands where it triggers the release of gastric juice. Hence sports competitors who chew gum to enhance their con-centration are usually doing a disservice to their stomachs by producing gastric juices when there is no food. Gastric juices have enough acidity and protein-splitting capacity to burn human flesh. The stomach has natural protection against this, although resistances can be lowered by alcohol or aspirin and by overproducing the juices when no food is available. A possible result is an open sore in the wall of the stomach, or a duodenal ulcer.

Lymph

From the Latin *lympha*, for water, this is a body fluid derived from the blood and tissue and returned to the circulatory system in *lymphatic* vessels. At intervals along the vessels there are lymph *glands* which manufacture antibodies and lymphocytes that destroy bacteria. The lymph system has no pump like the blood system and the movement of lymph is brought about largely by pressure from contracting skeletal muscles, backflow being prevented by valves.

    The lymph system doubles as the body's immune system in that it produces proteins called antibodies, lying at the surface of certain white blood cells (lymphocytes). When needed, antibodies and cells rush into the blood stream and "round up" the harmful bacteria and viruses. While the lymph system can make thousands of antibodies, its vital adversaries are constantly mutating so as to find ways of defeating it, as the Aids pandemic indicates.

Basically, the idea is to reduce the parts of the food that can be profitably used by the body (the nutrients) to molecular form and allow them to seep through the cells lining the long digestive tube, through the minuscule blood or lymph vessels in the stomach wall and into the blood or lymph. All the cells of the body are bathed in a fluid called lymph. Exchanges between blood and cells take place in lymph. Lymph is derived from blood, though it has a kind of circulatory system of its own, filtering through the walls of capillaries, then moving along channels of its own (lymphatics), which join one another and steer eventually to the veins, in the process surrendering their contents to the general circulatory system. Food is absorbed through the wall of the intestine which is covered in villi, tiny absorbant "fingers" that give the tube a vast surface area. Not all food passes directly into blood vessels: the lymphatics are responsible for collecting digested fats and transporting them to the thoracic duct which empties into one of the large veins near the heart.

    Once absorbed the nutrients are carried in the blood and lymph to each individual cell in the body where they are used up; that is, metabolized. The residue of indigestible or unabsorbed food is eliminated from the body by way of the large intestine. En route, bacteria in the large intestine feed on vestiges and, in return, produce certain vitamins which are absorbed and used. Some of the unwanted water is converted to urea and passed out via the bladder. The body has precise control over what it needs for nutrition, growth, and repair. One of the many functions of the liver is to store surplus nutrients and release them together to meet immediate requirements. This large abdominal organ receives digested food from the blood and reassembles its molecules in such a way as to make them usable to humans. Different cells need different nutrients, so the liver works as a kind of chef preparing a buffet for the blood to carry around the rest of the body.

A supply of glucose is needed by all body and especially brain cells, especially as they have no means of storage. If, after a sugar-rich meal, the body has too much glucose in the blood, the liver cells remove it and store it, later pushing it back into the blood when the glucose level drops. After a carbohydrate-rich meal, the level may increase briefly, but the liver will take out the surplus for later use. Muscle cells are also able to store large amounts of glucose molecules, packaged as glycogen, which is why endurance-event competitors, like marathon runners, try to pack muscle and liver cells with stored glycogen prior to competition in the expectation that it will be released into the blood when levels fall. After the glucose is used up, liver cells start converting amino acids and portions of fat into glucose and the body shifts to fat as a source of fuel.

Muscle-packing or muscle-loading

Carbohydrates (carbs) provide most of our energy and can be ingested in many forms, after which they are reduced to simple sugars before being absorbed into the bloodstream. Carbs are an economical source of fuel. Liver and muscles store carbohydrates in the form of glycogen, which converts rapidly to glucose when extra energy is needed. Mindful of this, endurance performers sometimes seek to "pack" or "load-up" their muscles with glycogen by consuming large amounts of carbo-hydrate foods such as bread, cereals, grains, and starchy products for about 72 hours preceding an event. The idea is to store as much glycogen as possible, making more glucose available when energy supplies become depleted.

Metabolism refers to all the body's processes that make food usable as a source of energy. The success of these depends on how effectively the body can get the nutrients and oxygen it requires to the relevant parts of the body and, at the same time, clear out the unwanted leftovers like carbon dioxide. The substance employed for this purpose is blood, but it's actually more than just a convenient liquid for sweeping materials from place to place. Cells, cell fragments (platelets), proteins, and small molecules float in a liquid plasma, which is mainly water (and makes up about 60 percent of the blood's composition). The plasma contains red and white blood cells; the latter are capable of engulfing bacteria and combating infections with antibodies. Red cells are more numerous and contain hemoglobin, a chemical compound with a strong affinity for oxygen.

Hemoglobin allows blood to increase its oxygen-carrying capacity exponentially. Long- and middle-distance runners have exploited the advantage of having more hemoglobin in their blood by training at high altitudes, where there is less oxygen naturally available in the air. Their bodies respond to the scarcity by producing a chemical that triggers the release of larger numbers of red cells in the blood. After descending to sea-level (or thereabouts), the body will take time to readjust and will retain a high hemoglobin count for some weeks, during which an athlete may compete and make profitable use of a generous supply of oxygen to the muscles (blood doping, as we will see in Chapter 8, involves extracting hemoglobin-packed blood during altitude training, saving it, and administering a transfusion to the athlete immediately prior to a race). At the other extreme, excessive bleeding or an iron-deficient diet can lead to anemia, a condition resulting from too little hemoglobin.

So, how do we manage to circulate this urgently required mixture throughout the body? The internal apparatus comprises the heart, blood vessels, lymph, lymph vessels, and some associated organs, like the liver. These form a closed system, meaning that the blood that carries the vital substances all over the body is confined to definite channels and moves in only one direction, rather than being left to swim about. It travels in three types of vessels. The thickest are *arteries* in which blood moves at high pressure from the heart to the body's tissues. These arteries split over and over again to form microscopic vessels called *capillaries* that spread to every part of the body. A single capillary is only about half a millimeter long and a single cubic meter of skeletal muscle is interlaced with 1,400 to 4,000 of them. Laid end-to-end the length of all the body's capillaries would be about 60,000 miles, or 96,500 kilometers. While coursing around, oxygen and nutrient-rich liquid, plasma, seeps through the ultra-thin walls of the capillary. At the same time, capillaries, like vacuum cleaners, suck up waste products from cells. Gradually, capillaries merge together to form larger vessels that turn out to be *veins*; these keep blood at a lower pressure as they deliver it back to the heart.

A fist-sized muscle weighing less than a pound, the heart is a four-chambered pump that pushes blood into the arteries, gets it back from all parts of the body (except the lungs), pumps it out of the lungs, takes it back from the lungs, then returns it to the body. The chambers of the right side of the heart consist of one atrium and one ventricle. Connected to the right atrium are two large veins, one of which brings blood from the upper body and one from the lower. Blood flows from the right atrium into the right ventricle via a one-way valve; it leaves this chamber through a pulmonary artery that branches and services the lungs. Another valve stops any backflow. Blood returns from the lungs via pulmonary veins which drain into a left atrium and, then, to a left ventricle.

From here, the blood is squeezed into the aorta, the single largest artery of the body, which runs into several other arteries connected to head, arms, and the upper chest, and, later, to abdominal organs and body wall. In the pelvis, the aorta branches and sends arteries into the legs. Blood returns to the right atrium of the heart through veins. The direction of the blood is ensured by a series of valves (blood, controlled by the valves, moves in one direction only). We call the movement away from ventricles systole and its opposite diastole. At any one time, there are about 1.5 gallons of blood in the mature human body. It takes less than a minute for the resting heart to pump out this amount and considerably less for the exerting sports performer, who can push out as much as 6.6 gallons per minute when active.

As mentioned before, the heart muscle has inherent rhythmicity and the pump acts independently of our volition. It will (given a suitable atmosphere) pump even outside the body, and with no stimulation; this makes heart transplants possible. Not that the heart is indifferent to outside influences; a sudden shock, for example, can cause sufficient stimulation to slow down, or skip, the heartbeat.

During exercise or competition the action may accelerate to over 200 beats per minute. The heart muscle itself would stretch and automatically increase its strength of contraction and flow of blood. Athletes work at increasing blood flow without the corresponding heartbeat. The extra blood flow results in a heightening of the pressure of blood in the arteries of the chest and neck, which are detected by special sensory cells embedded in their walls. Nerve impulses are sent to the brain, resulting in impulses being relayed back to the heart, slowing its beat rate and lowering potentially harmful blood pressure levels. So, the brain has to monitor or feed back what is going on during intense physical activity.

The rate of heart action is also affected by hormones, the most familiar in sports being adrenaline which causes an immediate quickening of the heart in response to stressful situations. The reaction is widespread; amongst other things, blood vessels in the brain and limbs open up, and glycogen is released

---

Heart Rate Monitor (HRM)

A device comprising a chestband transmitter and a wrist-worn receiver
that indicates how fast the heart is beating. The principle of exercising within a certain percentage of maximum heart rate has been
known for years; but, only with the advent of the HRM has the ability
to apply those benefits been available to athletes. It is necessary to
know the maximum heart rate (MHR) of the athlete and the threshold
heart rate, the point at which exercise moves from aerobic effort to
anaerobic. By exercising at slightly below the threshold, one can gradually force it up. Olympic 4,000-meter pursuit cycling champion, Chris
Boardman, used an HRM in competition as well as training: in setting
the world hour distance in Bordeaux in 1994, he had to cope with
severe heat – which makes the heart beat faster – so adjusted to ride
at six beats faster than he had planned.

---

from the liver. In this type of situation, the skeletal muscles might receive up
to 70 percent of the cardiac output, or the total blood pumped from the heart.
Under resting conditions, the liver, kidneys, and brain take 27, 27, and 14
percent respectively. Immediately after eating, the digestive organs command
great percentages (to carry food away), thus reducing the supply to the
muscles. So, activity after a meal tends to be self-defeating; you can't get as
much blood to the muscles as you would if you waited for three hours or so.

I mentioned before that food alone does not give the body energy, but
needs the addition of oxygen, which is, of course, inhaled from the surrounding air, taken to the lungs, and then transferred to all parts of the body via the
blood. Once it arrives at cells, the oxygen reacts with glucose, supplied by
courtesy of digested carbohydrates, and produces energy at the mitochondria
sites. During this process of respiration, unwanted carbon dioxide and water
are formed in the cells. Exhaling gets rid of them.

Lungs and windpipe make up the respiratory system, though the actual
process of breathing is controlled by the contractions of muscles in the chest,
in particular the diaphragm muscle beneath the lungs and the muscles
between the ribs. Space in the lungs is created by the diaphragm moving down
and the ribs expanding. Air rushes in mainly through the nostrils where it is
filtered, warmed, and moistened, and then into the lungs via the windpipe, or
trachea. To reach the lungs, the air travels along tubes called bronchi which,
when inside the lungs, divide into smaller and smaller tubes, ending in small
bunches of air sacs called alveoli. Oxygen seeps out of the alveoli and into
surrounding capillaries which carry hemoglobin, a compound which, as we

noted, readily picks up oxygen. While oxygen leaves alveoli, carbon dioxide, produced by the body cells, enters ready to be exhaled, a motion initiated by a muscular relaxation of the diaphragm and ribs. Air rushes out when we sigh "Phew!" to denote relief and relaxation; the ribs close in and diaphragm lifts up.

The motions are more pronounced during continuous physical exertion; the body makes a steady demand for more oxygen and to meet this we breathe more deeply and more fully. The heart responds by pumping the oxygen-rich blood around the body faster. The process involves sustained use of oxygen in the breakdown of carbohydrates and, eventually, fats to release in the mitochondria of cells where the raw fuel ADP is energy charged up as ATP. This is why the name *aerobic* (meaning "with air") is applied to continuous activities, such as cycling, swimming, and running over distances. In contrast, weight-lifting, high jumping, and other sports requiring only short bursts of energy are *anaerobic*. In this case, food is not broken down completely to carbon dioxide and water, but to compounds such as alcohol or lactic acid. An incomplete breakdown means that less energy is released, but what is released can be used immediately. "Oxygen debt" affects many sports competitors, particularly ones whose event requires explosive bursts, but over a reasonably sustained period. Four hundred-meter runners often tie up in the home straight; they can't get the oxygen and glucose round their bodies fast enough, so their muscles use their own glycogen stores for releasing ATP anaerobically (without oxygen).

The product of this process is lactic acid, which needs oxygen to be converted into carbohydrate to get carried away. As runners need all the oxygen they can process for the release of energy they "borrow" it temporarily, allowing the lactic acid to accumulate in the muscles and cause fatigue. After the event, the debt has to be repaid, so rapid breathing invariably carries on. Shorter-distance sprinters also incur oxygen debts, but the buildup of lactic acid in their muscles is not usually great enough to hinder contraction. Longer-distance performers tend to get second winds: an increase in heart beat rate and breathing enables the runner to take in enough oxygen to convert and dissipate the lactic acid without over-extending the oxygen debt.

Communications and control

Let's return to Aleksandr Popov for a moment. We now have an idea of how his movements are possible: how the supporting scaffold of his skeleton is urged into motion by the contraction of muscles; how those muscles are fed a supply of fuel to turn into energy; and how that fuel, in the form of food and oxygen, is pushed to its destination by blood which, at the same time, picks

Hyperventilation

Carbon dioxide (CO_2) is a waste product and needs to be flushed out of the blood. Even a small increase in CO_2 content of the blood stimulates deep and, later, more rapid breathing to reduce the CO_2. The action is brought about involuntarily, usually during physical activity because of the fast breakdown of carbohydrates to release energy (impulses are sent to the medulla, resulting in increased breathing). Occasionally, this can lead to an over-reduction and a loss of consciousness. When this happens, hyperventilation is said to occur.

up waste products to dispatch. Although we have examined these processes separately, this is a device; in actual performance, all the processes are closely connected and dependent on each other.

The digestion of food, for instance, would be of no value without a bloodstream to absorb it and to distribute the products; release of energy in a contracting muscle would cease if the lungs failed to supply oxygen via the circulatory system; a contracting muscle has to be connected to articulated bone to get a movement. The workings together of these is no haphazard affair. During strenuous activity, when muscles need to lose excess carbon dioxide and take in more glucose and oxygen, the rate of breathing increases automatically and the heart beats faster, so sending a greater amount of oxygen-rich blood to the muscles.

Crudely stated, the information we receive about the environment arrives by way of cells called *receptors*, which respond to changes in, for example, light and sound. They produce pulses of electricity which travel along nerves to the brain, which quickly interprets the meaning of the changes and issues instructions to the relevant other parts of the body (e.g. "loud noise – cover ears"). Some of the information received by the brain is stored for future use, a facility of crucial importance in the acquisition of skill, which involves the capacity to react in precisely the same way to similar stimuli time after time.

The two components of the whole nervous system are: (1) the central nervous system (CNS), comprising the control center of the brain and its message conduit, the spinal cord; and (2) the peripheral nervous system (PNS), which is the network of nerves originating in the brain and spinal cord and which is responsible for picking up messages from the skin and sense organs (sensory nerve cells) and carrying messages from the CNS to the muscles (motor nerve cells).

Nerves are spread throughout the entire body; each one consists of a bundle of minute nerve fibers and each fiber is part of a nerve cell, or *neuron*, of which there are about 100 billion woven into each body in such a way as to bypass the packed body cells. To do this, the network needs a shuttle service provided by connector neurons which carry signals back and forth. Further physical facts about signals are, first, that the nerve fibers that pick up sensations from receptors and deliver them to the CNS, do so with electrical impulses that are chemically charged; changes in the balance of the minerals sodium and potassium in the cells cause the impulse. Second, the speed of the impulse varies from fiber to fiber and with environmental conditions. And third, fibers covered in sheaths of myelin (a fatty substance) conduct impulses faster than naked fibers.

Perhaps the clearest way of depicting the role of the nervous system is by tracing its stages. Suppose you are a gun marksman (or woman); you must use primarily the senses of sight and touch when focusing on the target and aligning the gun and make adjustments to these environmental factors. A first step is made by bringing the target into focus: the eyes are, of course, sense organs (i.e. an assembly of receptors) and their surface, known as the retina, will react to rays of light by changing its chemical structure; this triggers off an electrical impulse that travels along nerve cells, or neurons, to the brain. There are no direct connections between neurons, so the impulse may have to travel a circuitous route. The tiny gaps between neurons are *synapses* and these are bridged by a chemical *neurotransmitter* that takes the impulse across the synapse to the next neuron. The points of connection with the next neuron are called *dendrites*, which are in effect short, message-carrying fibers. One long fiber, called an *axon*, carries messages away from one neuron to the dendrites of the next. It takes only fractions of a second for the impulse to make its way through the synapses and neurons to the brain.

The fine web of nerves running through most of the body pale beside the densely complex mesh of neurons in the brain. Senses gleaned from our contact with the environment provide inputs which are sent to the brain; this processes the information before sending out instructions to muscles and glands. Most of our behavior in and out of sports is controlled in this way. A fast pitcher in a baseball game may choose to do many different things on the basis of his sense impressions, mostly picked up by his vision and touch. He may notice a shuffle in the hitter's gait; he may feel moisture rising in the air that may affect the trajectory of his ball. His brain sends messages to his muscles so that he deliberately bowls a short, rising delivery.

But not all of our behavior is produced by such a process: the receiving hitter may not expect the fast ball which zips sharply toward his head, prompting him to jerk his head away almost immediately to protect it from damage – as we would withdraw a hand inadvertently placed on a hot iron. This type of reflex action is controlled by the spinal cord section of the CNS.

The nervous impulse defines an arc that short-circuits the brain, so that the message never actually reaches it. The behavior resulting from the reflex arc is sudden and often unco-ordinated because all the muscle fibers contract together to avoid the danger. A boxer drawing away from a punch, a goal-keeper leaping to save a short-range shot, a volleyball player blocking an attempted spike; all these suggest automatic responses that need not involve conscious will for their successful completion. We hear much about reflex movements in sports and, clearly, sports in which fast reaction is crucial do exhibit such responses. But most sports action is governed by the brain and, for this reason, we need to look in more detail at the structure and functions of this most vital of organs.

While the brain itself is an integrated unit which, like any other living organ, needs a continuous supply of food and oxygen to produce energy, it can be seen in its component parts, each of which has specific functions. The medulla, for instance, controls involuntary activities that we can't control consciously, but which are essential for survival (such as breathing and heartrate). Also of interest for sporting performance is the cerebellum which receives messages from the muscles, ears, eyes, and other parts and then helps co-ordinate movement and maintain balance so that motion is smooth and accurate. Injury to this component does not cause paralysis, but impairs delicate control of muscle and balance; for instance, the ability to surf or skate would be lost. All voluntary and learned behavior is directed by the cortex, the largest portion of the brain; this forms the outer layer of the area known as the cerebrum lying at the fore of the brain.

The cerebrum is divided into two halves, or hemispheres, each of which is responsible for movement and senses on its opposite side. Nerves on the two sides of the body cross each other as they enter the brain, so that the left hemisphere is associated with the functions of the right-hand side of the body. In most right-handed people, the left half of the cerebrum directs speech, reading, and writing while the right half directs emotions; for left-handers, the opposite is true. So, Goran Ivanisevic's service would have been controlled by the right side of his brain, while his emotional outbursts against umpires would be associated with the left. Physical movement is controlled by the motor area: motor neurons send impulses from this area to muscles in differ-ent parts of the body. The more precise the muscle movements, the more of the motor area is involved; so a hammer thrower's actions would not use up much space while a dart player's would, as he or she would be utilizing fine movements of the fingers.

The only other zone of the brain I want to note at present is the thala-mus, which is where pain is felt. Pain, of course, is principally a defensive phe-nomenon designed to warn us of bodily danger both inside and outside the body. Impulses originating in the thalamus travel to the sensation area so that

---

Brain types

Concept derives from the theories of Jon Niednagel, who believes there are inherited designs to brains which affect our mental and physical skills and predispose us to certain events. By knowing what sort of brain type sports performers have, it is proposed that they can be matched to training schedules that will allow them to excel. Those dominated by the right side of the brain are represented by *P* and by the left *J*; extroverts by *E* and introverts by *I*. Those whose dominant functions are sensing and feeling are *SFs* and those who rely on sensing and thinking are *STs*. *NFs* have intuition and feeling, while *NTs* are both intuitive and intelligent. Sports performers are grouped by their brain-type characteristics. For example: Mary Jo Fernandez, *INTP*; Seve Ballesteros *ESTP*; Tonya Harding, *ENTJ*.

---

a localization of danger can be made. This is a mechanistic account of our reactions to pain: it is actually affected by all manner of intervening factors, including self-belief. In other words, if people do not believe they will feel pain, they probably won't – at least under certain conditions. There are also cultural definitions of pain: we learn to interpret pain and react to it and the thresholds may differ from culture to culture.

Such is the nature of competitive sports nowadays that few concessions to pain are allowed. Inspirational coaches encourage performers to conquer pain by developing what's often called "mental toughness," just ignoring pain. Chemical ways of "tricking" the brain have been developed. Some drugs, for example, cause nerve cells to block or release a neurotransmitter (the chemical that carries nerve impulses across synapses to the dendrite of the adjacent neuron), the idea being to break the chemical chains linking brain to cell. We will look at the use of drugs more closely in Chapter 8. The point to bear in mind for now is that the CNS generally, and the brain in particular, play a central role, not only in the process of movement, but in the delicate sensory adjustments that have to be made in the operation of all sports, even those such as power lifting, which seem to require pure brawn. The lifter's cerebellum enables him or her to control the consequences of the lift; without this, initiation might be possible but corrective feedback co-ordination would be absent. In short, there would be no balance and no instruction to the opposing (antagonistic) muscles to make a braking contraction on the lift's completion. The whole operation would collapse.

While we exert a large degree of control over our bodies through the CNS, many vital activities, such as heartbeat, peristalsis, and functioning of the kidneys simply can't be controlled voluntarily. Handling these is a secondary system of nerves called the autonomic nervous system (ANS). Many of the cell bodies of the ANS lie outside the brain and spinal cord and are massed together in bunches, each bunch being a *ganglion*. These ganglia receive information from receptors in the various organs of the body and then send out the appropriate instructions to muscles, such as the heart, and glands, such as salivary glands. The instructions are interesting in that they are twofold and antagonistic.

Unlike skeletal muscle which is either stimulated to contract or not (it needs no nerve impulse to relay), cardiac muscle and the smooth (as opposed to striated) muscle of other organs must be stimulated either to contract more than usual or to relax more than usual. To achieve this the ANS is divided into two substrata: the sympathetic system (more centrally located) and the parasympathetic system (more dispersed). The parasympathetic system constricts the pupil of the eyes, increases the flow of saliva, expands the small intestine, and shrinks the large intestine; the sympathetic system has the opposite effect. Impulses are propagated continuously in both systems, the consequences of which are known as *tone* – a readiness to respond quickly to stimulation in either direction.

Tone is rather important in certain sports: for instance, a panic-inducing visual stimulus will cause an increase in sympathetic impulses and a decrease in parasympathetic impulses to the heart, eliciting a greater response than just a sympathetic stimulation. Impulses from the two systems always have antagonistic effects on organs. The name *autonomic* nervous system implies that it is independent and self-regulated, whereas, in fact, the centers that control ANS activity are in the lower centers of the brain and usually below the threshold of conscious control. The appeal of bringing ANS functions under conscious control is fascinating; yogi have for centuries been able to slow heartbeat quite voluntarily, with corresponding changes to the entire body. The potential for this in sports, particularly in the areas of recovery and recuperation, is huge.

In sports, responses to change in the environment have usually got to be swift and definite. Consequently, our treatment of the nervous system has focused on its ability to direct changes and issue instructions to the relevant parts of the body in order that they react quickly. The quickest communication system is based, as we have seen, on electrical impulses. But the body's response to an *internal* change is likely to occur over a period of time and be brought about by chemical adjustments. The substances involved are hormone molecules and they are manufactured by a group of cells called endocrine glands, the most important of which is the pituitary attached to the hypothalamus on the underside of the brain. This produces a growth hormone by regulating the amount of nutrients taken into the cells. Hormones themselves are messengers, secreted into the blood in which they travel to all body parts, interacting with other cells and effecting a type of fine-tuning.

Because some hormones have very specific effects – many of them local rather than body-wide – they have been of service to sports performers seeking to enhance performance (as we will discover in later chapters). The male testes secrete the hormone testosterone, which regulates the production of sperm cells and stimulates sex drive. Testosterone has been produced chemically and the synthetic hormone introduced into the body of competitors. Among the alleged effects are an increase in muscle bulk and strength and a more aggressive attitude.

Adrenaline is another example: as we have seen, it pours into the blood, stimulating the release of glycogen from the liver, expansion of blood vessels in the heart, brain, and limbs, and contraction of vessels in the abdomen. Fatigue diminishes and blood coagulates more rapidly (which is why boxers' seconds apply an adrenaline solution to facial cuts). Competitors pumped-up with adrenaline will usually have a pale complexion, on account of their blood being diverted from skin and intestine, and dilated pupils; hearts will be pounding and the breathing will be fast. The muscles will have the capacity to contract quickly and effectively either for, as the expression goes, *fight or flight*. This is an unusually fast hormonal change and most influences are long *term*, concerning such features as growth and sexual maturity. When they pass through the liver, the hormones are converted to relatively inactive compounds which are excreted as waste product, or urea, by the kidneys; this is why urinalysis is the principal method of detecting proscribed substances – it determines hormonal products in urine.

The chemical fine-tuning of the body is extensive and, in the healthy body, works continuously to modify us internally. Sweat glands are largely responsible for our adjustment to heat and, as many sports activate these, we should recognize their importance. The glands' secretions cover the skin with millions of molecules of water and they begin rising to the surface (epidermis) when external temperatures exceed about 25°C/77°F, depending on weight of clothing or the rigor of the activity performed. When blood reaching the hypothalamus is 0.5–1°C/35°F above normal, nerve impulses conveyed by the ANS stimulate sweat glands into activity.

Fluid from the blood is filtered into the glands and passes through their ducts so that a larger amount of moisture is produced on the skin surface. As it evaporates, the heat in the molecules escapes, leaving coolness. The internal temperature of the body is kept within acceptable limits, as long as the sweat continues to take away the heat. (When temperatures drop, a reflex action is to shiver, which is a spasmodic muscular contraction that produces internal heat.) Most, but not all, sweating results from the eccrine glands; secretions around the armpits and nipples of both sexes and the pubic area of females come from apocrine glands, which discharge not only salt and water, but odourless organic molecules that are degraded by skin bacteria and give off distinct smells. In mammals, the smell has a sexual function, though the lengths to which humans go in trying to suppress or disguise the smell suggests that the function has been discarded in our species.

A general point here is that sweat is not just water but a concentration of several materials and profuse sweating may deprive the body of too much salt. Heat prostration and sunstroke are curses to marathon runners and triathletes and their efforts to conquer them include swallowing salt tablets before the race, drinking pure water at stages during the race, and taking Gatorade or other solutions of electrolytes (salt and other compounds that separate into ions in water and can therefore help in the conduction of nerve impulses and muscle contraction). Problems for these athletes multiply in humid climates where the air contains so much vapour that the sweat can't evaporate quickly enough to produce a cooling effect; instead, it lies on the skin's surface forming a kind of seal. The result is known as heat stagnation.

Even more dangerous is the situation when, after prolonged sweating due to activity in hot atmospheres, sweat production ceases and body temperatures soar to lethal levels. Sweat glands perform a vital compensatory function in minimizing the effects of heat during physical activity and, under instruction of the brain, try to stabilize body temperature at around 37°C/86°F. But their thermostatic powers have clear limitations when tested by athletes, for whom 26 miles is but the first station of the advance toward the boundaries of human endurance.

The journalist who coined the now-clichéd term "well-oiled machine" to describe some highly efficient football team actually, and perhaps unwittingly, advanced a rather accurate description of the collection of trained and healthy individuals in question. Machines in the plural would have been more correct because, when examined in one perspective, that's what human beings are: a functioning series of systems made of cells and based on principles that any engineer, biologist, or chemist would find sound. But this is a partial and inadequate description and this chapter has merely set up a model; now it must be set in context and seen to work. We now have a grasp of the basic equipment and capabilities of the body; we still know little of its properties and motivations. Sport as an activity, derives from natural faculties, but the particular form or shape it has taken and the way it has been perpetuated and mutated over the centuries is not understandable in purely biological terms. It needs explanation all the same and this will be the task of the following chapters.

FURTHER READING ━━━━━━━━━━━━━━━━━━━━━━━━━━━

Biology, 3rd edn, by Eldira Solomon, Linda Berg, Diana Martin and Claude Villee (Saunders College Press, 1993) was recommended as auxiliary reading for Chapter 2; it is so encyclopedic that it functions as a useful adjunct to this chapter too. The sections on the organization of life and on energy production are of particular importance to students concentrating on the physical (i.e. rather than social) aspects of the body

Principles of Human Anatomy, 6th edn, by Gerard Torto (HarperCollins, 1992) is a clear, illustrated introduction to students of the human body; it uses a systems approach similar to the one favored in the present book; this has the advantage of unifying concepts that contribute to our understanding of the way the body works. It is appended with explanations of key terms.

An Imaging Atlas of Human Anatomy by J. Weir and P. Abrahams (Mosby-Wolfe, 1992) is one of a collection of publications that illustrate the human bodily systems using various imaging techniques, the others being a series of Imaging Anatomy Wallcharts (1994) and A Slide Atlas of Human Anatomy (1994) same publishers.

Physiology of Sport and Exercise by Jack Wilmore and David Costill (Human Kinetics, 1994) reviews the major body systems and examines the body's response to exercise; its strength is in emphasizing the role of the environment in affecting how the body responds – as such it complements the approach taken in this book.

In the seventeenth century, the French philosopher René Descartes tried to explain living processes like digestion, growth, and reproduction in terms of a mechanical model, i.e. the human as a machine. Repeat the exercise: break the human body down into its component parts and analyze the relations between them as if you were studying a machine, then do a specification sheet (rather as car manufacturers do), incorporating dimensions, safety ratings, replacement parts, insurance, maintenance costs, unique features, etc.

Finally, create some copy for a possible advertisement, for example: "Beneath the sleek contours of its outer shell is an engine incorporating all the latest technological advances – from electronic microchip management systems controlling fuel injection and timing through to the latest 16-valve system with turbo charger and intercooler together with 170-brake horsepower. With an acceleration of 0–60 mph in 7 seconds and a top speed of 140 mph the machine runs well without adjustment on unleaded or leaded fuel. The fully independent multi-link suspension, disc brakes on all wheels, power steering, and electronically controlled 4-wheel antilock brake system combine to offer precise handling."

Chapter four

Animal spirits
A history of sports

The mystery of ancestry

Can we recognize anything in the following activity that merits description as a sport? Time: early-1800s. Place: Birmingham, England. Players: a tethered bull and a ferocious dog.

> Sometimes the dog seized the bull by the nose and "pinned" him to the earth, so that the beast roared and bellowed again, and was brought down upon its knees ... The people then shouted out "Wind, wind!" that is, to let the bull have breath, and the parties rushed forward to take off the dog ... However, the bulls were sometimes pinned between the legs, causing [them] to roar and rave about in great agony.
>
> (Holt 1990: 16)

The quotation is from Richard Holt's book, *Sport and the Working Class in Modern Britain*, which is full of other lurid details of what passed as sports in the eighteenth and nineteenth centuries (1990). As well as bull-baiting, as the above activity was known, there was cock-fighting, which involved pitting two highly trained cocks together, and dog-fighting, which goes on in Britain and the USA today, albeit in an illicit

way. Legislation made such contests illegal, though cruelty to animals has by no means disappeared. The persistence of fox-hunting in the face of protests confirms this.

These types of activities in which animals were made to fight, maim and often kill each other, were regarded as sports. Before the reader rushes to deny any connection between such barbaric contests and what we now recognize as sports, consider some of the similarities. *Competition* for no reason apart from competition itself: unlike animal fights in other contexts, there were no evolutionary functions (such as "survival of the fittest") served by the fights. *Winning* as a sole aim: spectators were interested in a result rather than the actual process of fighting, and animal contests typically ended with one either dead or at least too badly injured to continue. Holt adds to his description of the Birmingham bull bait that, "blood would be dropping from the nose and other parts of the bull" (1990: 16). *Spectators*: the tournaments were set up with an audience in mind – in specially dug pits around which a crowd could stand, in barns, or other public places where the action was visible to spectators.

Gambling: the thrill of watching the contest was enhanced by wagering on one of the animals and money frequently changed hands among the spectators. *Animals* were trained and used: although the contests were unacceptably cruel by today's standards, we still train and employ animals in sports, such as horse- and dog-racing, pigeon-racing, polo, and (though repugnant to many) bull-fighting. Perhaps the most remarkable legacy is the Iditarod, a 1,180-mile race through Alaska featuring packs of huskies pulling a person in a sled. The original trail was forged by dog-sleds carrying freight to miners and prospectors; the latter-day contest recreates the hunger and exhaustion of driving for eight days and nights at temperatures of –60 degrees. Competitive and recreational fishing remains one of the world's most popular pursuits.

All these elements are present in human cultures that extend far beyond the Industrial Revolution of the late eighteenth and early nineteenth centuries, which is the conventional starting point for studies of sport. True, the distinct shape or form of sport developed in that crucial period and the organizational structure that distinguishes sport from mere play was a product of the industrial age. But I believe we can go back much further: in fact, given the right conceptual approach and historical direction, it's possible to trace the origins of contemporary sports back to primitive matters of survival; which is precisely what I intend to do in this chapter.

The methods we once used for getting nutrition have been reshaped and refined, but are still vaguely discernible. Track and field events such as running and throwing are virtually direct descendants of our ancestors' chase of prey and their attempts to stun or kill them with missiles; some events still consciously model themselves on the disciplines and aptitudes associated with hunting, modern pentathlon (riding, fencing, shooting, swimming, and running) being the clearest example. More advanced tool use, which enhanced the ability to survive and improved nutrition, also generated a new adaptation that we see reflected in current sport. Tools that were once used for killing or butchery have been transformed into symbolic instruments like bats, rackets, and clubs and used in a fashion which disguises the functions of their predecessors. The origins of others, such as epées, are more transparent.

The purpose of this chapter is to provide an account of the beginning of sports and its subsequent development up to the last century. In the perspective I choose to view sport, the entire phenomenon has human foundations that were established several thousand years ago. It follows that any chronicle must track its way back through history to discover the reasons for the human pursuit of what are, on analysis, mock hunts and battles and the purposes they serve at both individual and social levels. The latter point will be answered in the next chapter, but the immediate task is to unravel the mystery of ancestry: how did sports begin? It's a question that requires an ambitious answer, one which takes up deep into history for a starting point.

Blood Sports

Recreational pursuits that involved inflicting harm on animals were of three types, all very popular between 1780 and 1860 and modestly popular beyond. *Baiting* involved chaining, tethering or cornering an animal and setting trained dogs to torment or attack it: this was favored by the British and American plebeian or working class. Typically, a bull would be brought by a butcher or farmer who would be paid to have it secured to a post while specially trained dogs were allowed to snap at and bite it. The bull, having been ripped by the dogs, would be slaughtered and its meat sold cheaply. Badger-baiting involved releasing dogs down a badger's set to chase it out. *Fighting* consisted of goading trained dogs or cocks into fighting each other until one rendered the other unable to continue. This was a more commercialized activity followed by the English aristocracy, according to Holt. *Hunting* for amusement was also popular in the period, the quarry being ducks, cats, bullocks, among other animals. Needless to say, some of these activities persist to the present day.

Between 1.5 to 2 million years ago, *Homo erectus* arrived on the scene in East Africa and, later, spread to Asia and Europe. A highly successful creature in evolutionary terms, *Homo erectus* survived up to about 100,000 years ago and instituted some significant adaptations. According to some theories of evolution, *Homo erectus* evolved into the earliest members of our species *Homo sapiens*, who were succeeded in Africa by the anatomically modern *Homo sapiens sapiens* and in Europe by *Homo sapiens neandertalensis*, or Neanderthals. *Homo erectus* was a respectful and cautious scavenger, though much evidence points to males banding together in predatory squads and becoming proficient hunters of large animals like bears, bison, and elephants and using equipment such as clubs and nets. Layers of charcoal and carbonized bone in Europe and China have also suggested that *Homo erectus* may have used fire. Physically, the male of the species might have stood as tall as 5 feet 11 inches (1.8 meters) and, while the brain was smaller than our own, the animal had enough intelligence to make primitive tools and hunting devices.

Neanderthals, who were well-established in Europe by 70,000 BC, certainly had sufficient intellect to use fire on a regular basis and utilized a crude technology in making weapons which, as predatory creatures, they needed. As their prey were the large and mobile bison, mammoth, and reindeer, they made good use not only of physical weapons but also of tact, or stealth. They would hunt in packs and allocate assignments to different members.

Other hints of social life are found amongst Neanderthals. Evidence of burials, for example, indicates an awareness of the significance of death; ritual burials are not conducted by species other than humans. There is also something uniquely human about the rapport with other species: the relationships humans have with other animals is an unusual one and Neanderthals may have been the first to forge this special link. It's possible that Neanderthals attempted to domesticate as well as hurt other species. The cartoon depiction of Fred Flintstone adorned in bearskins is actually more accurate than it seems: it's quite probable that the wearing of skins was thought to invest the wearer with some of the animal's qualities (such as strength of the mammoth or speed of the deer). The close association between many sports and animals is undoubtedly connected to this type of belief.

Some see Neanderthals as distinct from and having no breeding with *Homo sapiens*, while others see them gradually replaced by *Homo sapiens* after long periods of genetic mixing. Whether or not they were replaced or just became extinct, two facts are clear: one is technological, the other social. Neanderthals exploited raw materials for tool manufacture and use; they also displayed collective behavior in the division of labor they used to organize and co-ordinate their hunts. Related to these two activities is the fact that the reciprocal obligations systems used in hunting were carried over into domestic life. Neanderthals were cave dwellers and so used a home-base arrangement; this leads to the suggestion that they most probably constructed a stable pattern of life, possibly based on role allocation.

Homo sapiens shared these features: they used tools, hunted in groups, and had division of labor at the home base and especially in the hunting parties. Accepting responsibility for specific duties had obvious advantages for survival: co-ordinating tasks as a team would have brought more success than pell-mell approaches. Signals, symbols, markers, and cues would have been important to elementary strategies. Complementing this was the sharing of food at the central home base. Maybe this awakened humans to the advantages of pair-bonding and the joint provisioning of offspring: the mutual giving and receiving, or reciprocity, remaining the keystone of all human societies.

The hunter-gatherer mode of life is central to our understanding of the origin of sport. It began with foraging and scavenging as much as 3 million years ago; hunting as a regular activity followed a period of feeding off carcasses or spontaneous picking. Including more meat in the diet brought about nutritional changes, but also precipitated the invention of more efficient means of acquiring food. The response was to hunt for it – and this had widespread behavioral repercussions, not only in terms of social organization but also in physical development. Covering ground in pursuit of quarry required the kind of speed that could only be achieved by an efficient locomotion machine. The skeleton became a sturdier structure able to support the weight of bigger muscles and able quickly to transmit the force produced by the thrust of limbs against the ground. Lower limbs came to be more directly under the upper body, so that support was more efficient in motion; leg bones lengthened and the muscles elongated. enabling a greater stride and an ability to travel further with each step. The human evolved into a mobile and fast runner, and, though obviously not as fast as some other predators, the human's bipedalism left upper limbs free for carrying.

Where quarry was near enough to be approached, but also near enough to be disturbed, hunters would need short bursts of explosive speed, an ability to contract muscles and release energy anaerobically. In short, they needed the kind of power which modern sprinters possess. Hunts might take up an entire day and would demand of the hunter stamina, endurance, and the capacity to distribute output over long periods – precisely the type of aerobic work performed by middle-distance and marathon runners, not to mention triathletes.

Effective synthesis of ATP from ADP and the removal of waste lactic acid was enhanced by respiratory evolution. Ribs expanded and the muscles between them developed to allow the growth of lungs, which permitted deeper breathing to take in more and more air. Since the sustained release of energy depends on a supply of glucose and other foods, the hunter's diet was clearly important. While we can't be certain exactly what proportion of the diet was taken up by meat, we can surmise that this protein-rich food source played a role in balancing the daily expenditure of energy and providing enough fats and proteins for tissue repair.

Habitual meat-eating was not unqualified in its advantages; it introduced the very severe disadvantage of bringing humans into open competition with the large mammalian carnivores and scavengers like hogs, panthers, and tigers which roamed the savannahs looking for food. Ground speed was, in this instance, a requisite quality for survival, the clawless, weak-jawed biped being ill-equipped to confront the specialist predators. In time, evolution yielded a capacity to make and use not only tools but also weapons like clubs and stones, which at least evened up the odds. The physical clash with other animals continues to fascinate elements of the human population, a fact witnessed in such activities as bear-baiting, boxing kangaroos, and the type of man vs horse races in which Jesse Owens performed during the undignified twilight of his career (as we will see in Chapter 6).

A momentous change in the period, as we have noted, was the increase in the human's most important asset. The larger brain, with its larger neurons and denser, more complex circuitry of dendrite branches, may well have been related to the long days spent beneath the hot sun, hunting in comparative safety while the bigger predators sought shade and rest. Obscure as the relationship between brain growth and behavioral change may remain, we should at least recognize that neither are independent of the environment in which the processes take place. For instance, survival success would have depended on the ability to identify in the surrounding environment things that were needed: rocks for tools and weapons, tracks of game and competitive predators, sources of vegetable. The need to discriminate perceptually encouraged larger brains and better communication skills, which in turn occasioned bigger and better brains; these more complicated organs needed nourishment in terms both of food and social stimulation, and this would have been reflected in subsistence methods and social arrangements. The process had no "result" as such, for the brain constantly developed in response to behavioral change but at the same time triggered new thoughts that were translated into action: a continuous feedback motion.

Hunting, gathering, and, to a decreasing degree, scavenging were the main human adaptations. Among their correlates were division of labor, basic social organization, increases in communication, and, of course, increase in brain size. Slowly and steadily the species evolved ways of satisfying basic biological drives and needs: food supply, shelter against the elements and predators, sex and reproduction. In the process a prototype emerged: "man the hunter" (and I choose the phrase with care, as evidence suggests that the more robust males assumed most responsibility in catching prey). The species' greater brain capacity gave them the advantage of intellect, an ability to devise methods of tracking and capture, to utilize cunning and stealth as well as force. Concentration became important; intelligence enabled our ancestors to ignore distractions and fix attention on the sought-after game. Hunts, especially for large animals, would be more effectively performed in squads and these required a level of co-ordination, synchronization, and communication. Co-operation and reciprocity were qualities of great utility in hunting and at the home base, where the spoils would be shared.

The accumulated experience of the hunt itself would impart qualities – like courage in the face of dangerous carnivores who would compete for food. Risks were essential to reproductive success; if they had not been taken the species would still be picking fruit! Among the specific skills refined in this period would have been an ability to aim and accurately deliver missiles, a capacity to judge pace in movement, and to overwhelm and conquer prey when close combat was necessary. We might also take note of the fact that humans became impressively good swimmers and divers, evolving equipment and functions that aided deep diving and fast swimming; this aquatic adaptation may have been linked to hunting for fish.

All these features are responses to the manner in which the species procured its food: this is essential to life and so has a strong, if not determining effect on every aspect of both lifestyle and personality. If an existing method of obtaining food does not yield enough nutrition, then bodies suffer and the species either perishes or makes new adaptations, perhaps formulating alternative methods. In the event, what seems to have happened in the case of *Homo sapiens* is that they hit upon a novel way of guaranteeing a food supply which eliminated the need for many of the activities that had persisted for the previous 2 million years or more, and had carved deeply the features of human character and capacities. As recently as 10,000 years ago, *Homo sapiens* devised a way of exploiting the food supply which was to remove the necessity of hunting and release humans to concentrate on building what is now popularly known as "civilization."

Instead of exploiting natural resources around them, the species began to exploit its own ability. In short, the ability to create a food supply. This was accomplished by gathering animals and crops together, containing them in circumstances that permitted their growth and reproduction, then picking crops or slaughtering animals as necessary, without ever destroying the entire stock. In this way, supply was rendered a problem only by disease or inclement weather. The practice of cultivating land for use, rather than for mere existence, gave rise to farming.

Recreating the hunt

Although now open to debate, the beginnings of agriculture are seen in orthodox teaching to coincide with the end of what is called the paleolithic age. The transition was seen by some as swift and dramatic, though the view has been challenged by others who accentuate the uneven process of development over periods of time. For example, in Europe, following the recession of the ice age, there appears to have been an interlude in which certain animals, especially dogs, were domesticated, some cereals were harvested, and forms of stock management were deployed, but without the systematic approach of later agriculturalists.

Obviously, regions differed considerably ecologically, and the period characterized by the transition from hunter-gatherer to farmer was neither smooth nor uniform. But it was sudden – in evolutionary terms, that is. Only as recently as 10,000 years ago do we see the systematic domestication of animals – a process central to agriculture. It may have taken the form of controlled breeding or just providing fodder to attract wild herds, but the insight was basically the same: that enclosing and nourishing livestock was a far more effective and reliable way of ensuring food than hunting for it.

Paleolithic age

From *palaios*, the Greek for ancient times, and *lithos*, meaning stone, this describes the period in which primitive stone implements were used. Beginning probably 2 million years ago when our ancestors put an edge on a stone, pressed its thick end against the palm of the hand and realized its power to strike and cut, this age saw the arrival of the hunter-gatherer, as opposed to the simple forager cultures. It ended as recently as 10,000 years ago, when the domestication of animals and cultivation of plants started.

Complementing this discovery was the realization that planting and nurturing plants and harvesting only enough to meet needs so that regrowth was possible was an efficient exploitation of natural resources compared to the cumbersome and less predictable gathering method. The breakthroughs spawned all manner of toolmaking and other technologies that added momentum to the agricultural transformation that is loosely referred to as the neolithic age (from the Greek *neo* meaning new and *lithos* meaning stone: a period when ground and polished tools and weapons were introduced).

What we need to remind ourselves of is that hunting and gathering had been dominant for more than two million years before. During that period the lifestyle and mentality it demanded became components of our character. Chasing, capturing, and killing with their attendant dangers were practiced features of everyday life. The qualities of courage, skill, and the inclination to risk, perhaps even to sacrifice on occasion, were not heraldic but simply human and necessary for survival. What we would now regard as epic moments were in all probability quite "ordinary." The coming of farming made most of these qualities and features redundant. The hunting parties that honed their skills, devised strategies and traded on courage were no longer needed. Instead, the successful farmer needed to be diligent, patient, responsible, regular, and steadfast. A farmer was more interested in breeding animals than in hunting them. The switch was bound to introduce strains.

Hunting and gathering affected us not only socially but perhaps even genetically, so long and sweeping was its reign. No organism is a product purely of hereditary nature or of environmental experience. Humans are no different in being products of the interaction between genes and the environment. But the kind of evolutionary change we are interested in proceeded at different levels: the human way of living changed, but not in such a way as to incur an automatic switch in human beings themselves. After all, even rough arithmetic tells us that the 10,000 years in which agriculture has developed represents at most 0.5 percent of the period spent hunting and gathering. Sport, in this scenario, is the evidence that we are still catching up with the changes. It is as if cultural evolution sped ahead of biological evolution: we did not completely change from one type of organism into another as quickly as the cultural pace required. There was still too much of the hunter-gatherer in us to permit an easy settling down to breeding animals and sowing crops.

One response to this strain was to re-enact the hunt: imitate the chase, mimic the prey, copy the struggle, simulate the kill, and recreate the conditions under which such properties as bravery and resolution would be rewarded. It was a fairly minor but important adaptation in which the customary skills, techniques, and habits were retained even when their original purpose had disappeared. It made far more sense to enclose, feed, and domesticate animals than to hunt them, as it did to sow crops rather than gather wild fruits and grains. It was perfectly possible to acknowledge this, while craving the *frisson* the hunts used to bring. How could the spirit of the hunt be recaptured? The answer was: let it continue. Hunt for its own sake rather than for food. No matter that hunting served no obvious purpose any longer, let people engage in it for the sheer pleasure or excitement it generated. In this way, people played at hunting: they did not direct their efforts to meeting the immediate material needs of life, or acquiring necessities. Hunting became instead an *autotelic* activity, having no purpose apart from its own existence.

> **Autotelic**
> From the Greek *auto*, meaning by or for itself, and *telos*, meaning end. An autotelic activity is one which has an end or purpose in itself and is engaged in for no external purpose.

Once it became detached from the food supply, the activity took on a life of its own. When survival no longer depended on killing game, the killing became an end; what was once an evolutionary means to an end became an end in itself. The new hunt no longer had as its motive the pursuit of food but rather the pursuit of new challenges. Although in behavioral terms much the same activity as hunting, the new version was an embryonic sports or at least an expression of the drive or impulse underlying sports right to the present day. Stripped of its original purpose, the processual aspects of the activity came to prominence. Team co-ordination, stealth, intelligence, daring, physical prowess, and courage in the face of danger were valued more than the end product and, over time, these became integrated into a series of activities, each in some way mimicking the original activities.

It sounds trite to say that the roots of sports lie in our primeval past when so many of today's sports operate not in response to survival but as adjuncts to commercial interests. At the same time, we should recognize that the impulses that make sports attractive enough to be commercially exploited are part of our evolutionary make-up. Sport was the result of the attempt to reintroduce the excitement and thrill of the hunt into lives that were threatened with mundane routines in unchallenging environments. As such it was and remains both precious and profound. It may owe nothing to the hunt nowadays; but it still owes a good deal to the attempts at replacing the hunt with something comparably as exciting. So, there is perfect sense in Gerhard Lukas's claim that "the first sport was spear throwing" (or *speer worfen*) (1969). Darts, blowguns, and bows and arrows were modifications of the basic projectile and unquestionably featured in mock as well as genuine hunts. The use of the bow is interesting in that it stimulated the construction of an artifact, the target, the bull's eye, which, as its name implies, represented the part of the animal to be aimed at. Archery, as a purely autotelic behavior, actually had the quality of compressing a symbolic hunt into a finite area and allowing a precise way of assessing the results. As such, it had potential as an activity that could be watched and evaluated by others, who would not participate except in a vicarious way (that is, they might experience it imaginatively through the participants – which is what most sports spectators do, even today).

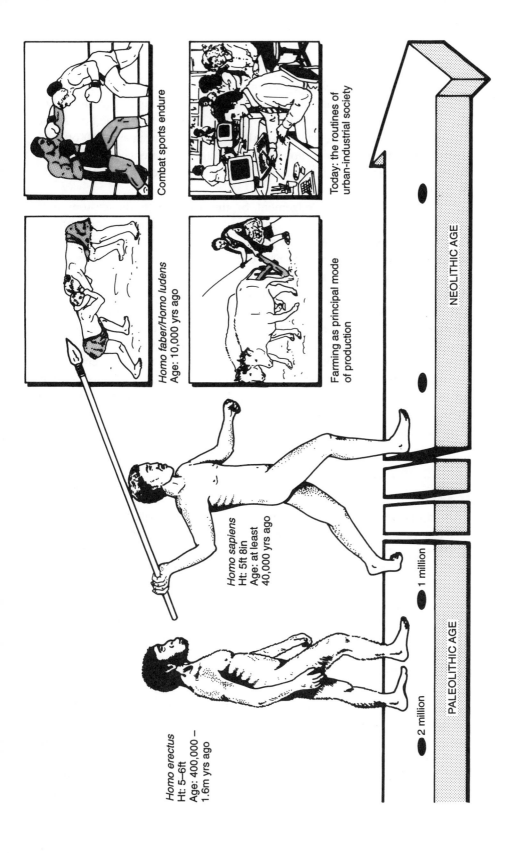

Homo erectus
Ht: 5–6ft
Age: 400,000 –
1.6m yrs ago

Homo sapiens
Ht: 5ft 8in
Age: at least
40,000 yrs ago

Combat sports endure

Homo faber/Homo ludens
Age: 10,000 yrs ago

Today: the routines of
urban-industrial society

Farming as principal mode
of production

2 million

1 million

PALEOLITHIC AGE

NEOLITHIC AGE

This vicariousness was, as we now realize, absolutely crucial to the emergence and development of sport. The facility for bringing the rationality and emotion of a hunt to a home base made it possible to include dozens, or hundreds, of people in the whole experience. Just witnessing an event offered some continuity, however tenuous, within change: spectators could "feel" the drama and tension of a supposed hunt from another age, through the efforts of the participants.

The obvious acknowledgement of this came with the custom-built stadia. These came with the clustering together of human populations and the creation of city-states. Irrigation was crucial to farming, of course, so most of the earliest known civilizations had their urban centers near rivers, as in China, India, and the Near and Middle East. Richard Mandell, in his *Sport: A Cultural History* (1984) urges caution in gleaning evidence of what we now call spectator sports in ancient civilizations. But he does show that the Mesopotamians, for example, left traces of evidence that suggest physical competitions. These might have been tests of strength and skill; though they may also have been more military training regimes than amusements for the masses. The seminal Egyptian civilization of some 5,000 years ago left much material in the form of documents, frescos, tombs, and bric-a-brac. In these we find depicted one of the most essential, enduring, and unchanging activities, and one which we will consider in the next section: combat.

State
An organized administrative apparatus in which a single government is empowered to rule. Governments may change, but the bureaucracy stays essentially intact, giving a stability and continuity to the state and its main institutions. See Chapter 12 for an analysis of the contemporary state's intrusion in sport.

In pursuit of *agon*

At some stage in ancient history, the idea of rivalry seems to have struck chords. The straightforward drive of the hunt, in which packs pursued game, acquired a provision. The object was not merely the climax of a kill, but in administering the kill faster or more effectively than others. Competition between individuals or groups added a new and apparently appealing dimension to an already perilous activity, turning it into a game with some semblance of organization and a clear understanding of what constituted an achievement. The amusement value, it seems, was boosted by the introduction of a human challenge and by spectatorship.

It is probable, though undocumented, that physical combat activities between humans and perhaps animals coexisted with the autotelic hunts. We need not invoke the Cain and Abel fable to support the argument that intra-species fighting, for both instrumental and playful purposes, existed throughout history. It is one of the least changeable aspects of *Homo sapiens*. Combat has many different forms, ranging from wrestling to fencing; stripped to its basics, it expresses the rawest type of competition. As such, it seems to have held a wide appeal both for participants seeking a means to express their strength and resilience and for audiences who to this day are enraptured by the sight of humans disputing each other's physical superiority.

The hunt, or at least the mimetic activity that replaced it, would have satisfied a certain need for those closely involved, but the actual behavior would have been so fluid and dispersed that it would not have been closely observed, certainly not as a complete and integrated action. Spectators would have been much more easily accommodated at a home base where fighting could be staged in much the same way and with a similar purpose to mock hunts: to break up tedious routines and raise emotions with brief but thrilling and relatively unpredictable episodes of violent action. The emphasis may well have fallen on animal fighting, unarmed human combat and, possibly, armed humans pitched against large animals such as bears or tigers. Given the purpose of this type of combat, some loose structure or framework governing the fight was likely; combatants fighting to kill or disable an opponent in order to save themselves in any way possible would be warring rather than engaging in a sport.

A fresco excavated from the tomb of an Egyptian prince and dated to about 4,000 years ago looks similar to a modern wall chart and shows wrestlers demonstrating over a hundred different positions and holds. Mandell suggests that there may have been professional wrestlers in the Egyptian civilization. Artwork shows fighters also using sticks about one-meter long; even today, stick fighting persists in parts of Egypt, though in a more ritualized form. It is quite possible that the proximity to the Nile encouraged competitive swimming and rowing. In the plains of the Upper Nile region, hunting of large game, including elephants, was commonplace, the chariot being an effective vehicle for this purpose. Pharaoh Tutankhamun (fourteenth century BC) is shown on one fresco hunting lions from his chariot. Amphibian Nile dwellers like crocodiles and hippopotamuses were also hunted. Crete had trade contacts with Egypt and some kind of cultural cross-fertilization is possible. Certainly, Cretans were avid hunters and their relics suggest they were combat enthusiasts also, though the form of fighting they favored seems more akin to boxing than wrestling. We also have evidence of a version of bull-fighting, and a type of cattle wrestling that resembles the modern rodeo in the United States.

The mythical and the mundane are intertwined in our knowledge of Greek civilization, popularly and justifiably regarded as the first culture to incorporate sports or, more specifically, competition, into civic life. The compulsion to pursue public recognition of one's supremacy through open contest with others was known by the Greeks as *agon*. Athletic excellence achieved in competition was an accomplishment of, literally, heroic proportions. Myths of Hercules sending discuses into oblivion and Odysseus heaving boulders are important signifiers of the high value Greeks placed on physical feats, but the less spectacular evidence shows that they approached, organized, and assessed the outcomes of activities in a way which is quite familiar.

Their approach was to win, and here we find the almost obsessional drive for success that characterizes much of modern sport: winning was quite often at any cost and scant respect was paid to such things as "fairness." Some may argue that the search for supremacy is a primordial competitive instinct. It is more likely that particular social arrangements in which inequality and distinct strata are key components encourage individuals to strive hard and "better themselves" by whatever means they can. Athletic prowess was one such means in the ancient civil society of Greece – the *polis*. Victors could acquire *arete* (excellence), the ultimate attainment.

In terms of organization, Greeks created events which exist today without major modification. They are credited with being the first organizers of sports on a systematic basis, the Olympic games, which began in 776 BC, being the clearest expression of this. This event integrated sports into a wider festival, drawing disparate competitors and spectators together at one site every four years in an effort to convince themselves they were in some sense united. Greeks were also influential in their attempts to determine outcomes. Despite aphorisms about competing being more important than winning, victory was crucial and systems were designed to ensure accurate assessment of performance.

Exact distances were measured and staggers were introduced on racing circuits. Tallies of points were kept in multi-discipline events like the pentathlon. Records of performances were kept (each Olympiad took the name of the victorious sprinter at the previous festival). The games may have been less important as a spectacle than they were as a focal point around which to organize training. Physical fitness, strength, and the general toughness that derives from competition were important military attributes, and so the process was tuned to producing warriors as much as sports performers. Sparta is the best-known city-state in this context: it was a site of phalanx training in which youths would be taken from their families and reared in an austere garrison where they would be honed for combat. There was also a religious element to competition, for the Greeks believed that athletic victory indicated that the victor would be favored by the capricious gods in whom they believed.

Whatever the motivation in striving to achieve, we can be sure that the Greeks went to great lengths in their preparations and so provided something of a prototype for what we now call training. Spartans in particular used a cyclical pattern of increasing and decreasing the intensity of preparations which is used in most modern sports. The very concept of preparation is important: recognizing that excellence does not spring spontaneously but is the product of periods of heavy labor and disciplined regimes prompted the Greeks to provide facilities. So, in the sixth century BC, we see a new type of building called a gymnasium (meaning, literally, an exercise for which one strips).

By the time of the Greeks' refinements, sports had undergone changes in purpose and, indeed, nature. While the content showed clear lines of descent connecting it with more basic hunting and combat, the functions it served were quite novel: it was seen as a military training activity, as a vehicle for status-gaining, or what we might now refer to as social mobility, and as a way of securing divine favor. This does not deny that the impulses associated with hunting and gathering were present, but it does highlight the autonomy of sports once separated from its original conditions of creation and growth. The Greek adaptation was a response to new material and psychic requirements. Powerful Greek city-states needed defense against outside attacks and they ensured this by encouraging and rewarding warriors. Accompanying the development of the *polis* was the growth of the state's control over human expressions of violence; sophisticated social organization and internal security were impossible without some regulation of violence. The state's response was to obtain a legitimate monopoly over violence and establish norms of behavior which discouraged the open expression of violence by citizens and encouraged saving violence for the possible repulsion of attacks from outside powers. Contests, challenges, and rivalries were ways in which the impulse could reassert itself, but in socially acceptable forms.

The value of sports earned it a central place in Greek civilization and the importance of this is reinforced by writers such as Huizinga and Elias, who stress that the process of becoming civilized itself implicates a culture in controlling violence while at the same time carving out "enclaves" for the "ritualized expression of physical violence." We will return to the theory in the next chapter, but should note the basic observation that sport serves as a legitimate means through which primitive, violence-related impulses and emotions can simultaneously be engendered *and* contained. Much of what the ancients would have regarded as expressions of civilization would be seen as barbarous from the standpoint of the late twentieth century. Gouging, biting, breaking, and the use of spiked fist thongs were all permissible in Greek combat. But these were occasions for the exhibition of warrior-like qualities and mercy was not such a quality. While victory was a symbolic "kill" it was also, at times, a quite literal kill.

For Romans, part of the appeal of sports lay in the climax of killing. One of their innovations of Greek sports was in establishing preparatory schools exclusively for gladiators, who would sooner or later be publicly feted or slaughtered. The actual events would be staged in hippodromes, cavernous stadia where spectators would joyously witness the death of one human being either by another or by a beast. Influenced in large part by Greek activities, Romans held foot races, chariot races, and many types of one-to-one combat in the centuries either side of the start of the Christian era. They were also aware of the immense military advantages of having a fit, disciplined, and tempered population. It was expensive to train gladiators, especially if they were all to be killed, so convicted prisoners and slaves were virtually sacrificed.

Adding to the extravagance was the cost of importing animals: wild beasts from throughout the world were captured, transported, and nourished. For five or more centuries, hundreds of thousands of beasts were brought into the coliseum and other stadia and, watched by massed audiences, pitched against each other or against humans. Death seems to have been an accepted part of this activity. There was nothing curious about the Romans' apparent lack of interest when it came to hunting (no artifacts to suggest much interest). They had no need to leave their cities: the hunts were effectively transferred to the stadia where audiences could satisfy their appetites for violence, or their "blood lusts," as some might say. Gladiatorial conflicts featuring wild animals were comparable to the primitive hunts; the comparisons between human combat and today's fighting sports are clear.

Nowadays, there are few deaths to observe in sporting combat, and when tragedy does strike it leads to a period of earnest self-reflection as well as attacks from medical authorities on the "barbaric" nature of such activities. The fact remains: audiences are amused and excited by the prospect of human combat, as they are by animal conflict – about which there is much less restraint, as the slaughter in bull-fighting, cock-fighting, and hare-coursing suggests. The threshold of tolerance has dropped, but this is largely a function of the cultural forces that emanate from civilization: the human proclivity to watch, enjoy, and appreciate the infliction of damage during combat does not seem to waver. Perhaps we are not so dissimilar to our Roman ancestors who wallowed in the bloodletting and cheerfully pointed their thumbs to the floor to answer the question, life or death.

The gladiatorial schools finally closed after Christian opposition in AD 399. In the following century, the combat grew less deadly and was superseded as an entertainment by less expensive chariot racing, which was arguably the first mass spectator event, drawing crowds of up to 250,000 to the Circus Maximus. Chariot racing required teams, each team wearing different-colored uniforms and the winners receiving prize money as well as garlands. There is a stunning recreation of a Roman chariot race in the William Wyler movie from 1959, *Ben-Hur*; the race sequence remains one of the most exhilarating film depictions of sport.

It has been argued that Roman sports assumed a political character in this period. With no genuinely democratic means of representation, the populations may well have grown restive and demanded change were it not for the diversionary effect of the combat and racing. The entertainment that drew crowds in their hundreds of thousands diverted their attention, if only temporarily, from their grievances and so served the function of maintaining the *status quo*. Masses were distracted and amused, if not by bread by circuses. The theme was updated in the Schwarzenegger movie *The Running Man* set in a totalitarian future in which "have-nots" are kept docile by a competition in which convicted criminals are pursued through a maze by "stalkers" – athletes trained to kill. "The public wants sports and violence," observes the competition's MC. "We give them what they want." We will consider the scholarly attempts to portray today's sports in a similar way later.

Sports and spectacle

Beside the civilizations of Egypt, Greece, and Rome, other cultures emerging in the pre-Christian era had activities resembling sport, though in this historical context we should observe Mandell's caveat that "the boundaries that we moderns use to separate 'sport' from other areas of human endeavor have been indistinct or not worth noticing in other cultures" (1984: 93). So, we can't be certain that the swimming, diving, and combat, armed and unarmed, practiced by inhabitants of South Asia around 2,500 years ago approached what we would recognize as sport; they may have had a more specific traditional significance, possibly bound up in the caste system.

Similarly, the equestrian pursuits of the Chinese, together with their competitive archery, may have been based less on recreation or amusement and more on military training. Yet as with Greeks and Romans, the activities themselves have been adapted to suit changing circumstances. For example, the sport we call polo almost certainly started life as a Chinese method of target practice. Many of China's martial exercises, which could be used competitively, were functional and were used to maintain a high level of fitness amongst the working population. Japanese industries have successfully adopted this ancient policy, holding exercise sessions before work in modern factories.

The Chinese were probably the first to employ a ball effectively, though there is evidence that the Egyptians experimented. In northern China there was a primitive kicking game. The Chinese invented a projectile that was the forerunner of the shuttlecock and, presumably, propelled it by means of some sort of racket or bat.

The military importance of the horse, especially fast and maneuverable breeds, is obvious and the Japanese perhaps more than any other population recognized this in their sporting traditions. Their competitive shows of speed and intricacy have clear counterparts in today's horse-oriented events, including dressage. Japan's legacy of martial arts is large and well known; combat in the feudal age of the *samurai* was based on several ancient disciplines and included the mastery of horses, weapons, and unarmed conflict.

Many of the skills survive, though with modifications. The pattern that emerges in Japan as elsewhere is the use of sport as a military exercise as well as a pursuit to retain interest and capture enthusiasm while preparing its participants for the more practical discipline of defense. Wherever we find a cavalry, we almost invariably discover some form of competitive endeavor involving the horse. Typically, the competitors would be something of an elite, with resources and possibly patronage enough to compete and serve; they may well have been lionized as Greek heroes were. Certainly in medieval Europe, armed knights were the basis of the continent's supremacy and glory. The knights would be served by peasants and would enjoy status, though in material terms they may not have been much better off.

Practice fights between mounted knights gave rise to a form of combat known as jousting and, as modern fans are drawn by sparring sessions or exhibition games, spectators stood in line as the combatants galloped toward each other, lances extended. The object was to tilt the lance at the adversary in an attempt to unseat him. As the jousts gained popularity they were surrounded by pomp and ritual, and formal tournaments were lavish affairs attended and heavily patronized by nobility. Jousting became an expensive pursuit quite beyond the reach of the peasantry, and indeed beyond all apart from the wealthy landowners whom the jousters served. Peasants would merely look on as the often huge and elaborate tournaments unfolded. The combat was frequently along territorial lines, as in a 1520 tournament in northern France between King Henry VIII of England and King Francis I of France. A truly "international" event, it was spread over three weeks and attended by dozens of thousands.

Jousting, as with the many other forms of combat, had the military purpose of keeping knights in good fighting shape, but may have been transformed into an alternative to warring. Disputes could be settled less expensively and more enjoyably by tournaments than by costly internecine battles. From the twelfth to sixteenth centuries, tournaments became more organized and orderly, as did European society as a whole. Accommodation was made for spectators, scaffolds and stands being built as the jousts grew more popular and attracted large crowds. After the sixteenth century, the grand tournaments faded and rural events emerged, though tilts were often at targets, not humans. The tournaments gradually changed character from being hard-edged and competitive; "from sports to spectacle" is how Allen Guttmann describes the change in his book *Sports Spectators* (1986). The process is familiar to anyone who has witnessed the transmutation of wrestling after it became a popular spectator "sport."

Hunting and archery coexisted with jousting and outlasted it, though never attracting comparable numbers of spectators. Archery survived virtually intact and is today an Olympic event; the old longbows have been considerably modified, of course. Civic festivals were organized around competitions and were grand occasions, drawing vast crowds to pageants all over Europe. The stag- and fox-hunts were direct predecessors of the modern fox-hunts, with the rich amusing themselves by setting free their hounds and giving pursuit; the poor would amuse themselves by pursuing them all.

Cock-fighting

This probably has origins in ancient China and Persia. Greeks may have become aware of it after their victory over Persia at Salamis in 480 BC and, in turn, introduced it to the Romans. For Greeks, the courage of fighting birds was regarded as exemplary: youths were encouraged to watch and emulate the birds' tenacity and valor in combat. Later, it became a mere source of entertainment, especially for gamblers. It first appeared in England in the twelfth century, though its popularity waxed and waned until the sixteenth century when Henry VIII built a royal cock-pit at his palace. In the eighteenth and nineteenth centuries, cocks were bought and sold, bred and trained in a more organized way, one trainer, Joseph Gulliver, acquiring quite a reputation. Cock-fighting was banned in 1835 but is known to persist in the USA and Britain.

Hunts and other "blood sports" continued to enjoy popularity among lower classes, whose penchant for watching tethered bears prodded with sticks and then set upon by fierce dogs is similar to that of the spectators who gathered at the Roman coliseum centuries before. Cock-fights, which have almost universal appeal, were held in England from about the twelfth century and attracted audiences from the various classes. As we saw from the description at the beginning of this chapter, the activities frequently ended in dead, dying or seriously hurt animals. Hugh Cunningham, in his *Leisure in the Industrial Revolution*, relates a Sunday morning meeting in London in 1816 at which several hundred people were assembled in a field adjoining a church yard. In the field, "they fight dogs, hunt ducks, gamble, enter into subscriptions to fee drovers for a bullock." The Rector of the nearby church observed: "I have seen them drive the animal through the most populous parts of the parish, force sticks pointed with iron, up the body, put peas into the ears, and infuriate the beast" (1980: 23).

Although condemned systematically from the eighteenth century, blood sports persist to this day, most famously in the Spanish bull rings and in the streets of Pamplona. England's bull ring, in Birmingham, reminds us that such events were not always confined to Spain; bull running ceased in England in 1825, a year after the founding of the Royal Society for the Prevention of Cruelty to Animals (RSPCA). The same organization brought pressure against cock-fighting, which was banned in 1835, only to go "underground" as an illicit, predominantly working-class pursuit.

The decline of cock-fighting, bull-baiting and the like coincided with cultural changes that brought with them a range of alternative leisure pursuits. The whole spectrum of changes were part of what some writers have called the civilizing process – which we will cover in more detail in the next chapter. But, before we are tempted into assuming that barbaric tastes and activities have completely disappeared, we should stay mindful of Holt's caution: "The tendency by members of all social classes to maltreat animals for excitement or gain is by no means dead even today" (1990: 24). Dog fighting in particular persists in the West to this day and dogs are bred for the specific purpose of fighting. In the early 1990s, amid a panic over the number of ferocious breeds proliferating, the British banned the import of American pit bulls (such animals are required to be registered in Britain under the Dangerous Dogs Act, 1991; there are about 5,000 unregistered pit bulls trained for fighting rather than as pets). And, as if to remind us of our retrograde thirst for blood, a police operation in County Durham, north-east England, in 1995 yielded six arrests, the recovery of 14 dead cockerels and 40 live birds and implements, including sharpened spurs (probably imported from the USA), weighing machinery and a board that listed names, weights and betting odds on the birds.

Blood sports in general and fox-hunting in particular are seen as having central importance by Norbert Elias and his collaborator Eric Dunning. The "civilizing" of society demanded greater personal self-control and a stricter constraint on violence, but the process of hunting or just observing allowed "all the pleasures and the excitement of the chase, as it were, mimetically in the form of wild play" (1986). While the passion and exhilaration associated

> **Mimetic**
> From the Greek *mimesis* for imitation, this describes an activity that imitates or resembles another, and which is carried out especially for amusement. A child may mimetically play cowboys-and-indians or adult members of Round Table organizations may imitate battles, albeit in a mock way.

with hunting would be aroused, the actual risks would be absent in the imagined version (except for the animals, of course) and the effects of watching would be, according to Elias and Dunning, "liberating, cathartic."

The comments could be applied without alteration to all of the activities considered so far. They are products of a human imagination ingenious enough to create artificial situations that human evolution has rendered irrelevant. But, once created, they have seemed to exert a control and power of their own, eliciting in both participants and audience a pleasurable excitement that encapsulates the thrill or "rush" of a hunt, yet carries none of the attendant risks.

History shows that activities which at least resemble sports are rarely purely autotelic and can be augmented with other purposes. From ancient to medieval ages, the tendency was to imbue supposed sporting activities with a military purpose, often encouraging qualities within participants that were of obvious utility in serious combat. We also find a subtheme in sports history in which many of the main roles were occupied by privileged or elite groups who performed, while most of the supporting roles were played by peasantry or plebeians who watched. The public provision of entertainment by the powerful had a latent political function in diverting attention away from *realpolitik* and animating sentiments and emotions that were not challenging to the established order of things.

> **Realpolitik**
> This refers to political realities based on material needs rather than on, for example, the ambitions and ideals to which sports appeal.

Human relationships with other animals have been peculiarly ambivalent. Dogs, for instance, have been domesticated and cared for, and used to hunt other more vulnerable creatures and to retrieve birds which have been killed. Many other animals have simply been used as expendable prey, an observation that gives credence to the view that, while the hunt as a survival mechanism has receded, the violent impulses that it once fostered remain. Animal abuses very gradually declined in the long period under review and, though they have been under pressure this century, they certainly have not disappeared in the modern era. Animal uses, as opposed to abuses (though the distinction may not be acceptably clear-cut for everyone), are still very much with us, as dog-racing and horse-racing, remind us. The previously mentioned Iditarod in which packs of huskies pull a sled for eight days and nights in temperatures of –60 degrees is an organized competition in which the driver talks to, becomes as tough as, and even sleeps with his dogs, according to Gary Paulsen (1994).

This close relationship with animals suggests a continuity in sports and one which, if traced back, has its origins in the transition from hunter-gatherer to farmer. While the connecting thread appears at times to be only tenuous, we can infer that there is surely some human property that elicits a desire for a form of autotelic enterprise based on competition. The way in which it manifests itself differs from culture to culture, and in this chapter I have pulled out only fragments from history to illustrate the general argument. The impression is still clear enough to draw a plausible scenario and one in which a basic impulse continues to operate in widely different contexts. In most of these contexts, some spectacle was made of violence. Despite the ostensibly civilizing forces at work, physical cruelty and the infliction of damage on others continued to attract and entertain people. But, in the nineteenth century, very sharp and dramatic changes took place, particularly in Europe, that were to affect the sensitivity to, and public acceptance of, violence, and this was to have an impact on the entire shape and focus of sport. It was also to establish the framework of what would now legitimately pass for sport.

FURTHER READING

Sports in America: From wicked amusement to national obsession edited by David Wiggins (Human Kinetics, 1995) collects 19 essays organized into five parts: (1) Pre-1820; (2) 1820–70; (3) 1870–1915; (4) 1915–45; (5) 1945–Present. The third part, dealing with industrialization and urbanization is especially relevant; in this, various writers focus on the period 1870–1915.

History of Sport and Physical Activity in the United States, 4th edn, by Betty Spears and Richard A. Swanson (Brown & Benchmark, 1995) is one of the most respected and durable histories of North American sport and should be read in conjunction with *Sports Spectators* by Allen Guttmann (Columbia University Press, 1986) which is densely packed with historical detail on the emergence of sport. Guttmann's focus is far wider than that implied by the title and actually provides a basis for understanding sport. "We are what we watch," writes Guttmann toward the end of the book that captures how sports can be used as a barometer of historical change and one which should be read by any serious student of sport.

Richard Holt's books, *Sport and the Working Class in Modern Britain* (Manchester University Press, 1990) and *Sports and the British* (Oxford University Press, 1989), examine what now seem to be crude forms of sports and reveal the links between these and today's versions. Older activities gradually faded as industrialization encroached and cultural patterns changed, but Holt emphasizes the continuities and "survivals" from old to new. Complementing these is Hugh Cunningham's *Leisure in the Industrial Revolution* (Croom Helm, 1980).

Combat Sports in the Ancient World by Michael Poliakoff (Yale University Press, 1987) describes in fine detail the early forms of combat, such as the Greeks' pankration ("total fight") and Egyptian wrestling. "The will to win is a basic human instinct, but different societies give varying amounts of encouragement (or discouragement) to the individual's attempt to measure himself against others," observes Poliakoff in his chapter entitled "The nature and purpose of combat sport." Elliott J. Gorn's *The Manly Art: Bare-knuckle prize fighting in America* (Cornell University Press, 1986) updates the argument.

ASSIGNMENT

Cock-fighting and boxing: these are two sports that have deep historical roots, but which have aroused controversy. Cock-fighting is illegal; and both American and British Medical Associations lobby for a ban on boxing. Despite its illegality, cock-fighting persists underground. Defenders of boxing argue that, if banned, boxing would also go underground, making it more dangerous. But, one might contend that drug-taking is a widespread underground activity and that does not mean we should legalize it. Compare boxing and drug-taking, taking into account that both cost lives, yet both are engaged in by young people on a voluntary basis. If one is legal, should the other be?

The Great Debates I
Is fox-hunting a sport?

Elias's historical research shows us that, at one stage, fox-hunting was the quint-essential sport, embodying all the elements that were later to become refined into organized sport. But, today, it seems an anachronism.

Those who say it *IS NOT* argue:

- It is cruel, inflicting unnecessary suffering on foxes.

- The hunt deliberately prolongs the process of killing.

- It is an activity practiced only by those rich enough to indulge themselves.

- It bears little resemblance to contemporary sports.

Those who say it *IS* argue:

- Hunting is, by comparison with other methods, a humane way of killing foxes.

- Thousands of hounds bred purely to hunt would have to be put down.

- Foxes are rural pests, preying on fowl and other forms of wildlife.

- A ban on hunting is a "thin end of the wedge" leading to bans on other sports involving animals.

Chapter five

The hunt for reasons
Theories of sports

Tenor of life, tempo of work

One of the fashionable haunts of the nobility and upper classes
in the early eighteenth century was James Figg's amphitheatre
in London. Figg, himself a swordsman and all-round fighter,
opened the venue in 1719 and attracted large crowds to watch
displays of animal baiting as well as human contests, featuring
swords, fists, and staffs. No sexism, here: Figg held contests
between and amongst men and women. Figg's cachet brought
him appointments as a tutor to the gentry, instructing in the
"art of self-defense," which was regarded in those days as very
much a gentleman's pursuit.

There was very little gentlemanly restraint in the actual
contests, which were bare-knuckle affairs without either a
specified number of rounds or a points-scoring system. A match
was won when one fighter was simply unable to continue. Three-
and four-hour contests were commonplace, with wrestling
throws, kicks, and punches all permissible. Such types of
combat were rife in England in Figg's time (he died in 1734)
and drew on what was ancient tradition, as we have noted.
(Homer's *Iliad* makes reference to competitive bouts.) No
doubt similar forms of combat took place in other parts of the
world in the eighteenth century though, in England, fighting
was to undergo a special transformation.

71

At about the same time as Figg's venture, another combat activity was gaining popularity, at least in parts of Great Britain. Ball games such as Cornwall's "hurling" and Wales's "knappan" were local exercises, very loosely organized according to customs rather than central rules and were played with an inflated animal bladder. Ancient Greeks and Romans also used pig or ox bladders, though they tended to fill them with hair and feathers, more suited to throwing than the fast kicking games that became popular much later. In the intervening centuries ball games were always peripheral to activities such as combat, racing, or archery, but in the nineteenth century they seemed to "take off."

I describe ball games as different to "combat activity" although it seems that at least some variants of what was to evolve into football allowed participants to complement their delicate ball-playing skills with cudgels and other instruments that Mr Figg and his associates would have been adept at using. Meetings would have resembled an all-out struggle much more than a practiced, rule-bound game with clearly defined goals and final results.

But violence was popular and the rough and wild "folk games," as Eric Dunning and Kenneth Sheard call them in *Barbarians, Gentlemen and Players* (1979), were "closer to 'real' fighting than modern sports." The authors suggest that football's antecedents reflected the "violent tenor of life in society at large" and also the low threshold of repugnance "with regard to witnessing and engaging in violent acts." Sometimes, the distinction between witnessing and engaging became blurred and spectators would join in the action.

It's rather artificial to link these pursuits of the eighteenth century with modern boxing or wrestling and soccer or rugby football; first, because of the regional variations and, second, because of combinations of rules and characteristics that made any systematic differentiation of games impossible. Yet, somehow, the essentials of both activities have dropped into the stream of history and arrived in the 1990s as well-ordered, highly structured, and elaborately organized sports. I use the two examples because they embody currents and changes that have affected the entire assortment of activities that have become modern sport. The decline in spontaneity and open brutality in sports mirrored trends in society generally.

The new rules of prize-fighting, instituted in 1838, introduced some measure of regulation, including a "scratch" line which was a mark in the center of a 24-foot square ring which competitors had to reach unassisted at the start of each round, or else be judged the loser (that is, "not coming up to scratch"). It was a small but significant modification that removed the necessity of a beating into submission or a knockout to terminate a bout. In 1886, Queensberry rules were devised to reduce the degree of bodily damage possible and to increase the importance of skill as a decisive factor in the "noble art."

The same forces affecting combat helped reshape football, taking out some of its ferocity and establishing sets of rules in what was previously a maelstrom. In 1863, the Football Association was formed to regulate the kicking form of the sport. The version that stressed handling was brought under the control of the Rugby Union, which was created in 1871. The Union split into distinct amateur and professional organizations in 1895, the latter being known as Rugby League (which remained confined to the northern counties of England).

In both cases, the organizations were responses to demands for orderliness and standardization. England had metamorphosed into an industrial society where the valued qualities were discipline, precision, and control. Sport not only absorbed these qualities, but promoted them, gradually influencing perceptions and expectations in such a way as to deepen people's familiarity with the industrial regimen.

Industrialization drew populations to urban centers in search of work; not work quite as we know it today, but uncomfortable, energy-draining activities performed for long hours often in squalid and dangerous conditions. This type of work needed a new mentality. People were expected to arrive at work punctually and toil for measured periods of time. Their labors were planned for them and their efforts were often highly specialized according to the division of labor.

Behavior at work was subject to rules and conditions of service. Usually, all the work took place in a physically bounded space, the factory. There was also a need for absoluteness: tools and machines were made to fine tolerances. Underlying all this was a class structure, or hierarchy, in which some strata had attributes suited to ruling and others to being ruled. The latter's shortcomings were so apparent that no detailed investigation of the causes was thought necessary: their poverty, or even destitution was their own fault.

All these had counterparts in the developing sports scene. Time periods for contests were established and measured accurately thanks to newer, sophisticated timepieces. Divisions of labor in team games yielded role-specific positions and particular, as opposed to general, skills. Constitutions were drawn up to instill more structure into activities and regulate events according to rules. They took place on pitches, in rings and halls – in finite spaces. Winners and losers were unambiguously clear, outright, and absolute. And hierarchies reflecting the class structure were integrated into many activities. Captains of teams, for example, were "gentlemen" from the upper echelons. The sense of order, discipline, location, and period which sport acquired helped it both complement and support working life. *Homo faber* and *homo ludens* were almost mirror images of one another. As the form and pace of sport imitated that of industry, so it gained momentum amongst the emergent working class seeking some sporadic diversion from its toil, something more

THE IMPORTANCE OF MEASURED TIME

PORTABLE INSTRUMENTS TO MEASURE TIME ACCURATELY WERE INDISPENSABLE TO THE TRANSITION FROM PREINDUSTRIAL CULTURE TO MODERNITY. WATCHES, THEN CHRONOGRAPHS AND COMPUTERS ENABLED SPORTS TO QUANTIFY, RECORD AND ORGANIZE ACTIVITIES.

impulsive and daring than the routine labors that dominated industry. While sport was assuming a symmetry with work, it still afforded the working class an outlet, or release from labor; it was pursued voluntarily, at leisure.

Homo faber/homo ludens

From *homo*, the zoological name of the human genus; *faber* being the Latin for work, *ludens* for play. These describe two images of the supposed natural state of humans. In *homo faber*, work is the primary activity and the human existence is based on productive activity; humans express their creativity through the objects they make. Marx's stress on the liberating potential of unfettered labor did much to popularize this. The Dutch historian Johan Huizinga opposed this view, advancing the concept of *homo ludens*, in which irrational play is a primary human capacity that is often stifled by the demands of work, especially in contemporary society. Self-realization comes through free, perhaps frivolous, play.

Yet there were trends to offset this. Despite the popular beliefs that public schools in the nineteenth century were upholders of the virtues of sport, they actually echoed many of the sentiments of the Puritans, who disapproved utterly of any activity that seemed frivolous, including dancing, blood sports, and wagering (betting). Such entertainments were seen by Puritans as the mindless pleasure of *flâneurs* and, of course, such idlers were ripe for the devil's work. In the thirteenth and fourteenth centuries, Puritans suppressed any activity resembling a contest in their attempts to create an atmosphere of strict moral discipline. In the sixteenth century, the universities of Oxford and Cambridge banned football.

Public school masters initially tried to prevent the development of football in particular, believing it to be disruptive of order and morally debilitating. There was also the feeling that it was demeaning for the sons of the upper classes to practice activities that were, as one headmaster of the day described them, "fit only for butcher boys . . . farm boys and laborers" (quoted in Dunning and Sheard 1979: 47). Gentlemen scholars became the new Corinthians in sharp contrast to the laboring commoners.

Intellectual trends in Germany and France were influenced by the philosopher J. J. Rousseau whose treatise *Emile* (first published in 1762) argued that physical training and competitive sport would yield positive results in the overall education of a child. Ideas drifted across to English

Corinthians
From the ancient Greek city of Corinth, site of the Isthmian games, which was known for its wealth, luxury and licentiousness, Corinthians being its inhabitants. In the early nineteenth century, this took on sporting connotations when it was appropriated by wealthy gentlemen amateurs, who could afford to ride their own horses, sail their own yachts and pursue sports for no financial gain – in contrast to the professional players. The self-styled Corinthians believed they embodied the true spirit of sport for its own sake.

public schools, so that, by the 1850s, two main revisions were made to the original ideas on sport. Expressed by Peter McIntosh in his *Fair Play:* "The first was that competitive sport, especially team games, had an ethical basis, and the second was that training in moral behavior on the playing field was transferable to the world beyond" (1980: 27). Together, the ideas formed the core of "Muscular Christianity." Unselfishness, justice, health: these were the type of ideals that were manifest in sport, but also in any proper Christian society. Public schools, influenced by the doctrine, began to integrate a program of sport into their curricula. Team games were important in subordinating the individual to the collective unit and teaching the virtues of alliances. It was often thought that England's many military victories were attributable to the finely honed teamwork encouraged by public schools. Again, we glimpse the notion of sport as a preparation for military duty: the playing fields of public schools were equated with battlegrounds (Eton and Waterloo, for example). Thomas Hughes's classic, *Tom Brown's Schooldays* is full of allusions to the role of public schools in producing populations suited to rule over an empire.

Muscular Christianity
A doctrine about the positive moral influence of physical exercise and sport, which had its intellectual roots in the philosophy of J. J. Rousseau in France and Gutsmuths in Germany, and which was approvingly adopted by the public schools of England in the late nineteenth century.

The physically tough and toughening version of football, as practiced by Rugby School under the headship of Thomas Arnold and his assistant G. E. L. Cotton, gained acceptance in many public schools. Its toughness was useful in sorting out those fit enough to survive and perhaps later prosper in positions of power. The frail would either strengthen or perish. Its appeal to the prestigious public schools bent on turning out "great men" was soon apparent as the sport of rugby spread through the network and, in time, to a number of "open" clubs in the north of England (which admitted *nouveaux riches* and working-class members).

Muscular Christianity was also instrumental in carrying the other principal variant of football to the working class. "Socker" was encouraged by churches. A quarter of today's Football League clubs were founded and, for a while, sustained by churches eager to proselytize in urban centers which by the 1880s were humming with the sound of heavy machinery. Industry itself wasn't slow to realize the advantages of possessing a football team comprising members of its workforce. Places like Coventry, Stoke, and Manchester can boast enduring Football League clubs that were originally works outfits. Arsenal was based at Woolwich Arsenal, a London munitions factory. Matches which were only held on designated holy days and other festive occasions became more and more regular, routine, and organized. We might stretch the point and describe the early works teams as "para-industrial": organized much as an industrial force and intended to supplement the strictly industrial. It was a very deliberate policy pursued by factory owners in much the same way as their European counterparts of the day and contemporary Japanese industries. In some ways, sport was a foil for industrial order; a potent instrument for instilling order in the workforce.

Exporting its sports has been a major trade for England over the decades. Versions of the football played at Rugby and other public schools were popular among college students at North America's principal universities in the 1880s. The throwing and passing, as opposed to kicking, game was played at a competitive level. As early as 1874 there is a record of a game between Harvard and McGill. Interestingly, Wilbert Leonard documents a game of soccer between Rutgers and Princeton back in 1869. Baseball's origins are mysterious, probably evolving out the English games, base-ball and rounders, in which players struck a ball with a bat and ran through a series of bases arranged in a circle, or a "round." Baseball was the first fully professional sport in America, charging admissions to ballparks in the 1860s and attracting a predominantly blue-collar following.

If sport was an instrument, it had two cutting edges for as well as carving out new patterns of order it was also responsible for outbreaks of disorder. Work and leisure were cut in two to the imperatives of industry. The more fluid way of life in which the manner in which one earned a living blended imperceptibly with the rest of one's life disappeared as the factory system issued its demands, which were a workforce ready to labor for a set amount of time at a specific site. During that time workers operated under virtual compulsion; outside that time they were free to pursue whatever they wished (and could afford). Sport was a way of filling leisure time with brief, but exhilarating periods of uncertainty: the questions of who or which team would win a more-or-less equal competition was bound to prompt interest and speculation, as, it seems, it always has. The spell of physically competitive activity, far from being broken, was strengthened by the need for momentary release from a colorless world dominated by the monotonous thuds and grinds of machinery. Competitions, whether individual combats, ball games, or animal baits, drew crowds; but public gatherings always carried the potential for disruption.

Public gatherings and festivals, and other staged events attracted a working class which was in the process of becoming industrialized but which had not yet done so by the mid- to late nineteenth century. It was still adjusting to what John Hargreaves in *Sport, Power and Culture* (1986) calls the changes in "tempo and quality of industrial work." Hargreaves argues that the English church's efforts in building football clubs had the effect of controlling the working class so that it would be more pliant for ruling groups. In fact, Hargreaves's entire thesis revolves around the intriguing idea that sport has helped integrate the working class into respectable "bourgeois culture" rather than struggle against it.

But the integration was never smooth and police or militia were regularly called to suppress riots and uprisings at football matches, prize fights, footraces, cock-fights, and so on, as large groups spontaneously grew agitated and unruly. Boxing events to this day employ whips who are promoters' chargés d'affaires responsible for most of the minor business. But as the etymology suggests, the original whips were employed to encircle the ring, cracking their whips or lashing at troublesome members of the audience. Local laws were enacted, prohibiting meetings in all but tightly policed surroundings, sometimes banning sports completely. The rise of the governing bodies within individual sports represents an attempt to absorb working-class energies within a formal structure, thereby containing what might otherwise have become disruptive tendencies.

As the nineteenth century drew to an end, most sports took on a much more orderly character: both participants and spectators came to recognize the legitimacy of governing organizations, the standards of conduct they laid down and the structures of rules they observed. The whole direction and rhythm of sport reflected the growing significance of industrial society. Richard Mandell sums up: "[L]ike concurrent movements in law and government, which led to codifications, and rationalization, sport became codified, and civilized by written rules which were enforced by supervising officials (the equivalent of judges and jurors)" (1984: 151).

The reasons for concentrating on nineteenth-century England are: (1) it is here we find something like a factory's smelter shop where organized sport appears as an extract from the molten historical trends; (2) the English experience radiated out amongst the imperial colonies and ex-colonies, including North America, with sports, as well as trade, "following the flag"; and (3) it is this period of history that has excited many writers sufficiently to produce grand theories of the purposes or functions of sport in the modern world. We'll now consider three of the major functions.

The "civilizing spurt": Elias

"Sportization" is how Norbert Elias refers to the process in which precise and explicit rules governing contests came into being, with a strict application to ensure equal chances for competitors and supervision to observe fairness. He acknowledges that this took place in the nineteenth century and accompanied the English Industrial Revolution. Yet, he is wary of theories that explain one in terms of the other. "Both industrialization and sportization were symptomatic of a deeper-lying transformation of European societies which demanded of their individual members greater regularity and differentiation of conduct," he writes in "An essay on sport and violence" (1986b: 151).

The "transformation" had roots as far back as the fifteenth century and involved the gradual introduction of rules and norms to govern human behavior and designate what was appropriate conduct in a given situation; it also involved the rise of impersonal organizations to maintain rules. These reflected a general tendency in Europe toward interdependence: people began to orient their activities to each other, to rely less on their own subsistence efforts and more on those of others, whose tasks would be specialized and geared toward narrow objectives. In time, chains of interdependence were formed: a division of labor ensured that each individual, or group of individuals, was geared to the accomplishment of tasks that would be vital to countless others. They in turn would perform important activities, so that every member of a society depended on others, and no one was an "island." The pattern of relationships that emerged is called figuration. For this kind of system to operate with reasonable efficiency, people would have to be discouraged from pursuing their own interests and whims in an unrestrained way. There had to be a method of control over emotions and behavior, particularly violent behavior. The need for control grew more acute in eighteenth-century England, where, in the aftermath of civil strife, many people feared a recurrence (Elias and Dunning 1986: 171). The state was the central authority responsible for internal orderliness and overall organization and planning. With the formation of state control came what Elias calls a "civilizing spurt."

Here we come across Elias's more general historical account, *The Civilizing Process* (1982), which describes a sweeping trend, or even evolution, in which human societies have controlled the use of violence and encouraged an observance of manners. The two aspects are part of one general tendency. So, for example, the decline of dispute settlements through violence and the rise of social prohibitions on such things as spitting and breaking wind are not unconnected in Elias's scheme. They both represent new standards of conduct in changing figurations. The level of acceptable violence drops as the emergent state takes over the settling of disputes and monopolizes the legitimate use of violence. As rules and conventions develop, they spread to all areas, so that standards are imposed, both externally and internally as well as being controlled by the state; individuals control *themselves* according to accepted or "correct" codes of conduct.

Figuration

While, in a general sense, this refers to the form, shape, or outline of something, Elias has applied it to interdependent relations between people and used it to represent "chains of functions" between them. Some have found in the concept a new approach to study, while others, like Bauman (in *Sociology* vol. 13, 1979) have found it reminiscent of more orthodox notions, like "pattern" or "situation," and question the value and originality of the concept.

Since the days of the ancient Greeks, which is Elias's starting point, civilization has progressed with the state's power and therefore control over violence within the family and between neighbors, clans, and fiefdoms, increasing at a pace roughly equivalent to our internal controls over emotions and behavior; in other words, self-restraint. (The similarity to Freud's conception of society taming our more primitive urges through the super-ego is quite pronounced here.)

The civilizing process is a vast world trend, but not a completely linear one: there are phases in history when a figuration may "decivilize" and regress to barbarism, tolerating a higher level of violence and ungoverned behavior. This is described by Elias as a "reverse gear." Equally, there is allowance for sharp accelerated movements "forward," such as in the civilizing spurt Elias believes is so crucial to our understanding of modern sport.

While it would caricature the civilizing process to equate it with changes in self-control this particular aspect of the wider development acted as an agent in generating "stress-tensions" which, in turn, agitated the need for organized sport. How does Elias see this happening? First, an abstract observation: "In societies where fairly high civilizing standards all round are safeguarded and maintained by a highly effective state-internal control of physical violence, personal tensions of people resulting from conflicts of this kind, in a word, stress-tensions, are widespread" (1986a: 41). Next, most human societies develop some countermeasures against stress-tensions they themselves generate and "these activities must conform to the comparative sensitivity to physical violence which is characteristic of people's social habits (customs and dispositions) at the later stages of a civilizing process" (1986a: 41–2).

So, the ways in which people "let off steam" mustn't violate the standards that have become accepted by society at large. Watching humans mauled by wild animals might have provided stimulating and enjoyable release for the ancient Romans, as might burning live cats or baiting bulls for the English in the last century. But, the civilizing process, according to Elias, changes our threshold of revulsion for enacting and witnessing violence, so that, nowadays, some cultures in the West find a sport like boxing – relatively mild in historical terms – intolerably violent. The methods we choose to discharge tension closely reflect general standards and sensitivities.

Fox-hunting is Elias's favorite example. Once synonymous with the word "sport," fox-hunting is now an anachronism and pressure against it would have no doubt prompted its demise were it not a pursuit practiced exclusively by England's landowning elite. Developing in the late eighteenth century, this peculiarly English sport was quite unlike the simpler, less regulated, and more spontaneous forms of hunting of other countries and earlier ages where people were the main hunters and foxes were one amongst many prey (boar, red deer, and wolves being others). Fox-hunting (itself an example of a figuration) was bound by a strict code of etiquette and idiosyncratic rules, such as that which forbade killing other animals during the hunt. Hounds were trained to follow only the fox's scent, and only they could kill, while humans watched.

The fox itself had little utility apart from its pelt; its meat wasn't considered edible (not by its pursuers, anyway) and, while it was considered a pest, the fields and forests were full of others which threatened farmers' livestock and crops. The chances of anyone getting hurt in the hunt were minimized, but each course in the wall of security presented a problem of how to retain the immediacy and physical risk that were so important in early times. Elias believes that the elaboration of the rules of hunting were solutions. The rules served to postpone the outcome, or finale of the hunt and so artificially prolong the process of hunting. "The excitement of the hunt itself had increasingly become the main source of enjoyment for the human participants" (Elias and Dunning 1986: 166). What had once been foreplay to the act of killing became the main pleasure. So the fox-hunt was a virtual "pure type" of autotelic hunt: the thrill for participants came in the pace and exhilaration of the chasing and the pleasure of watching violence done without actually doing the killing.

But, the influence of the civilizing spurt is apparent in the restraint imposed and exercised by the participants. The overall trend was to make violence more repugnant to people, which effectively encouraged them to control or restrain themselves. Elias stresses that this should be seen not as a repression but as a product of greater sensitivity. The fox-hunters didn't secretly feel an urge to kill with their own hands; they genuinely found such an act disagreeable, but could still find pleasure in viewing it from their horses; what Elias calls "killing by proxy."

Despite all attempts to abolish them, hunts persist to this day, probably guided by appetites similar to those whetted by the sight of humans being masticated by sharks. Hundreds of millions of *Jaws* fans can attest to the enjoyable tension provided by the latter, albeit through the medium of film. While Elias doesn't cover the modern hunts, we should add that their longevity reveals something contradictory about the civilizing trend and the impulse to condone or even promote wanton cruelty. To ensure a long and satisfying chase, and to be certain that foxes are found in the open, "earth stoppers" are employed to close up earths (fox holes) and badger sets in which foxes may take refuge. Many hunts maintain earths to ensure a sufficient supply of foxes through the season (foxes used to be imported from the continent). The hunt does not start until after 11 a.m. to allow the fox time to digest its food and ensure that it is capable of a long run. During the course of a hunt, a fox may run to ground and will either survive or be dug out by the pursuant dogs, a virtual baiting from which even the dogs emerge with damage. New hounds are prepared by killing cubs before the new season, a practice observed and presumably enjoyed by members of the hunt and their guests.

In Elias's theory, fox-hunting was a solution to the problems created by the accelerating trend toward civilization and the internal controls on violence it implied. The closing up of areas of excitement, which in former ages had been sources of pleasurable gratification (as well as immense suffering), set humans on a search for substitute activities and one which didn't carry the risks, dangers, or outright disorder that society as a whole would find unacceptable – what Elias, in the title of one of his books, calls the *Quest for Excitement*. The English form of fox-hunting was only one example of a possible solution, but Elias feels it is an "empirical model," containing all the original distinguishing characteristics of modern sport. Other forms of sport, such as boxing, soccer, cricket, and rugby showed how the problem was solved without the use and abuse of animals; the first two of these were appropriated by the working class. All evolved in a relatively orderly manner, well matched to the needs of modern, bureaucratic society with its accent on organization and efficiency and ultimately in line with the general civilizing process.

The explanation of sport is but one facet of Elias's grand project which is to understand the very nature and consequences of the civilizing process. It follows that critics who are not convinced by his general model are certainly not by his specific one. The actual idea of a civilizing process has the tinge of a theory of progress in which history is set to proceed through predetermined stages which can't be altered. Elias's mention of the irregularity of the process and the "reverse gear" are rather peripheral to the main thesis which suggests that, as Paul Hoggett puts it, "civilization seems to march onwards fairly straightforwardly without any collapsing back into barbarity" (1986: 36).

Many modern observers of sport might want to argue that "collapses" are quite commonplace and point fingers in the direction of soccer stadia, often the sites of open, almost ritualistic violence between rival fans. Elias and his devotees would recommend a more detailed examination of history to appreciate that violence has for long been related to soccer; only the media's amplification of it has changed. Presumably the same could be said about fox-hunting which continues unabated today. However, this response is only partially satisfactory, as many other sports have developed violent penumbra quite recently and it is hard to establish any historical connections with, say, boxing, cricket, and rugby, all of which have experienced major crowd disorder over the past two decades.

It is interesting that the nucleus of Elias's model has not been attacked. A basic proposition is that "pleasurable excitement . . . appears to be one of the most elementary needs of human beings" (1986b: 174). Elias never documents the sources of such "needs" and, considering that the entire theoretical edifice rests on them, one might expect some expansion. This is mysteriously absent. Is it a biological drive? Part of a survival instinct? A deep psychological trait? Elias's treatment seems to suggest that the need for "pleasurable excitement" is of a similar order to the need for food, shelter, sex, and other such basic needs. I agree that it *appears* as basic as these, but I would want to look closely at the changing contexts, social and ecological, in which such needs manifest themselves.

This may seem a small quibble with what is after all a hugely ambitious attempt to illuminate the nature and purpose of modern sport by connecting its changing character to the civilizing transformation of the past several centuries. Far from being an autonomous realm separated from other institutions, sport is totally wrapped up with culture, psyche, and the state. Human "stress-tensions" are linked to large-scale social changes. Yet the analysis still seems caught in a timewarp; as Vera Zolberg concludes, it does "not devote adequate attention to one of the most striking features of sport in modern society, that of the *business* of sport" (1987: 573). The way in which sport has been seized upon by commercial organizations in recent years has tended to show Elias's theory as adequate at a certain level, but unable to cope with the developments imposed on sport by the pressures of professionalism in recent years. The state may once have played a key role in precipitating organized efforts to satisfy basic needs for excitement, but private business has become a powerful force. Alternative theories have tried to link the two.

Marxism I: Sport as a new opiate

Sport is a remarkably ironic thing, its chief characteristic being that it provides an entertaining relief from work while at the same time preparing people for more work. This is the central insight of a group of theorists who have, in one way or another, been influenced by the work of Karl Marx. Although Marx himself didn't write about sport, his theories have great relevance. The focus of his work was the development of modern capitalism, an economic system based on a split of the ownership of the means of production (factories, land, equipment, etc.). Owners of the means of production are bosses, or bourgeoisie, in whose interests capitalism works and who are prepared to milk the system to its limits in order to stay in control.

The working class, or proletariat, are forced to work for them in order to subsist. As the system doesn't work in their interests, they have to be persuaded that it *could* if only they were luckier, or had better breaks, or worked harder. In other words, the system itself is fine; it's actually the workers who need to change for the good. As long as workers are convinced of the legitimacy of economic arrangements, then capitalism is not under threat. So the system has evolved methods of ensuring its own survival. And this is where sport fits in.

John Hargreaves identifies four main areas. First, organized sport helps train a "docile labor force": it encourages in the working class an acceptance of the kind of work discipline demanded in modern production; hard work is urged in both sport and work. We've noted before how the organization and tempo of industry became reflected in sport and Hargreaves sees the symmetry as almost perfect. Compare the features of sport and industry: "a high degree of specialisation and standardisation, bureaucratised and hierarchical administration, long-term planning, increased reliance on science and technology, a drive for maximum productivity, a quantification of performance and, above all, the alienation of both producer and consumer" (1982: 41). Major events, like the Olympics and Super Bowl, are given as examples of the final point. Second, sport has become so thoroughly com-mercialized and dominated by market forces that events and performers are treated as – or perhaps just *are* – commodities that are used by capitalist enterprises: "Sport is produced, packaged and sold like any other commodity on the market for mass consumption at enormous profits" (1982: 41).

The transferring or trading of players typifies the "commodification." The third area in which sport fits in is in "expressing the quintessential ideology in capitalist society." What Marxist theorists have proposed here is that sport works in subtle ways at indicating qualities or imperatives in people; all these qualities have counterparts in society at large. Aggressive individualism, ruthless competitiveness, equal opportunities, elitism, chauvinism, sexism, nationalism: all these are regarded as admirable. Their desirability isn't ques-tioned in sport and the uncritical approach to them is carried over to society. Fourth, there is the area of the state: this bureaucratic administration repre-sents capitalist interests in the West and the state-capitalist societies of the Soviet bloc. It follows that every intrusion into sport by the state must be seen as some sort of attempt to link sports participation with the requirements of the capitalist system.

Four areas, then, but hardly a theory; they are really only lowest common denominators for all those favoring a Marxist conception of sport. Beyond these, there are a variety of interpretations all taking their lead from Marx in the sense that they see the split over the means of production as central. In other words, sport has to be analyzed in terms of class relations. Paul Hoch has advanced one of the most acerbic Marxist critiques of sport, which he likens to the mainstream religions about which Marx himself wrote much. Religion was regarded as little more than a capitalist convenience, absorbing workers' energies and emotions and supplying a salve after the week's labors. Sport has much the same significance. Both religion and sport work as an opiate that temporarily dulls pain and gives a false sense of well-being, but which is also a dangerous and debilitating narcotic that can reduce its users to a helpless state of dependence. The attraction of sport is as compelling as that of religion and its effects are comparable: it siphons off potential that might otherwise be put to political use in challenging the capitalist system.

Jean-Marie Brohm has added to this approach a book of equal astring-ency whose title describes sport as "a prison of measured time." By this, Brohm means that the institutional, rule-governed, highly organized structure of modern sport has been shaped by capitalist interest groups in such a way as to represent a constraint rather than a freedom. Sport is in no sense an alternative to work, less still an escape from it "since it removes all bodily freedom, all creative spontaneity, every aesthetic dimension and every play-ful impulse" (1978: 175). The competitor is merely a prisoner, whose performances are controlled, evaluated, and recorded, preferably in quantitative terms. Capitalism as a system stifles the human imagination and compresses the human body into mindless production work; and as sport is but one part of that system, it can do little more than reproduce its effects. It just obeys the "logic" of the system. As Richard Gruneau writes: "For Brohm, capitalism has shaped sport in its own image" (1983: 38). Others, like Gerhard Vinnai and Bruno Rigauer agree with the basic assumptions and emphasize how corporations have penetrated, or completely taken over sport. It is as if sport has been appropriated by one class and used to bolster its already commanding position in the overall class structure. For Rigauer, sport has aided the economic system by improving the health of workers and so minimizing the time lost at work through illness (we presume he would interpret the British Sports Council's "Sport for all" campaign in such terms).

Like Brohm, he sees a "technocratic" take-over of sport, with performances being subject to rationalization and planning and training becoming more time-absorbing and important than performance itself. Initiative and creativity are stifled, rendering the human performer as the "one-dimensional man," so called by the Marxist philosopher Herbert Marcuse (from whom Brohm and Rigauer draw insights). In all accounts, the human beings are depicted as passive dopes, pushed around by factors beyond their control. But are humans just like hockey pucks? Do they really respond so readily and easily? Those who think not find the work of Hoch and Brohm rather too deterministic – all thoughts and behavior are determined by outside forces emanating from the capitalist system. Sport is but one instrument for maintaining the domination and exploitation of the working class. In contrast, other writers prefer to see the working class playing a more active role. Certainly, there is a complementarity between the way in which modern sport is organized and the functions it fulfills on the one hand, and the requirements of capitalism on the other. But this doesn't deny that different groups (classes) are involved in different sports *and* at different levels at different stages in history.

Sport is not, as Hargreaves puts it, "universally evil." Its meaning and significance have to be investigated more closely. Other Marxist writers, including Richard Gruneau and Hargreaves himself, have attempted to do this. All would go along with the more orthodox Marxist approach, but only so far. Sport is much more multifaceted than the others acknowledge. It may give substance to wider ideologies and slough off working-class energies, but it can also be useful as a builder of solidarity within working-class groups which are brought together with a common purpose. "It is precisely this type of solidarity that historically has formed the basis for a trenchant opposition to employers," observes Hargreaves (1986: 110).

Public gatherings at sports events have always generated a potential for disorder and have attracted the state's agents of control. Some writers have even inferred a form of political resistance from the exploits of soccer hooligans. So, involvement in sport can actually facilitate or even encourage challenge rather than accommodation. Far from being a means of controlling the masses, sport, on occasion, has needed controlling itself. On the issue of sport as a preparation for work, Hargreaves reminds us that not all sports resemble the rhythms and rationality of work. Fishing and bowling provide relaxation and relief in very stark contrast to work.

Hargreaves (1986) argues against a firmly negative view of sport as providing only "surrogate satisfactions for an alienated mass order ... perpetuating its alienation" and instead argues for a more flexible, spontaneous interpretation. Sport may perform many services in the interests of the *status quo*, amongst them a belief in the ultimate triumph of ability ("if you're good you'll make it" – in sport or life generally). It also helps fragment the working class by splintering loyalties into localities, regions, etc. But it can also provide a basis for unity and therefore resistance to dominant interest groups: "Part mass therapy, part resistance, part mirror image of the dominant political economy," as David Robins puts it (1982: 145).

Marxism II: Cultural power

Even those who stick valiantly to Marx's first principles are embarrassed by the literalism of this type of approach: staying true to Marx and applying his class-based formula to virtually any phenomenon is like trying to vault with a pole made of timber: not only is it heavy, but it's rigid. Other writers have opted for more flexibility, taking basic Marxist ideas as they have been reinterpreted by later theorists, in particular Antonio Gramsci. Two oft-neglected writers, Mark Naison and Brian Stoddart have offered theories of sports that draw on Gramsci's concept of hegemony and its role in supporting empires.

Naison's early article, "Sports and the American empire" (1972) and Stoddart's analysis of the "Sport, cultural imperialism, and colonial response in the British empire" (1988) advance our understanding of the economic and political utility of sports in stabilizing what might otherwise be disruptive colonial situations. Both writers acknowledge the work of C. L. R. James, whose historical analysis of cricket showed how the values supposedly embodied in the sport were disseminated throughout the Caribbean and how these were of enormous benefit to a colonial regime endlessly trying to manage the local populations.

Sport for both Naison and Stoddart is a means of cultural power, not direct political power as suggested by the others. "Athletic events have increasingly reflected the dynamics of an emergent American imperialism," writes Naison (1972: 96). "As the American political economy 'internationalized' in the post-war period, many of its most distinctive cultural values and patterns, from consumerism to military preparedness, have become an integral part of organized sports." And Stoddart: "Through sport were transferred dominant British beliefs as to social behavior, standards, relations, and conformity, all of which persisted beyond the end of formal empire" (1988: 651).

Hegemony
From the Greek *hegemon*, meaning leader, this refers to leadership, supremacy or rule, usually by one state over a confederacy, or one class over another. It has been used in a specifically Marxist way by Antonio Gramsci, who sought to understand how ruling, or leading groups in a capitalist society maintain their power by indirect rather than direct economic or military means. They do so by creating a culture that is shared by all but which favors one class over another, usually the most deprived. It is a domination, but of intellect or thought rather than body, though ultimately there is a relation because the labor of subordinate groups is exploited. It is important to appreciate that hegemony is not some artificial contrivance: it is a genuinely felt set of beliefs, ideas, values and principles, all of which work in a supportive way for the *status quo* and hence appear as common sense. According to Gramsci, an entire apparatus is responsible for diffusing ideas that complement and encourage consensus. These include the Church, education, the media, political institutions and, if Stoddart, Naison and others are to be accepted, sports.

By participating in sports, populations who came under American and British influences were taught teamwork, the value of obeying authority, courage in the face of adversity, loyalty to fellow team members (especially the captain) and, perhaps most importantly, respect for rules. Stoddart writes of cricket, though it could be applied to any sport: "*To play cricket* or *play the game* meant being honest and upright, and accepting conformity within the conventions as much as it meant actually taking part in a simple game" (1988: 653). Ruling over colonies in far-flung parts of the globe could have been achieved by military force; indeed, it was initially. But coercion is not cost-effective, especially so when the geographical distance between the metropolitan centers and the peripheral colonies was as great as it was, particularly in the British case. But, if a population could be persuaded that the colonial rule was right and proper, then this made life easier for the masters. Sport provided a way of inculcating people with the kind of values and ideas that facilitated British rule and a "vehicle of adjustment to American imperialism, its popularity an index of America's success in transmitting adulation of its culture and values" (Naison 1972: 100).

None of this suggests a passive acceptance of the rule of America or Britain. As Thomas Sowell writes in his *Race and Culture: A world view*: "Conquest, whatever its benefits, has seldom been a condition relished by the conquered. The struggle for freedom has been as pervasive throughout history as conquest itself" (1994: 79). By exporting institutions as strong as sport it was possible to create shared beliefs and attitudes between rulers and ruled, at the same time creating distance between them.

Organized sports, remember, were products of the imperial powers, most of the rules being drawn up and governing bodies being established between the 1860s and 1890s, exactly the period when the imperialism was at its height. The rulers, having experience with sport, were obviously superior and this reinforced the general notion they tried to convey – that they were suited to rule, as if by divine appointment. The rules of sports were codified at a central source, transferred to all parts of the vast imperial web, then adhered to by people of astonishingly diverse backgrounds. The colonial experience in general was not unlike this: ruling from a center and engineering a consensus among millions.

Impoverished groups over whom Americans and British ruled were introduced to sports by their masters. When they grew proficient enough to beat them, that posed another problem. West Indian cricketers became adept at repeatedly bowling fast balls which were virtually unplayable. South Africa developed a style of rugby that made it almost invincible. Australia beat England regularly at cricket. The problem as it was seen on British soil was that such achievements might be "interpreted as symbolic of general parity," as Stoddart puts it (1988: 667). Baseball was "popularized by the increasing number of American corporate and military personnel" in Puerto Rico, the Dominican Republic, Venezuela, Mexico and elsewhere, writes Naison (1972). Now, many players from those countries play in US leagues.

The concept of sport as a purveyor of imperial culture is a powerful one, especially when allied to a Marxist analysis of the role of ideas in maintaining social structures. Sport, in the eyes of critics like Naison and Stoddart, is not the blunt instrument many other Marxists take it to be. For them, its value to ruling groups is in drawing subordinate groups toward an acceptance of ideas that are fundamental to their control. This was appropriate in the empires of America and Britain, where orders and directives came from a central source; just like the rules of any sport.

Imperialism
From the Latin *imperium*, meaning absolute power or dominion over others, this refers to the political and economic domination of one or several countries by one other. The union of the different countries, known as colonies, is the empire. There is an unequal relationship between the ruling sovereign country, sometimes known as the metropolitan center, and the peripheral colonies which are reduced to the status of dependants rather than partners. Technically, the USA's colonial dependencies have been few compared to, say, Britains or those of other European powers in the nineteenth and early twentieth century. But its indirect political influence and its economic pre-eminence over a vast network of other countries have convinced many that there is a North American imperialism.

For theorists influenced by Marxism, sport can never be seen as neutral. It can be enjoyed; indeed it must be for it to be effective. If we spotted the surreptitious purposes of sport, we could hardly enjoy it at all. For it to work, sport must be seen as totally disengaged from the political and economic processes. In the colonial situation, it was crucial that sports were enjoyed and transmitted from one generation to the next. Yet, according to Marxism, this should not deflect our attentions totally away from the valuable functions it has served – and probably still serves – in the capitalist enterprise at home and abroad. This gives a different slant to the variety of Marxism that sees sport in a one-dimensional way: as a politically safe channel, or an outlet for energies that might otherwise be disruptive to capitalism. Yet, it clearly complements it in identifying the main beneficiary of sports as capitalism.

Unlike Marxist writers who see the dissatisfaction resulting from capitalism as having potential until it is diverted into sport, ethologists (analysts of animal behavior) see the dissatisfaction, or more correctly, frustration, as having *natural* sources. Whereas Marxists would see that frustration possibly transformed into political protest should sport disappear, ethologists would insist that it would lead to humans fighting each other. Sport is a vent; a system through which we release violent behavior. We will now examine one ethological approach.

An ethological approach: Morris

While he dismisses most of the Marxist approaches to sport as "political claptrap," Desmond Morris discerns a "small grain of truth" in the idea that events that fascinate, excite, and entertain people also distract them from "political terrorism and bloody rebellion." But, on examination, this aspect of sport "is not political after all, but rather has to do with human nature" (1981: 20). Morris, as a student of animal behavior and who affords humans pride of place in his perspective, has turned his sights to sport in his book *The Soccer Tribe*. He begins from an observation of the 1978 World Cup Final between Argentina and Holland, an event comprising 22 brightly clad figures "kicking a ball about in a frenzy of effort and concentration" on a small patch of grass, and watched by something like one-quarter of the entire world's population. "If this occurrence was monitored by aliens on a cruising UFO, how would they explain it?" asks Morris. His book is a kind of answer.

Morris adopts the role of the puzzled, detached observer, recording notes in the ship's log in an effort to discover "the function of this strange activity" and, while his sights are fixed on soccer, his records have relevance for all sports. His rejection of the Marxist "social drug" approach is under-standable, for Morris's ethology follows that of Konrad Lorenz, who believed that aggression is instinctive in all animals, including humans. Sport is truly a "safe" diversion from violent behavior. But were political systems to change, the aggression would still exist and would still need an outlet. Political frustrations may aggravate aggressive tendencies, but they do not cause them. This removes the need for any detailed social or psychological theory: sport in general and soccer in particular are grand occasions for venting instinc-tively violent urges. But Morris goes on to expose several interesting facets, the first being the *ritual hunt*. Morris's initial premise is much the same as the one offered in this book: that the predecessors of sport were activities that "filled the gap left by the decline of the more obvious hunting activities" (Morris 1981). The activities passed through a series of phases, the final one being symbolic in which players represent hunters, the ball is their weapon and the goal the prey. Footballers "attack" goals and "shoot" balls. Sport is a disguised hunt, a ritual enactment.

Morris calls modern players "pseudo-hunters" whose task of killing the inanimate prey is deliberately complicated by introducing opponents to obstruct them, making it a "reciprocal hunt." Goalkeepers of a soccer team resemble "claws" of a cornered prey "lashing out to protect its vulnerable surface." Its parallels with hunting have given soccer global appeal. Some sports, such as archery, darts, bowling, billiards, snooker, skeet, skittles, curling, croquet, and golf, all concentrate on the climax of a hunt in the sense that they all involve aiming at a target. They lack the physical risks and exer-tions of a headlong chase and the necessary co-operation between members of the hunting pack. Tennis and squash are more physical, but, unless played in doubles, lack teamwork. Some sports, especially motor racing, capture the chase aspect of hunting and also retain dangers. Basketball, netball, volleyball, hockey, cricket, baseball, lacrosse, and rugby football have plenty of fast-flowing movement and a climactic aiming at targets. Yet the risk of physical injury isn't too high. Morris believes that, apart from soccer, only Australian rules football and ice hockey approach what he calls the "magic mixture." The former has been isolated geographically and the latter suffers because the small puck (the "weapon") makes it difficult for spectators to follow the play. Soccer seems to capture all the right elements in its ritual and has the potential for involving spectators to an intense degree, which makes watching all the more satisfying.

For all its ritual, soccer – and for that matter many other sports – has a tendency to degenerate into what Morris calls a *stylized battle*. At the end of play there is usually a winner and loser, and this is not a feature of hunts. Soccer caricatures many other sports in arousing its spectators; fans seethe and fight, they are outraged at bad play or decisions, and euphoric at good results. Other sports engender similar reactions, but at a milder level. At least one piece of research has put this to the test, focusing on hooliganism at football grounds as "ritualized aggression" in that it is not typically violent in a destructive way, but conforms to an "order" with unwritten rules and codes of behavior. As befits an ethological approach, comparisons are made with nonhuman species which use ritual displays of aggression for various purposes, but do so without transgressing boundaries. The stylized war for Peter Marsh *et al.* (1978) is bounded by *The Rules of Disorder*.

In a similar vein, Morris argues that sport serves as a safety valve through which people vent their spleen in a way which would be unacceptable in many other contexts. But attending an emotional event, as well as providing an outlet for anger and frustrations built up during the week's work, may add a new frustration if the result isn't satisfactory and so make the spectators and players feel worse than before. So, the fan (who happens to be male in Morris's example) "goes home feeling furious. Back at work on Monday, he sees his boss again and all the pent-up anger he felt against the soccer opponents wells up inside him" (1981: 20). So, every match is therapeutic and inflammatory "in roughly equal proportions."

Another ambiguous function of sport is its capacity to act *as a status display*. Again, Morris writes about soccer, but in terms that can be adapted to fit other sports: "If the home team wins a match, the victorious local supporters can boast an important psychological improvement, namely an increased sense of local status" (1981: 20). Soccer, like most other organized sports, developed in a period of industrialization; as we have noted, many British clubs began life as factory teams. A successful side conferred status not only on the team, but on the firm and even the area. Winning teams and individuals are still held in esteem locally because a victory for them means a victory for the community or region.

The conferment of status is quite independent of objective material positions. Since the publication of Morris's book, this aspect of his argument has become more relevant, as depressed areas in which local manufacturing industries have collapsed or in which communities have been destroyed have yearned for success through sport. The troubled West Midlands city of Coventry was boosted by the local football club's first-ever English Football Association (FA) cup win in 1987. Northern Ireland gained respite from destruction and bloodshed on fight nights when boxing occupied centerstage in the sports world.

Morris's fourth function of sport *as a religious ceremony* is arguably the most underdeveloped in his assessment, but others before him have expanded on this concept. Like a religious gathering, a sporting event draws large groups of people together in a visible crowd; it temporarily unites them with a commonly and often fervently held belief not in a deity but in an individual sports performer, or a team. Sport is a great developer of social solidarity: it makes people feel they belong to a strong homogeneous collectivity which has a presence far greater than any single person. Morris equates the rise of sport with secularization: "As the churches . . . emptied with the weakening of religious faith, the communities of large towns and cities have lost an important social occasion" (1981: 23). The function has been taken over by sport.

This argument has been expressed by a number of writers, perhaps most famously by Michael Novak, whose book *The Joy of Sport* (1976) is a reverent acknowledgement of the ecstatic elements of sport. Certainly, the general view that sport has assumed the position of a new religion is a persuasive one and is supported by the mass idolatry that abounds in modern sport. (For the most complete study of the relationship, see Shirl Hoffman's *Sport and Religion*, 1992.) We need look no further than the opening or closing ceremonies at the Olympic games, or half-time at the Super Bowl, to see the most stupendous, elaborate displays of ritual and liturgy. These are precisely the type of rituals that have been integral to mass religious worship in the past. The purposes they serve would be similar. In measurable terms, one could suggest that sport is more popular than religion: *far* more people watch sport than go to church; sport gets *far* more media attention than religion. Sports performers are better-known than religious leaders. In all probability, people discuss sport more than they do religion. So, it seems feasible to say that sport occupies a bigger part of people's lives than does religion.

But religion is intended to provide transcendental reference points beyond everyday experience; it gives moral guidelines; it instructs, informs, and enlightens. Some fanatics may believe sport does all these things. Realistically, it doesn't, though this isn't the thrust of the argument. Do religious believers follow the guidelines or learn from the enlightenment? Some might respond that sports fans do. Otherwise, why ask Michael Jordan to tell

THEORIES OF SPORTS

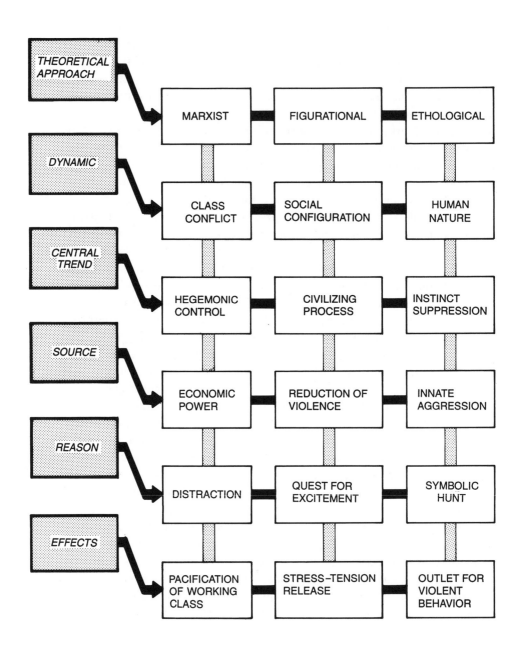

people to drink Gatorade, or any number of American sports stars to drink Coca-Cola? People *follow* sports with much the same zeal and commitment as active church-goers follow religion and, although it might seem insulting to religious adherents, sports fans do pursue a faith, albeit in their own way.

The comparison between sport and religion extends beyond superficial resemblances when we recognize that sport has become a functional substitute, supplying for the follower a meaningful cause, an emblematic focus, and a source of allegiance, even belonging. But there is still another way in which sport fills a vacuum left by religion and here we move on to the concept of sport *as a social drug*. Morris, who is dismissive of Marxist theories of sport, fails to make the connection between the two functions. The "opiate thesis" we encountered earlier, when applied to sport shows how sport can function to keep workers' minds off political revolt and so preserve the *status quo* – which is, according to Marx, what religion was supposed to do. Morris, in rebutting this, states the argument rather crudely, making sport seem a "bourgeois-capitalist plot," a conspiracy orchestrated by the bosses. As we saw in the previous section, this isn't quite the intention of Marxist writers.

There are two residual functions, both of which Morris concedes are exaggerations. As *big business* sport is commercialized and run effectively as if making money was the sole organizing principle. This is partly true, but misses the reason for the involvement of the "vast majority" which is because they "love" sport. "Money is a secondary factor", according to Morris. As *theatrical performance* showbusiness influences are very evident in sport nowadays and the suggestion is that sport has become a mass entertainment. This is true for football, boxing, baseball, and other sports, but not for bowls, netball, judo, and many other minority sports. Even then, sport, by definition, can never be pure entertainment for as soon as the unpredictable element of competition is gone, it ceases. It then becomes pure theater.

Morris's treatment is not a formal theory, but a catalog of functions which soccer serves, as indeed do all sports at various levels, from the psychological to the political. There is no attempt to link the functions together, nor much evaluation of which functions are most effective. Its minor strengths lie in drawing our attention to the many ways in which sport has embedded itself in modern culture and the modern psyche. Try thinking of something that can simultaneously function as a stylized battle, a religious ceremony, and a status display. Morris offers what is really no more than a preamble to his "dissection" (as he calls it) of soccer, but even in this he dismantles the notion that sport is "only a game" and indicates that a match is "a symbolic event of some complexity."

So much for attempts to make sense of sport through grand theories, all of which have merits yet none of which is without problems. At least they provide frames of reference within which we can operate when investigating some of the more specific issues concerning sport. In the following chapters we will do exactly that, in each case looking at popular ideas that circulate in sport and exposing some of their shortcomings.

FURTHER READING

Sport and Leisure in Social Thought by Grant Jarvie and Joe Maguire (Routledge, 1995) is an interesting attempt to select a number of traditions in social thought and examine what light they shed on the development of sports. Many of the classical social theorists had little or nothing to say about sports, so the authors try to explicate.

Sport and Leisure in the Civilizing Process edited by Eric Dunning and Chris Rojek (Macmillan, 1992) is probably the best collection of essays devoted to a critical appreciation of the contributions of Elias to the understanding of sports. Rojek's introduction is perhaps the clearest exposition of the figurational approach available. This may profitably be read in conjunction with *Sport, Leisure and Social Relations*, edited by John Horne, David Jary and Alan Tomlinson (Routledge & Kegan Paul, 1987).

The Sports Process: A comparative and developmental approach edited by Eric Dunning, Joseph Maguire and Robert Pearton (Human Kinetics, 1993) has 13 valuable contributions from a panel of international scholars; while the book is not specifically about theories of sports, the discussions on sports history and comparative physical culture bring Marxist and figurational analyses to the fore.

Rip Off the Big Game by Paul Hoch (Anchor Doubleday, 1972) has been criticized as a rather too crude Marxist account, but still packs a punch as a powerful critique of modern sport. At the time of its publication it was a landmark that influenced other approaches to the study of sport. Now out of print, it is available only through libraries, but it repays reading.

ASSIGNMENT

Consider ways in which sport reflects almost perfectly changes in technology, patterns of work, and people's values and attitudes in a manner **not** suggested by any of the theories covered in this chapter.

Chapter six

Behind on points
How black sports
performers are made

A million dreams, one star

In March 1995, two of the most potent black sporting symbols were released, one from prison, the other from baseball's backwaters. Mike Tyson and Michael Jordan were the most successful African Americans in sports. They earned more money, more respect and, in Tyson's case, more notoriety than any black sports performer in history. Their absence from sport's big league was agonizing. Tyson's was enforced: he was found guilty of raping a beauty queen contestant in an Indianapolis hotel room and banished in ignomy. Jordan quit the Chicago Bulls with the plaudits ringing in his ears; he wanted to conquer his second sport, baseball, but fared poorly with Chicago White Sox. Their returns had promoters rubbing their hands and advertisers reaching for their checkbooks. It was a unique return to action of two black males who had defined their sports and inspired the dreams of millions.

But, are they realistic dreams, or just dangerous fantasies? In this chapter, we will address not only this question, but, perhaps more importantly, why we should be asking it at all. After all, whose business is it if someone wants to channel all his or her energy into the pursuit of an ideal? Sports themselves thrive off the zeal and ambition of millions of "wannabes," the vast majority of whom never approach the level where they can make a living, let alone a fortune, out of sports.

Tens of thousands of young African Americans and African Caribbeans who grew up in American and British inner cities in the 1970s are now reflecting on a sports career that never was. They, like literally millions before them, had watched television, listened to radios and read newspapers and magazines. There was the evidence before their eyes: black sports stars lauded all over the world, winning world titles, gold medals and making the kind of money that qualifies you for a place in *Fortune* magazine.

But appearances are often deceptive and these highly unrepresentative superstars unwittingly create an illusion. As American sports writer Jack Olsen observed in his 1968 book, *The Black Athlete*: "At most, sport has led a few thousand Negroes out of the ghetto. But for hundreds of thousands of other Negroes it has substituted a meaningless dream." While the time and effort demanded in trying to become another Jordan or Tyson is so great that it may ruin a young person's prospects of doing anything else, the actual chances of emulating them are infinitesimally small. Failed sports performers have quite frequently destroyed any other career possibilities they might have had. No sports performer can avoid making sacrifices; the black performers' sacrifices are just greater than most.

Tyson case

On 19 September 1991, heavyweight boxer Mike Tyson was indicted by a Marion County grand jury of raping Desiree Washington, a contestant at a Miss Black America pageant, who claimed Tyson had forcibly had sex with her in an Indianapolis hotel room. Tyson had attended the pageant. On 10 February 1992, Tyson was convicted of rape and sentenced to six years in prison. Washington later alleged that Tyson had given her a venereal disease. Tyson was released from prison in March 1995, and resumed his professional boxing career five months later under the guidance of Don King. During his imprisonment, the boxer converted to Islam.

But, the gains are greater too, the reader might argue. Even the black sports performers who don't spring to mind when we talk of riches are millionaires. Linford Christie, (the sprinter), Andy Cole, (the soccer player), Sandra Farmer Patrick, (the hurdler); sport is such a lucrative area, nowadays, that even modest success earns a lot of money. And, no matter how you interpret the evidence, many blacks achieve success relative to the number of blacks in the total population. African Americans account for about 13 percent of the total US populations; African Caribbeans are, by the largest estimate, only 2 percent of the British population. Yet, the NBA has 80–90 percent majority of black players, and one in five professional soccer players in Britain is black. Ninety percent of world boxing champions are black. We could marshal other figures to support what is an obvious fact: black people over-achieve in sports; it's also a fact that far more leave sport in failure and disappointment. We need to uncover some of the processes at work beneath these facts.

There are also questions to be asked about women, not a minority group in a numerical sense, but certainly a minority in terms of top jobs, wealth, income, and political influence. The position of women in sports is, generally speaking, quite unlike that of black people, for they have been discouraged from participating, often by means of convenient fallacies about their being physically incapable of withstanding the pressures of competition and naturally unsuited to the demands of sport. Their results have – certainly up to quite recently – shown this to be so. Women do not, by and large, compete head-to-head with men (and when they do, they are invariably beaten) and where performance can be measured, women are some way behind their male counterparts. Again, this is deceptive for there have been concealed processes at work for many decades and these have served to suppress women's success in sport.

Cast in a different light, women's experience is comparable with that of blacks. Being minorities, both have marginal positions, meaning that they are largely excluded from many of the key areas of society. Neither features prominently in politics, the professions, or other areas of society where important decisions are made that affect people's lives. Their exclusion is usually the product of an "-ism": as blacks are discriminated against and their accomplishments diminished through racism, so women are prohibited from competing on equal terms with men through sexism. Both remain on the underside of a lopsided structure of inequality and this has affected the involvement of both in sport in quite different ways, as we will see in this and the following chapters.

Escape attempts

There is quite a story to blacks' involvement with organized sport in the West. It begins in the late eighteenth century during the American War of Independence, when General Percy of the British forces captured the town of Richmond. Impressed by the fighting prowess of a slave who worked on the plantations there, Percy took Bill Richmond – as he named him – under his tutelage and groomed him for prize-fighting. While it couldn't have been an

> ## Racism
>
> A set of beliefs or ideas based on the assumption that the world's population can be divided into different human biological groups designated "races." Following on from this is the proposition that the "races" are ordered hierarchically, so that some stand in a position of superordinacy, or superiority, to others. This is a classic type of racism; nowadays, ideas of superiority are often veiled in arguments concerning culture, nationalism, and ethnic identity. Quite often, these contain connotations of racism that are not specific, but only inferred. When ideas, or beliefs, about racial superiority are translated into action, we speak in terms of racial discrimination, or simply *racialism*. Racism is the idea; racialism is the practice.

easy life, prize-fighting had its perks (like extensive travel in Europe) and must have seemed far preferable to plantation work. Richmond was something of a prototype, his modest success encouraging slave owners and merchants to scour for potential fighters whom they might patronize.

The celebrated Tom Molyneaux was one such fighter. Once a slave he was taken to England and trained by Richmond, eventually winning his freedom. Molyneaux built on his predecessor's success, hobnobbing with the nobility and generally mixing with the London beau monde. It was in his classic fight with English heavyweight champion Tom Cribb, in 1810, that he created his niche in sports history. Peter Jackson was born on the West Indies island of St Croix and travelled to Sydney and San Francisco before settling in England in the late nineteenth century. He, more than any pugilist of his day, embraced fame, though world champion John L. Sullivan's refusal to fight him denied him the ultimate title. Yet his decline was abrupt and he became a habitual drinker and was made to play in a stage version of Stowe's *Uncle Tom's Cabin*.

Some slaves continued to leave America to campaign as prize-fighters in Europe, but the majority were pitted against each other locally. The years on either side of emancipation in 1865 saw blacks filtering into other sports; they were most successful at horse-riding and baseball. In the latter, they were not permitted to play with or against whites. Ninety-eight years after the first Molyneaux–Cribb clash, a black man ascended to the apogee of sporting achievement. John Arthur Johnson in 1908 challenged and beat Tommy Burns, a white man, to become the heavyweight champion of the world. Fighting as "Jack Johnson," he broke the "color line" which segregated blacks from whites in all areas, including sport. In fact, after Johnson eventually lost the title in 1916, the line was redrawn and no black man was allowed to fight for the world title until 1937 when Joe Louis started a succession of black champions interrupted only by Rocky Marciano (1952–5), Ingemar Johannson (1959–60), and Gerrie Coetzee (1983–4). It's puzzling to wonder why Jack Dempsey is often acknowledged as one of the "greats" when he either refused or was prevented from defending his title against blacks.

Johnson and, in an entirely different way, Louis were black sports symbols, Johnson especially cultivating a reputation as a "bad nigger," a moral hard man who, as Lawrence Levine puts it, "had the strength and courage and ability to flout the limitations imposed by white society" (1977: 420). Johnson's imagery was based as much on his penchant for the company of white women as his boxing. This was a time when the Ku Klux Klan was in its ascendancy and blacks were lynched for far lesser deeds than consorting with white females. Far from being "bad," Louis was a virtual Uncle Tom character, obsequious, apolitical and exploitable – as his poverty, despite vast ring earnings, demonstrates. Yet, he too was a potent symbol for black Americans who were short of heroes or role models on whom to style their own lives. Both were anomalies: conspicuously successful black men in a society where success was virtually monopolized by whites.

The other outstanding black sportsman of this period was Jesse Owens who, like Louis, was "a credit to his race" – which meant he was self-effacing and compliant to the demands of white officials. Well, not totally compliant: after returning a performance of theatrical proportions at the 1936 "Nazi Olympics" in Berlin, where he won four gold medals and shamed Hitler into a walk-out, he was expelled from the American Athletics Union for refusing to compete in a Swedish tour. Owens was eventually reduced to freak show racing against horses and motorcycles. Other black sports performers were similarly brought to reduced circumstances. Johnson suffered the indignity of imprisonment, of fighting bulls in Barcelona, of performing stunts in circuses, of comically playing Othello, and of boxing all-comers in exhibitions at the age of 68. Louis ended his days ignominiously in a wheelchair, welcoming visitors at a Las Vegas hotel. The careers of all three followed a comet's elliptical path, radiating brilliance in their orbit, yet fading into invisibility. Plenty of other blacks have followed the same route. Sports history is full of dreams turning to nightmares. But black sportsmen seem particularly afflicted. Not even "The Greatest," Muhammad Ali, could maintain his dignity in later years.

While boxing was the first sport in which blacks were able to cross the color line and compete with whites, others followed the form. In 1946, when Joe Louis was nearing the end of his reign as heavyweight king (and the year in which Jack Johnson died), Jackie Robinson became the first black person to play major league baseball. He was sent death threats and his teams, Montreal and the Brooklyn Dodgers, were sometimes boycotted by opponents. The hostility of his reception may have initially daunted administrators from recruiting black players, but by the 1950s the numbers entering major league were multiplying.

Nowadays, basketball is dominated by black players. The trend began in 1951 when Chuck Hooper signed for Boston Celtics and precipitated a rush: within 16 years, over half the National Basketball Association players were black. The specter of freak show that had hung over Owens and the others visited basketball in the shape of the Harlem Globetrotters whose goals were more in making audiences laugh than scoring hoops. The comic Globetrotters' popularity with whites was probably because of the players' conformity to the image of blacks as physically adept, but too limited intellectually to harness skill to firm objectives. James Michener in *Sports in America*, wrote of the Globetrotters: "They deepened the stereotype of 'the loveable [*sic*], irresponsible Negro'" (1976: 145).

Civil rights legislation in 1964 and 1965 erased the color line, in a *de jure*, or legal, sense at least. As the segregationist barriers in education tumbled down, so black youngsters began to mix and play competitively with whites. College football came within reach of more blacks and this, in turn, translated into more black professional players. By 1972, African American players comprised 40 percent of the NFL.

Stereotype
An image or depiction of a group based on false or, at best, incomplete information, which can be used as the basis for gross generalizations about members of such groups. Typically, a stereotype extracts alleged features of a culture or a "race" and elevates these to prominence, making them into defining characteristics. The stereotype is usually insulting, frequently demeaning and occasionally hostile.

In Britain, the historical developments were similar, though compressed into a shorter timespan and with considerably fewer numbers, of course. The old prize-fighters Richmond and Molyneaux were followed by a succession of prize-fighters, one notable being Andrew Jeptha, who migrated from Cape Town, South Africa, in 1902 and became the first-ever black boxer to hold a British title in 1907 (this was before the formation of the British Boxing Board of Control). On the track, sprinters from the British Caribbean, like Arthur

Wharton, Jack London, McDonald Bailey, and Arthur Wint established reputations from the end of the nineteenth century to the 1950s.

Wharton transferred to professional soccer with Preston North End, thus becoming the first-ever black player; though the person popularly credited with that distinction is Lloyd Lindbergh Delaphena, who played for Middlesbrough and Portsmouth in the 1950s. This period was one of mass migration from the Caribbean and, as a consequence, many migrants, such as Trinidad's Yolande Pompey and Guyana's Cliff Anderson, were active in British rings. Hogan "Kid" Bassey, originally from Nigeria but based in Liverpool, won the world featherweight title in 1957.

But one boxer embodied all the elements of the black sportsman in this period. Born in the Midlands town of Leamington Spa in 1928, Randolph Turpin had a Guyanese migrant father and an English mother. Inspired by the example of his older brother Dick, who in 1948 won the British middleweight title, Randolph had a shimmering boxing career that came to a climax in 1951 when he upset Sugar Ray Robinson to become the world middleweight champion. Lacking any financial acumen, he ran into trouble with the Inland Revenue which filed a bankruptcy petition against him for unpaid tax on his considerable ring earnings. His career plunged to humiliating depths when he engaged in "boxer vs wrestler" bouts and even consented to a fully fledged comeback in an unlicensed boxing promotion at the age of 35. On 16 May 1966 he committed suicide by shooting himself, though rumors of a gangland murder were rife, according to his biographer Jack Birtley (1976: 140–53). His fall resembled that of other black champions.

Marilyn Fay Neufville broke the world's 400-meter record in 1970 when she was 18. Born in Jamaica, she ran for Cambridge Harriers, a London club, and became the first black female to make an impact on British sport. Sprint events were later virtually dominated by black women, but less conspicuously, judo and volleyball also benefited from the growing participation of black women.

Unlike the USA, Britain has never had formal segregation, so black school children have competed in sport with peers from a variety of ethnic backgrounds. Soccer, as the nation's most popular game, has been played in high schools throughout the country so it was not unexpected when, in the late 1970s and early 1980s, black players began appearing in Football League teams. First, the trickle: Albert Johanneson, a Leeds United player in the 1960s; Clyde Best, who played for West Ham United in the 1970s. Then the flood: dozens of professional players, including Viv Anderson, who in 1979 became the first black footballer to represent England, began to appear, prompting reactions from the racist fans, who frequently pelted them with bananas and targeted them for abusive chants. Through the 1980s, black footballers continued to make their mark on British soccer often to the ambiguous rejoicing of newspapers whose "Black Magic" and "Black Power" headlines were more than faintly reminiscent of a London paper's banner after a promotion in June 1946 when five black boxers posted wins: "Black Night for British Boxing" (quoted in Henderson 1949: 340).

At the close of the 1980s, a "second generation" of British-born blacks was established in British sport. Over half the British boxing champions were black as were more than 40 percent of the Olympic squad of 1988, and virtually every Football League club had two or three black players on its books. It is no coincidence that the major sports in which blacks have excelled – boxing, track and field, football, and basketball – are ones which demand little in the way of equipment. They can be practiced away from any formal organization and with minimal resources. A strong pair of legs, fast hands, sharp reflexes, and a desire to compete are basics. Much more than this is needed to progress in the club-oriented sports, like cricket, golf, and tennis, which tend to be accessible only to the middle class. It might be argued that cricket has some possibilities for players of working-class backgrounds – and blacks in the main come from such backgrounds – but the very structure of the sport and the educational institutions in which it is encouraged make it more available to the more affluent class. The same argument applies to Rugby Union.

In the more accessible sports, blacks have grown to a prominence that belies their numerical minority status in both the USA and Britain. Their sometimes overwhelming success in certain sports is quite disproportionate to their numbers within the total population. The ratio is most pronounced in boxing, track and field, and basketball. But in sports in which blacks have either been allowed to compete or have been attracted to, they seem to approach a mastery that is difficult to match. Blacks' apparent predilection for sport, and the high orders of success they have achieved, has been the subject of bar-room discussion and academic controversy. Why so many in sport and why so many champions? The answers are intertwined.

Second nature

One of the simplest and most influential explanations of black excellence has been supplied by Martin Kane in an article in the magazine *Sports Illustrated*; the article is entitled "An assessment of black is best" (18 January 1971). At the center of Kane's argument is the "insight" that blacks are endowed with a natural ability that gives them an advantage in certain sports. Around this lie a number of other related points, many culled from Kane's interviews with medical scientists, coaches, and sports performers. An important, though oddly dated, point is that there are race-linked physical characteristics.

Blacks as a "race" have proportionately longer legs to whites, narrower hips, wider calf bones, greater arm circumference, greater ratio of tendon to muscle, denser skeletal structure, and a more elongated body. Typically, they have power and an efficient body-heat dissipation system. Kane inferred these features from a small sample of successful black sportsmen – that is, a minority with proven excellence rather than a random sample from the total population. And he concludes that blacks are innately different and the differences, being genetic in origin, can be passed on from one generation to the next.

So, cold climates are said to affect all blacks badly, even ones who are born and brought up in places like Toronto. Weak ankle bones would account for the relative absence of black ice hockey players. The disadvantages are transmitted genetically, as are natural advantages which equip blacks to do well in particular sports where speed and power are essential. Kane argues that blacks are not suited to endurance events. Since the publication of the article, hundreds of African distance runners have undermined this point, though Kane tries to cover himself by claiming Kenyans have black skin, but a number of white features.

Kane's arguments border on the absurd, especially when we consider anthropologists' dismissal of the concept of race itself as having any analytical value at all. Black people are descended from African populations, but, over the centuries, their genetic heritage has become diversified and complicated by various permutations of mating. There is no "pure" race. Kane ignores this when he examines the area of psychology, emerging with a set of personality traits that are supposed to be determined by race. Blacks have the kind of yielding personality that puts them, as one coach told Kane, "far ahead of whites . . . relaxation under pressure" (1971: 76).

This has a common-sense authenticity about it, for coaches and spectators seem to associate black sports performers with a cool approach to competition, never stressing-out, or growing tense. But competitors themselves actually work at portraying this: they consciously try to convey an image that reflects coolness. That's all it is – image. Beneath the surface, black performers are as tense and concerned as anyone else. Possibly more so: sport for many blacks is not a casual recreation (as it may be for white youths), but a career path and every failure represents a possible sinking to obscurity. Every event has to be approached as if it were the most demanding of one's life; defeat is not easily assimilated as a result. Kane mistook impression management for deep psychological profiles.

Slavery is the key to the third part of Kane's argument. "Of all the physical and psychological theories about the American black's excellence in sport, none has proved more controversial than one of the least discussed: that slavery weeded out the weak" (1971: 80). Here Kane introduces some homespun Darwinism, his view being that, as only the fittest survived the rigors of slavery, those best suited to what must have been terribly harsh environments passed on their genes to successive populations, who used them to great effect in sport. There are two drawbacks to this. First, it's preposterous to suggest that blacks bred for generations in such a controlled way as to retain a gene pool in which specific genes related to, for instance, speed, strength, and agility, became dominant. Second, these properties were probably of less significance in matters of survival than intelligence, ingenuity, and anticipation and Kane considers none of these as essentially black features.

All three categories of Kane's theory gel into a formulation that states that blacks' achievements in sport are linked to their so-called race. Sport is seen as "second nature" to a black person. This implausible suggestion belongs in the realms of racist folklore and not scientific inquiry. Unfortunately, its simplicity and comprehensiveness have made it appealing to many who want to explain the success of blacks in sport as due to race. US writer Harry Edwards has even suggested that the explanation itself has effects for white competitors who, believing blacks to be innately superior, start off at a psychological disadvantage. "The 'white race' thus becomes the chief victim of its own myth" (1973: 197).

But its appeal disguises something more sinister because, if we accept as proof of the natural ability argument the outstanding results recorded by black sports performers then what are we to infer from the underachievement of blacks in formal education? That they are naturally limited intellectually? If so, it could be argued that they should be encouraged to develop their gifts and possibly neglect areas in which they haven't much aptitude. Sadly, this is what has happened in the past and it gives us the first clue in answering the question of blacks' sporting success all over again, this time with an entirely different approach.

Losers and still champions

History alone tells us that sport has been one of the two channels through which blacks have been able to escape the imprisonment of slavery and the impoverishment that followed its dissolution; the other being entertainment. In both spheres, blacks performed largely for the amusement of patrician whites. This holds true to this day: the season-ticket holder or cable television subscriber, no less than old-time slave masters, have decisive effects on the destinies of sports performers. For this reason, slaves were encouraged; the incentive might be freedom or at least a temporary respite from daily labors.

There is an adage that emerged during the 1930s depression in York-shire, England, a county famed for its cricket and its mining industry: "Shout down any coalpit and half a dozen fast bowlers will come out." The theme is similar: that material deprivation is an ideal starting point for sporting prowess. "Hungry fighters" are invariably the most effective. As we have seen, many fight their way out, only to return to indigence; but they're not to know that as they're striving for improvement. Blacks' supposed predilection for sport is more a product of material circumstances than natural talent.

Whether or not sport is a viable avenue from despair is not the issue: it has been seen as such by people who lacked alternatives. And the perception has stuck, and probably will continue to stick as long as obstacles to progress in other avenues remain. The argument here is that the early slave prize-fighters began a tradition by setting themselves up – quite unwittingly – as cultural icons, or images to be revered and copied; in today's parlance, role models. The stupendous success of blacks in such sports as boxing and athletics has clearly been inspirational to countless young blacks over the decades.

Racism and racial discrimination have worked to exclude blacks from many areas of employment, restrict their opportunities and, generally, push them toward the "marginal" or least important areas of the labor market. Experiencing this at first hand or anticipating it through the stories of others has set young people thinking about alternative sources of employment. "There aren't too many successful black tycoons, professionals, or politicians, so where should I look for an example?" black youths might ask themselves. Answers spring to mind readily: Shaq O'Neal (estimated earnings: $60 million [£38 million] and climbing), Lenda Murray (enjoys a status on par with a movie star), Emmitt Smith (stellar running back in the NFL); the list goes on. Blacks *can* make it, but only in certain areas. Evaporating into insignificance are the millions of other aspirants whose fortune never materialized and whose career ended shabbily. No matter how remote the chances of success may be, the tiny number of elite black sports stars supply tangible and irrefutable evidence that it can be achieved.

By their early teens, black youths showing potential become draught horses, drawing along the displaced ambitions of parents, sibling and human cargo of others who, for some reason, have had their own ambitions blighted and remain fixed in the underclass, their only hope of redemption lying in the success of the would-be champion. Encouraged, even cajoled, by physical education teachers at high school who might subscribe to the popular if mistaken view that blacks have "natural talent," young persons might, while running or fighting, discover new dimensions of themselves. Zealous scouts for colleges pump up the youths with inflated claims when they attempt to woo them into their programs. Many youths understandably find comfort in

> **Cultural icons**
> The term "icon" is from the Greek *eikon*, meaning image. Its applica-
> tion to culture refers to the image that is conferred, granted or attributed
> to an individual by a collection of others. In a sense, the cultural icon
> exists almost independently of the individual, who may be a sports or
> rock star: popular perceptions, expectations and beliefs define the icon
> much more powerfully than the person. Jack Johnson, for example,
> "was not merely a fighter but a symbol," as Levine puts it (1977: 430).
> In 1912, it was widely believed that Johnson had been refused passage
> on the doomed *Titanic*, and this enhanced his status even further.
> Contemporary cultural icons also have beliefs built around them
> that contribute to their status: Madonna and Michael Jackson are
> supreme cultural icons of the late twentieth century; there is a willing-
> ness to believe almost anything about either of them. Similarly, some
> contemporary black sports stars command iconic status.

the view that they do possess natural advantages. The fact that such views are
based on stereotypes not realities doesn't enter into it: beliefs often have a
self-fulfilling quality, so that if you believe in your own ability strongly
enough, you eventually acquire that ability. I can illustrate the point.

A few years ago, I received a call from a journalist from the British
Sunday Times. He was writing a story on black over-achievement in sports
and wanted to know why no one actually expressed what he felt was an
evident truth: that there is a natural edge that blacks possess. Was it because
of political correctness? he asked. Partly, I answered, but also because it has
racist implications and mainly because it is just wrong. Then, I qualified
my response: the fact that a journalist, who happened to be black himself,
writing for a prestigious newspaper was prepared to entertain the idea was
testimony to its power. It's not only whites who have bought the myth of black
natural talent in sport: black people have accepted and, in some cases, even
clung to a tinpot theory that has actually performed a disservice.

Actually, it's not the myth itself that has performed the disservice so
much as the culture in which it has stayed credible; that being one in which
blacks have been regarded as unsuited to or just unwanted for work that
demands intellect and imagination – cerebral rather than physical skills.
Study after study in the USA and Britain – and, more recently, in parts of
continental Europe – has chronicled the extent and intensity of racism in
today's society. We need not dwell on specific examples; suffice it to say that in
the post-war years in Britain and for many more years before that in the USA,

blacks have been systematically squeezed out of education and employment opportunities for reasons that derive from, in its rawest form, racist hostility.

The origins of this hostility lie in the European colonial expansion of the seventeenth century, the settlement of the West Indies, or Caribbean, and the expansion of trade in slaves, gold, and sugar between Africa, the Americas, and Britain. Slavery meant that whites maintained their domination over blacks and so kept a rigid inequality. The inequality has been modified and lessened in the decades following emancipation, but blacks have never quite shed the remnants of their shackles and whites have passed on their colonial mentality. Seeing blacks as great sports performers might seem a compliment, but, as Harry Edwards observes, "the only difference between the black man shining shoes in the ghetto and the champion black sprinter is that the shoe shine man is a nigger, while the sprinter is a fast nigger" (1970: 20).

Historically, sport, along with entertainment, was one of the areas in which blacks were allowed to maximize their prowess, and circumstances haven't changed sufficiently to permit a significant departure. Blacks still approach sport with vigor and commitment at least partly because persistent racism effectively closes off other channels. Even if those other channels have become freer in recent years, black youths have become accustomed to anticipating obstacles to their progress. So that, by the time they prepare to make the transition from school to work, many have made sports as a career their first priority.

With sights set on a future filled with championships, black youths fight their way into sports determined that, slim though their chances may be, they will succeed. And they usually do, though mostly in an altogether more modest way than they envisaged. Few attain the heights they wanted to conquer and even fewer surpass them. An unstoppable motivation and unbreakable commitment are valuable, perhaps essential, assets to success in sport and this is why so many possessors of these achieve some level of distinction. But titles are, by definition, reserved for only a very small elite and, while blacks are always well-represented among the elite of all sports in which they compete, there are never enough championships to go round. The majority inevitably fail.

Blacks' success in sports may look impressive, but, compared to the numbers of youths entering sport, their interest primed, their success is not so great, even when their chances are affected by "stacking" and other racialist maneuvers. Sheer weight of numbers dictates that a great many African Americans and African Caribbeans will rise to the top of certain sports. When the phenomenon is approached this way, the reasons are less opaque. There is no need to resort to imprecise ideas such as natural ability: blacks' sporting success is actually constructed in history and contemporary culture. Let me summarize.

> **Stacking**
> This refers to the disproportionate concentration of ethnic minorities in certain positions in a sports team. In American football, black players have been allocated to running-back and wide-receiver positions; in baseball, they have been stacked in outfield positions. This tends to exclude them from, for instance, quarterback and starting pitching positions – which are the most prestigious – and compels them to compete against other blacks for their team position. It could be argued that stacking is based on stereotypes and that such stereotypes are in the process of being dismantled by quarterbacks such as Warren Moon and Randall Cunningham, who show intelligence and judgement rather than power and speed in their play. Equally, evidence from baseball (Jiobu 1988) suggests that the stereotypes still operate. (Eitzen has studied stacking in depth, both with Sanford 1975, and with Yetman 1977; see also Curtis and Loy 1978.)

Cultures on both sides of the Atlantic have fostered strains of racism that, while less virulent now than 20 years ago, are still bitter enough to convince young black people that their future in mainstream society may be curtailed by popularly held stereotypes about their abilities. Weighing up the possibilities of a future career, many opt for a shot at sports, where it has been demonstrated time and again that black people can make it to the very top and command the respect of everyone, whites included. Respect is a sought-after commodity by people who have been denied it historically. Ideas of the *White Men Can't Jump* variety are conveyed to young black people by possibly well-meaning, but mistaken, coaches and high school teachers who enthuse over a career in sports. Then the story separates into two contrasting plots. Some tread the road to respectability, even stardom, making a living they can be proud of from professional sports. Others dissolve into oblivion, never to be heard of.

What this scenario doesn't seem to account for is the scarcity of black competitors, let alone winners, in certain sports. Their exclusion from more expensive pursuits like golf, shooting, skiing and so on is obvious: you need money to get started. But swimming, tennis or some field events pose more of a mystery. One might reasonably suppose that, over the years, a percentage of young blacks would gravitate toward areas not traditionally black-dominated. Perhaps they will, but so far the pull of the icons has been irresistible. Black stars today have been recast into idols by corporations, watchful of an emergent black middle class with plenty of disposable income.

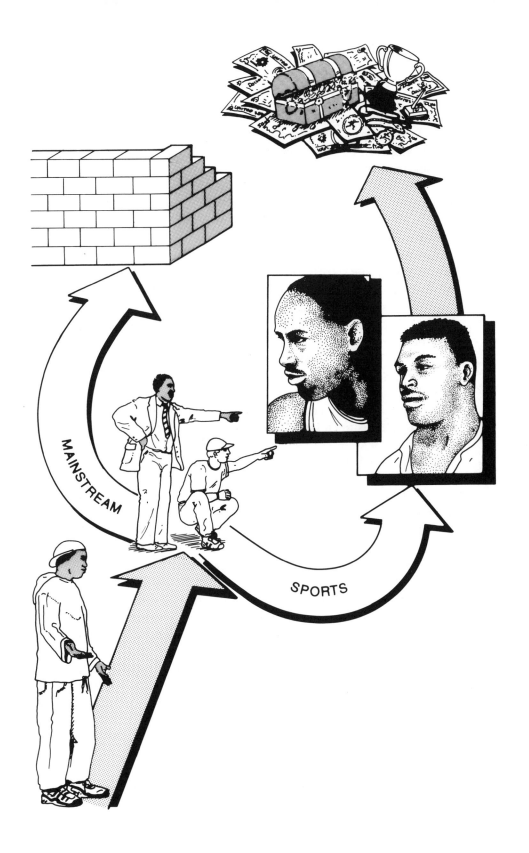

Having their products endorsed by successful blacks can help them gain a piece of the developing African American market.

As recently as 1987, Eitzen and Sage reported that world-ranked tennis players Lori McNeill and Zina Garrison were missing out on sponsors to inferior white players (1993: 339). Since then there has been a steady march of blacks into higher tax brackets. By 1995, it was possible for the Wall Street value of stocks in the five companies endorsed by Michael Jordan to swell by $2.3 billion (£1.4 billion) amid rumors that he would return to basketball. The endorsement of a recognizably successful sports performer can add enormously to the marketability of a product. Advertisers have been guided less by fine spirits, more by the argument that affluent blacks can be persuaded to part with their money by other, more successful blacks.

The result is the transformation of the likes of David Robinson and Barry Sanders into something much more than sports performers: they have become representatives of an aspirational culture in which people are prepared to emulate them in nearly every respect. If they chase the same dreams and seek the same praise, they might eat the same breakfast cereal or wear the same sneakers. If those dreams have long since gone, they might still buy the products they endorse. Whatever the logic behind the advertisers' ploy, the effect is to create a televisual pantheon for living sports stars. The majority of young blacks will structure their ambitions around the icons of success they see before them, all but deified by tv culture.

But, there is no natural reason why blacks should not excel in other sports – those historically reserved for whites. Charlie Shifford, along with several other black golfers, was shut out of the Masters, but a change in Professional Golf Association (PGA) rules in 1990 required that all tournaments be played only at clubs that did not discriminate. Ron Townsend became a reluctant celebrity in the same year when he became the first black member of the Augusta National Golf Club in Georgia, for long a bastion of southern white leadership. Fifteen years before, Lee Elder had been the first black player to compete at Augusta; but golf is a prohibitively expensive sport and few blacks have broken through to the pro ranks since. It will take years before Tiger Flowers and other prospects begin to win major titles.

Perhaps the most unlikely black professional emerged in Britain during the early 1990s. Spurning traditional routes, Oliver Skeetes applied himself to equestrian sport and became an accomplished rider. The apparent incongruity of a black male in hunting pink and jodhpurs made Skeetes a media darling, though British tabloids were typically interested in his sexual rather than sporting accomplishments. Golf and equestrian are hardly fertile areas for black progress. The fact that black players have made impressions, albeit at relatively low levels, suggests that more traditionally white-dominated sports will soon accommodate black performers.

Even swimming: for long seen as a taboo sport for blacks on account of their alleged heavy bones, swimming will begin to attract more black competitors. We will then see the sinking of one of the most durable myths in sport.

We know about the "before" part of the black experience in sports, how and why athletes make it to the pros, or fail in the process. The "during" phase can be read about in the sports pages of any newspaper. But, what happens "after"? Rags-to-riches and back-to-rags stories are legion. Boxers especially have a knack of earning and blowing fortunes: Razor Ruddock was one of many millionaires-cum-bankrupts when he was declared financially insolvent in 1995. Others go on to become sportcasters, movies stars and all-round media personalities; the most successful of these combined all three and became the most famous black sports star ever – but for the wrong reasons, of course.

Considering the heavy investment of black people in the playing side of sport, one might expect many to stay in sport and serve in officiating or administrative capacities Here there is an unevenness. Although, there has been a steadily growing number of black game officials since 1965 (when Burt Tolar became the NFL's first black official), the number of black coaches and administrators has been few. Dennis Green, who was the first African American head football coach when he joined Northwestern University in 1981, later went on to coach Minnesota Vikings. Art Shell was the first black NFL coach when he joined Los Angeles Raiders in 1989. In Britain, Viv Anderson successfully transited from playing to managing, first at Barnsley, then as assistant manager at Middlesbrough. Black people are certainly appearing in the front offices, but not in the numbers one might expect from a glance at the number of active players

Interestingly, there are (literally) one or two African Americans who have bypassed the salaried positions and headed straight for the seats of power. Beginning as a boxing promoter in the 1970s, Don King became one of the most powerful figures in sport: a man at the center of an extensive web of business interests stretching over a range of sports and sports-related areas. Peter Bynoe and Bertram Lee aspired to King-like powers in 1989 when they bought the Denver Nuggets of the NBA for $50 million (£31 million); they were the first African American owners of a major sports club. The deal went sour when Lee had cashflow problems and was made to sell his share. Bynoe also sold out in 1992, leaving the sports without a black owner, though Evander Holyfield and Hammer were prepared to spend $80 million (£50 million) on Houston Rockets.

There is a scene in the movie *Hoop Dreams*, in which a basketball coach addresses his protégés with some sobering statistics. Each year, 500,000 boys play high school basketball, he tells them. Of the 14,000 who progress to

---

Don King

The world's leading sports promoter has summed up his own rise thus: "I was an ex-numbers runner, ex-convict who received a full, uncondi-tional pardon. I am, what they would say in America, what everyone's supposed to be – when coming from the wrong side of the track to the right side of the track" (quoted in Regen 1990: 115). After serving a prison sentence for manslaughter, King's first promotional venture was in 1972 when he staged an exhibition by Muhammad Ali in an African Americans' hospital in Cleveland. His first major promotion in 1974 (when aged 43), also featured Ali, when he regained the heavyweight title from George Foreman in Zaïre. After this, King kept an interest in the heavyweight championship, either by promoting bouts or managing the champions. Mike Tyson left his manager Bill Cayton and entered into a business relationship with King. Tyson refused to criticize King, even when many of his boxers, like ex-champion Tim Witherspoon, turned against him. King has also co-promoted rock stars, such as Michael Jackson, and began his own ppv tv system, KingVision. His biggest pro-motion never materialized: Tyson's conviction and imprisonment for rape meant that a fight with Evander Holyfield (originally scheduled for 8 November 1991) fell through. It was expected to gross more than $100 million (£62 million), with the ppv operation alone drawing $80 million, foreign sales $10 million and the promotional fee from Caesar's Palace $11 million. Former heavyweight champion Larry Holmes once said of King: "He looks black, lives white and thinks green."

---

intercollegiate basketball, fewer than 25 percent ever play *one* season in the NBA. Don't reach for your calculator: it works out at about 1:143. Some American writers, like Jack Olsen and Nathan Hare, have looked at the underside of this "shameful story" (as Olsen calls it) which begins with visions of wealth and glamor but frequently ends in poverty, crime and, sometimes, insanity. Their conclusions concur with those of Edwards in the sense that they believe that young blacks are seduced into sport and, in the process, ignore their formal academic and vocational studies. They invest so much energy in sport that little is left for other pursuits. So, by the time dreams fade, they are left with few if any career alternatives and join the gallery of "also-rans."

Sports that attract blacks are always expensive in terms of people: wasteful, profligate even. If it takes 143 ambitious kids to make one NBA player for one season, how many to produce a Jordan? Entering sports is less a career choice, more a lottery. As I noted earlier, the idea of recruiting bowlers from Yorkshire coalpits might have proved workable in the 1930s. Now, young whites are told to enjoy their cricket, but, first, get a degree and qualify as a lawyer or a doctor. The same piece of advice doesn't reach as far as inner London, or South Central LA.

There are always a small number of outstanding performers with naturally endowed faculties, but there's no reason to suppose that the black population has a monopoly or even a majority of them. Success in sport is due much more to non-physical qualities such as drive, determination, and an ability to focus sharply. Given that blacks see the job market as a maze of culs-de-sac, they may well accrue more than their fair share of these qualities. Failure has potentially direr consequences for them than for their white, working-class counterparts who, while still having limited opportunities, at least escape racialism.

Returning to *Hoop Dreams*, we hear the familiar cliché from one of the school players: "Basketball is my ticket out of the ghetto." One can almost hear a chorus of others saying the same thing. It is explosive motivational fuel. Add the "push" of outsiders, the magnetizing influence of black icons and you have a heady mixture – one which sends young blacks into sport year after year. If and when this slows, it's been suggested that this would reflect a quickening of the rate at which opportunities arise in the job market. In other words, if racialism disappeared completely there'd be only a few black sports stars. That's not the case at present and, while discrimination persists, sport is bound to prosper from the contributions of blacks. This shouldn't disguise the practices and processes which effectively produce the black sports star, who is both a champion and loser – a symbol of the failure they, as champions, never experience. From the 1770s to the present, sport has been a route to fame and material fortune for thousands of blacks and will continue to be that in the future. For tens of thousands of others it will be only a route to nowhere. Sport conceals deep inequalities and, for all the positive benefits it yields, it remains a source of hope and ambition for blacks only as long as those inequalities remain.

FURTHER READING

A Hard Road to Glory by Arthur Ashe (Amistad/Warner Books, 1988) is a three-volume history of the participation of African Americans in sports. Ashe himself, during and after his tennis career, was a constant advocate of academic study over sports and spoke publicly on the need for black children to temper their sports ambitions.

Five Minutes to Midnight by Richard Lapchick (Madison Books, 1991) is a reflection on the author's arguments of two previous books. Broken Promises (St Martin's Press/Marek, 1984) begins with an account of the author's own beating-up by racists because of his vocal opposition to a Davis Cup tennis competition between the USA and South Africa. Later, the scope of the book broadens to include a general assessment of racism in American sport. The other book is Fractured Focus (Heath, 1986).

All in the Game? Sport, race and politics is a special edition of the journal Race and Class (vol. 36, no. 4 April–June, 1995) and may be read in conjunction with Winners and Losers by Gajendra Verma and Douglas Darby (Falmer, 1994) which is based on a two-year study in Manchester, England, designed to explore the orientations ethnic minorities have toward sports and the response of providers of sports facilities. The research focuses mainly on South Asian youth.

A Sociological Perspective of Sport, 3rd edn, by Wilbert Leonard (Macmillan, 1988) has a chapter "Sport and race" which is a useful summary of many of the issues and research findings relating to this subject. Complementing this is Participation by Blacks and Ethnic Minorities in Sport and Recreation: A review of the literature by Jose Parry (London Research Centre, 1988).

ASSIGNMENT

In 1947, psychologists Kenneth and Mamie Clark conducted a famous experiment: they asked 253 black children to choose between four dolls, two black and two white. The result: two-thirds of the children preferred white dolls. Conclusion: that black children had internalized the hatred society directed at all black people and so suffered from poor self-esteem. But this was before the rise of so many African American and African Caribbean sports icons. Repeat the experiment using a smaller sample of children, but use dolls in the likeness of famous sports stars: two black and two white. Document the results and draw out the implications, taking note of major social changes over the past 50 years.

The Great Debates II
Which is the toughest sport?

While there is no set of objective criteria available, we might list endurance, physical punishment sustained and demands on the body when we try to evaluate the toughest sport.

Pro cycling involves

- 155 miles covered in a 7-hour day's racing.
- Typically, 14 mountains climbed, none lower than 1,000 feet.
- Average 10,000 calories per day burned.
- Competition takes place in extreme weather conditions: rain, cold, debilitating heat do not cause postponements.

Rugby Union involves

- Two halves each of 40 minutes of continuous play.
- No protective padding apart from optional skull-cap-style headgear to protect ears.
- Tackles and hits allowable below neck by players usually 200-plus lbs.
- Injuries often caused by off-the-ball and, therefore, illegal hits, headbutts, raking (dragging cleats across face of felled player) and gouging.

Pro boxing involves

- 12 championship rounds, each of 3 minutes duration with 60-second interval between each.
- Only protection is padded cup covering groin and 8oz or 6oz gloves.
- Accelerated force of 50G from heavyweight's punch is equivalent to being hit with 14-lb padded hammer at 20 mph.
- Injuries include facial cuts and bruises, broken noses and brain damage.

Triathlon involves

- Swimming for 2.5 miles (4 km) without break; cycling continuously for 75 miles (120 km); running 19 miles (30 km). Distances vary.
- Losing about 4,500 fluid ounces (225 pints or 128 liters) of bodily fluids over six hours or more.
- Competitions take place in any weather conditions, with rough seas, heat, and humidity posing particular problems to competitors.
- All training (6 days per week at 6 hours a session) to be performed above the anaerobic threshold between 80–90 percent of maximum heart rate.

Chapter seven

The second sex
Why women are
devalued by sports

Ladies first

Imagine we have a DeLorean car like the one in the *Back to the Future* movies. We blast off, travelling backwards through time until we arrive at 1880, right in the middle of the period when most sports are acquiring sets of rules and institutional bodies to govern them. It is 32 years since Elizabeth Cady Stanton and Lucretia Mott met at Seneca Falls to launch the American Women's movement and two years since the 19th Amendment, which proposed votes for women, was first rejected by Congress. It will continue to be rejected in every session up till 1920. In Britain, women are poised to step up their campaigns: in 1903, they will become more militant in their attempts to secure political recognition for women. Emmeline Pankhurst's suffragettes will suffer indignity and violence in their ultimately successful efforts, but their only excursion into sports is horrific: in 1913, Emily Davidson will throw herself under a horse owned by King George V at the Derby race. It will take until 1918 before the franchise is extended and the shackles of Victorian Britain are left behind.

Women have no genuine involvement in sports save for watching men or playing somewhat gentle games such as skittles, quoits or croquet and their tennis seems relaxed and playful compared to the more competitive endeavors of men.

But we are going to change all that through a historical intervention: we have brought back a VCR and tapes of Steffi Graf to show how the game should really be played. And there's more: we have a video of Wang Junxia, of China, crossing the finishing line of a marathon with the clock showing 2:25. A game of women's rugby is a clincher, but, for good measure, we show the television show *American Gladiators* in which women flex their well-vascularized biceps and go head-to-head in combat.

This, we argue, is empirical proof that women, contrary to the Victorian ideal, are not as fragile, dainty or timid as they are made out to be. They can be tough, durable and combative; and they can be as muscular as their male counterparts. Sports' various governing organizations are convinced and immediately allow women admission into their activities, but not in separate events. Graf and the others look capable of playing and beating men, they say. This is not quite what we had in mind, but we let it pass. In one stroke, women are transformed from spectators to competitors: they run, play tennis, golf, football, they even venture into prize-fighting. We witness the first few contests. The female competitors get iced time and again. Yet, as we leave to return to the 1990s, we notice a slight but discernible improvement. What is happening in the present by the time we get back?

One answer to this is: no difference. Women will always come second and, usually, a very poor second to men. An alternative is: they are able to hold their own in virtually every sporting matchup in which raw physical strength is not the sole determining factor; that's most sports, of course. I have a definite answer, but, to arrive at it, need to explain the logic guiding the argument.

We can take the questions we asked about blacks' involvement in sport, invert them, and apply them to women. Why so few and why so little success compared to men? Both may draw objections on the grounds that women, nowadays, enter sport in considerable numbers and their achievements are many. But sportswomen are still a numerical minority and, in measurable terms at least, their performances do not match those of men. Pressed to offer an immediate explanation we might take the simple, but misleading, natural ability argument, suggesting that women are just not equipped to handle sports and are always carrying a physical handicap. But the argument has much the same failings as the "black is best" theory; it exaggerates physical factors and ignores social and psychological processes that either facilitate entry into or halt progress within sport. It replaces fact with myth, in this case a myth about women's inferiority.

In this sense, beliefs about women in sport have virtually exact parallels with those about women generally: they're not as capable intellectually or physically as men, their natural predisposition is to be passive and not active and their relationship to men is one of dependence. All three beliefs are sexist and have been strongly challenged since the late 1960s, of course, but their effect on sport is still evident.

Sexism

Like racism, a set of beliefs or ideas about the purported inferiority of some members of the population, in this case, women. The inferiority is thought to be based on biological differences between the sexes: women are naturally equipped for specific types of activities and roles and these don't usually include ones which carry prestige and influence.

Hunting has historically been a predominantly male pursuit, the early sexual division of labor ensuring that women, as bearers of children, had necessarily to spend more time at base camp while men sought food. This didn't prevent women's active involvement in sports and, as societies transformed, women took active roles. In ancient Greek and Roman times, they would hunt, ride, swim, and run, but not (usually) engage in combat. The medieval period saw some women, certainly noble women in parts of Europe, jousting. It's also probable that women competed in a forerunner of the modern game of darts which involved throwing 18-inch hand weapons at a barrel. Certainly, many women were adept archers.

As I've stated before, activities before the nineteenth century, while resembling sport in content, were not strictly sports in the contemporary sense of the word. By the time of the emergence of organized, rule-bound activities we now recognize as sports, women were effectively pushed out of the picture. The "age of chivalry" had made sure women were seen not as active agents but as objects to be placed on a pedestal, protected and revered. Frail of body and mind, women could not be expected to engage in any manner of physically exerting activity, save perhaps for dancing, horse-riding, bowling, and the occasional game of lacrosse. By the eighteenth century, the image of women as the "weaker sex" was well-established: their hair was to be worn up and their skirts to their ankles. Quite recent pictures of women playing tennis remind us that long skirts were *de rigueur*.

Tennis was actually one of the few areas where women were allowed to compete, though only those of means could afford to. As well as full skirts, they wore tight corsets, long-sleeved blouses, and boaters. It was a convention of Victorian society that women should appear decorative at all times. Not until 1931 did a woman break tradition: Lili de Alvarez of Spain caused a rumpus when she appeared in shorts at Wimbledon. The tradition she broke was one based on the Victorian ideal of women as gentle, delicate, and sub-missive. Women might let perspiration appear on their alabaster complexions, "glow" during exercise, but should never succeed in sport which was custom-arily associated with ruggedness, resilience, assertiveness, and a willingness to expend "blood, sweat, and tears." Women weren't capable of such feats and, even if they were, shouldn't attempt them on account of the harm they would inflict on themselves. Among the problems thought to result from physical exertion were an inability to conceive and 'masculinization' of body features.

Women, it was thought, were closer to nature than men: their duties should be confined to those nature conferred on them, like child-bearing and -rearing. Their role was to nurture. Far from being the product of a male conspiracy, this view was widely held and respected by men and women alike. Accepting that anything resembling strenuous exercise was detrimental to their well-being, women actually contributed, in a self-fulfilling way, to sexist beliefs about them. "The acceptance by women of their own incapacitation gave both a humane and moral weighting to the established scientific 'facts,'" writes Jennifer Hargreaves in her *Sporting Females* (1994: 47).

True, many women were campaigning forcefully and sacrificially in their quest for political suffrage, but their quest did not extend into sports. Women, particularly upper-middle-class women, sat ornamentally as they watched their menfolk participate in sports. But a closer inspection of women involved not so much in competitive sports but in active leisure pursuits, such as rock climbing or fell walking, would have revealed that women were as robust as men and their equals in endurance.

Pierre de Coubertin, to whom so much is owed for his vision of the modern Olympics, embodied Victorian sentiments when he urged the prohi-bition of women's participation in sport. The sight of the "body of a woman being smashed" was, he recorded, "indecent." "No matter how toughened a sportswoman may be, her organism is not cut out to sustain certain shocks" (quoted in Snyder and Spreitzer 1983: 155–6). The Olympics were to be dedicated to the "solemn and periodic exultation of male athleticism . . . with female applause as reward," said de Coubertin. Despite his reservations, women were included in the 1900 Olympics, four years after the inauguration, though in a restricted number of events and not in competition with men. Even as recently as 1980, Kari Fasting notes how women were not allowed to run a 3,000-meter event, the reason being that "it was too strenuous for women" (1987: 362).

Snyder and Spreitzer write about the types of sport women have been encouraged or discouraged from pursuing. "The 'appropriateness' of the type of sport continues to reflect the tenets of the Victorian ideal of femininity" (1983: 156). They go on to identify three types. The *categorically unacceptable* includes combat sports, some field events, and sports that involve attempts to

---

Women's rugby

In the 1930s, women from provincial badminton and tennis clubs in New Zealand got together and played rugby. It was planned to coincide with a men's matchup played on the same day and had no serious intentions: it was a sort of exhibition, almost a spoof of the men's game. Although women had played a version of rugby football in Wales in the nineteenth century, the NZ game was the first recorded competition played according to rugby union rules and, as such, was something of a breakthrough for women's sports. Rugby had traditionally been a byword for macho sport, the type of game for which women were thought ill-suited. After the Kiwi women had broken the taboo, women all over the world set about doing likewise. Organized matches in the USA and France started in the 1960s, leagues sprung up in Canada and all over Europe in the 1970s, and a Japanese women's league was established in 1983. The Women's Rugby Union was founded in 1983 in response to growing enthusiasm for rugby from women in Britain. It staged its first World Cup competition in 1991, Wales hosting a 12-nation tournament which was won by the USA "Eagles" who beat England in the final game.

---

subdue physically opponents by body contact, direct application of force to a heavy object, and face-to-face opposition where body contact may occur. *Generally not acceptable* forms of opposition include most field events, sprints, and long jump; these strength-related events are acceptable, the authors believe, only for the "minority group" women, particularly, we presume, ethnic minorities. Sports that involve the projection of the body through space in aesthetically pleasing patterns or the use of a light implement are *generally acceptable* for all women; no body contact is possible in sports such as swimming, gymnastics, figure skating, and tennis.

The long-standing beliefs about why some sports only are appropriate for women are almost certainly changing, as the inclusion of marathons and 10,000-meter races in the Olympics indicates. Women also competed in taekwondo, an exhibition event, at the 1988 games. Power-lifting and body-building, both of which necessitate intense resistance training, are now established events for women. Women have recently shown themselves as aggressive, robust, and resilient competitors capable of achieving levels of sporting performance comparable to those of men – when given the opportunity.

Black women, especially, have achieved excellence, presumably for the reasons advanced in the previous chapter and not because of any innate ability. The justification for denying women the opportunity to compete on equal terms with men combines biology with politics and common sense with illogicality. Women have been regarded as biologically incapable of the same physical feats as men; it has been seen as impolitic even to let them try. One result is that, over the years, they haven't achieved as much as men and that's obvious; yet the conclusion that women *can't* achieve the same levels doesn't follow logically from the original premise that they are biologically different. In fact, it could be argued that, if women had been regarded as equally capable as men physically, then they would perform at similar standards, and that the only reason they don't is because they've been regarded as biologically incapable for so long.

It barely needs stating that the experience of women in sport virtually replicates their more general experience. They have been seen and treated as not only different to men – which they manifestly are, of course – but also inferior in many respects. Feminists today have argued plausibly that, historically, women's position has been subordinate to that of men. They have been systematically excluded from high-ranking, prestigious jobs, made to organize their lives around domestic or private priorities, while men have busied themselves in the public spheres of industry and commerce. Being the breadwinner, the male has occupied a central position in the family and has tended to use women for supplementary incomes only, or, more importantly, as unpaid homeworkers, making their contribution appear peripheral. Traditionally, females have been encouraged to seek work, but only in the short term: women's strivings should be toward getting married, bearing children, and raising a family.

Since the late 1960s and the advent of legal abortion and convenient female contraception, women in the West have been able to exercise much more choice in their own fertility and this has been accompanied by feminist critiques of male dominance. Empirical studies showed wide discrepancies in earning power and this prompted legislation on both sides of the Atlantic designed to ensure equality in incomes for comparable jobs.

One of the loudest cries of feminists was about the abuses of the female body: women, it was argued, have not had control over their own bodies; they have been appropriated by men, not only for working, but for display. "Sex objects" were how many women described themselves, ogled at by men and utilized, often dispassionately. Against this, they recoiled. Even a "respectable" magazine like *Sports Illustrated*, ostensibly interested in what women do as opposed to what they look like, used to devote issues to photographs of women posing in swimwear.

Women are underrepresented in politics compared to their total number in the population. They consistently earn less than their equivalent males and are increasingly asked to work part-time. Despite recent changes in the number of places in higher education occupied by women, they tend to opt for subjects (like sociology and art) that won't necessarily guarantee them jobs in science and industry. When they do penetrate the boundaries of the professions they find that having to compete in what is, to all intents and purposes, a man's world, has its hidden disadvantages.

Some argue that this state of affairs has been brought about by a capitalist economy geared to maximizing profits and only too willing to exploit the relatively cheap labor of women who are willing to work for less than men, mainly because they've been taught to believe that their work is unimportant and subsidiary to that of men, and that their "real" work is domestic not industrial. Others insist that women's subordination has a larger resonance that transcends any political or economic system and is derived from *patriarchy*, a state in which men have continually sought to maintain the grip they have had on society and have found the deception that "a woman's place is in the home" a great convenience which they wish to perpetuate. Whatever the motivation behind the successful effort to keep women subordinate, its effects have been felt in sport, where women have for long been pushed into second place.

Patriarchy
From the Greek *pater*, father, and *arkhes*, ruler, this describes a set of social arrangements in which dominance in power and authority are male-centered and expressed in unequal gender relations. Its origins can be traced back to primitive sexual divisions of labor, resulting from the transition from hunting, perhaps 10 thousand years ago. Women, unable during pregnancy and periods of early child-rearing to engage in the more physically challenging game hunting and, later, subsistence agriculture, were assigned to alternative, more domestic chores. Male economic power was augmented with the domestication of animals, and male proprietorship of herds and their associated wealth was interwoven into political systems. In its contemporary meanings, it retains the emphasis on male control, but nuances this by adding *how* this is perpetuated. Male influence in most mainstream institutions, including the educational system and the mass media, makes it possible for patriarchal control to become pervasive. So, when the old apothegm "women are their own worst enemies" is brought into play, it reveals more about patriarchy's powers than it does about women's gullibility.

"Unladylike" is one of those words with a certain ring to it: the many activities to which it refers are to be avoided by any female who favors keeping her dignity. In a Victorian environment, the application of the term to behavior that involved some degree of physical exertion was commonplace, unless the behavior was performed by females out of necessity. Washing, cleaning, fetching coal, and emptying chambers were activities performed by working-class women, but they could have few pretensions to being ladies. These were typically the kind of women whose daily duties were so draining that they wouldn't have the inclination to add to their physical workload. Gentlewomen and the wives of the emergent bourgeoisie would have time for croquet, tennis and perhaps archery, but were self-consciously "ladies."

The situation reinforced the social perception of women as delicate creatures in need of men's protection, which manifested itself in terms of the treatment afforded women. But, as the nineteenth century passed and women were made to play a vigorous role in the 1914–18 war effort, the flimsy illusion of delicacy was eroded. A vocal and effective suffragette movement was prising open new areas in politics and education for women. The Second World War effort also drew women to factories, trucks and areas of work traditionally reserved for men. The war periods also left a gap in sports that women filled. The movie *A League of Their Own* and its sequel followed the fortunes of a women's baseball team.

As more women entered formal education, so they began to participate more fully in sport, often demonstrating high proficiency. This led to another set of spurious reasons, this time based on medical evidence, as to why women shouldn't be permitted to compete. But, before moving to this, we should consider the importance of debates over the nature of women's bodies.

Perverting nature

It was for long suspected that women had less energy available than men, so engaging in sport might lead, it was supposed, to an atrophy of reproductive organs as they would be deprived of necessary energy. This was cheap theory, of course, but one which raised doubts in the minds of some: could exercise have a detrimental effect on a woman's fecundity? No one knew the answer, but it was thought wise to err on the side of caution, which meant that women should abstain from sport. Tony Mason, in his *Sport in Britain*, mentions a bizarre conjecture. "Hockey," he writes "was said to inhibit breastfeeding." He adds that this wasn't just a false idea invented by men to keep sport exclusive: "Many women shared the idea that their role was primarily domestic, their natures inherently unsuitable for 'manly' physical exertion" (Mason 1988: 7–8).

Even more intimidating was the folk belief that involvement in sport not only interfered with fertility, but actually affected a woman's endocrinal system, possibly leading to *virilism*, the development of secondary male characteristics. The idea here was based on the fact that testosterone, the hormone responsible for facial hair, deep voice, broad shoulders, muscle mass, and other typically male features and which is produced primarily in testes, is found in both sexes, though significantly less in females' adrenal glands. Women, on the other hand, carry proportionately higher levels of estrogen and progesterone. Prolonged exercise, it was speculated, induced an imbalance in women's hormones causing an overproduction of testosterone and so resulting in "defeminization."

Among the advantages for a female competitor would be a reduction of subcutaneous fatty tissue and a proliferation of muscle cells. While this had no basis in scientific fact, scattered cases did seem to support this speculation. There was the mysterious gold medal winner at the 1936 Olympics, who, several years later, confessed that "she" was actually a man who had been pressured into competing for the glory of the Third Reich. In 1952, two French female medalists were later exposed as males. Speculation over the invincible Press sisters, Irene and Tamara, circulated in athletics. Were they actually "sisters" at all? They retired rather suddenly when sex testing was introduced in athletics in 1966 thus fueling more suspicion about their gender. (In all, six female competitors missed the European championships at Budapest after it was announced there would be sex tests; and of the 243 tests, no one failed.) Had the Press sisters somehow trained themselves into men? Had they experimented with synthetic testosterone so much that they had induced permanent sex changes? Or were they men in athletic drag? Whatever the answer, they were two of countless other Soviet bloc women who were thought to have undergone some sort of transformation or mutation.

Sex tests, such as the Barr Sex Test, which involved a microscopic examination of cells from the inside of the cheek or a hair follicle to identify a typical female chromosome pattern, could only determine effects, not causes. In 1967, the Polish sprinter, Eva Klobkowska, failed such a test because she showed an excess of male hormones; to her apparent surprise she was found to have internal testicles. This condition is not as uncommon as it may first sound, though in hindsight, the muscular bulk and power possessed by Soviet female athletes were the result of neither this nor excessive training, but anabolic steroids. Still, the "natural successor" to the Press sisters, Jarmila Kratotchvilova, of Czechoslovakia, never tested positive for drugs.

The mêlée of folk story and science that purported to explain what Linda Birke and Gail Vines (1987) call "the perversion of women's true nature" as caused by too much exercise was inconclusive. What evidence we

Barr sex test
The test requires that a sample of cells be scraped from the inside of a woman's cheek and subjected to a laboratory test to determine whether a minimum number contain what are called "Barr bodies" (collections of chromatins). Although the exact number of these chromatins varies from woman to woman and may change over time for any given woman, usually about 20 out of every 100 cells contain this characteristic. If the count drops below a minimum percentage, the competitor is disqualified.

have today contradicts the earlier speculations: vigorous exercise is beneficial for women in a general sense and may have a reciprocally positive effect on their reproductive functions. For example, Evelyn Ashford, of the USA, broke the 100-meter world record in 1984 and 40 weeks later gave birth; Ingrid Kristiansen, of Norway, did it in reverse order, first giving birth, then returning to the track to record the world's best times for 5,000 and 10,000 meters. Any number of women athletes today are mothers and many swear by the benefits of childbirth to sports performance.

Adrianne Blue, in *Grace Under Pressure* (1987), records how, in 1928, the first Olympic 800 meters for women was considered "dangerous." Now, it seems, every argument about the physical and mental improvements that men derive from sporting activity of any order applies with equal force to women, who have, particularly since the 1980s, trained harder, competed harder and improved performances with no apparent deficiency or fragility even in the most exacting events. From the vantage point of the 1990s, when women such as Portugal's Manuela Machado regularly grind out sub 2:27 marathons, it seems staggering that Katherine Switzer was disqualified from the 1968 Boston marathon for no reason other than that she was a woman. Women were simply not meant to be able to run such distances; this myth held sway despite the 3:40 run, in London, of a certain Violet Percy in 1926. Switzer became an active campaigner for women's marathons and convinced her employers Avon cosmetics to sponsor an all-women's marathon in London in 1980, an event that many feel made a strong impact on Olympic organizers. In 1981,the IOC voted to allow a women's marathon: Joan Benoit of the USA won in 1984 and, incidentally, earned over $400,000 (£250,000) in the following year, thanks to her unique success.

The marathon is rather an instructive case-study. Between Briton Dale Greig's first official run in 1964 and today, the world record for women has improved by 1 hour 5 minutes and 21 seconds. In the same period, the men's

Pregnancy and sports performance

The potential benefits of the hormones produced in early pregnancy have long been recognized by sports science: during the first three months, the mother's body generates a natural surplus of red corpuscles rich in hemoglobin. These assist cardiac and lung performance and improve muscle capacity by up to 30 percent. A pregnant woman also secretes increased amounts of progesterone to make muscles more supple and joints more flexible.

Olga Karasseva (now Kovalenko), a gymnastics gold medal winner at the 1968 summer Olympics, later revealed that she had become pregnant and had an abortion shortly before the games to prepare her body. She also claimed that, during the 1970s, females as young as 14 were ordered to have sex with their men friends or coaches in an effort to become pregnant (reported in the British *Sunday Times*, S1: 23, 27 November 1994). Suspicions that female athletes from the former Soviet Union planned abortions to coincide with competitions first surfaced in 1956 at the Melbourne summer Olympics, then eight years later at Tokyo. One estimate at the time suggested that as many as 10 out of 26 medal winners may have manipulated their pregnancies, though no conclusive proof ever came to light. In the mid-1970s, East German and Scandinavian women were accused by two magazines, *Il Mondo Nuoto*, of Italy, and *Aktuellt*, of Sweden.

record has been reduced by 5 minutes 2 seconds. The difference in the world's bests was 12 minutes 13 seconds in 1995 (or about 9 percent).

The moral of this would seem to be that, when women are allowed legally to compete in an event, they can perform at least on comparable terms with men. One wonders how great or small the marathon time differential would be had a women's event been allowed in the Olympics at the time of Violet Percy's run. "The same as it is today," might be the skeptic's answer, marshaling the support of significant differences in all women's and men's track records. But marathons, though separate events in major international meets, regularly pitch men and women together and, in this sense, they provide a meaningful guide. From the 1970s and the boom in popular marathons and fun runs, women have mixed with men, competed against them, and on many occasions beaten them. The gap shown in the marathon figure would surely have been narrower had television not intervened and insisted that women started their races prior to the men, thus removing the opportunity for females to test their mettle against the world's fastest males.

THE PROGRESSION OF MEN'S AND WOMEN'S MARATHON RECORDS

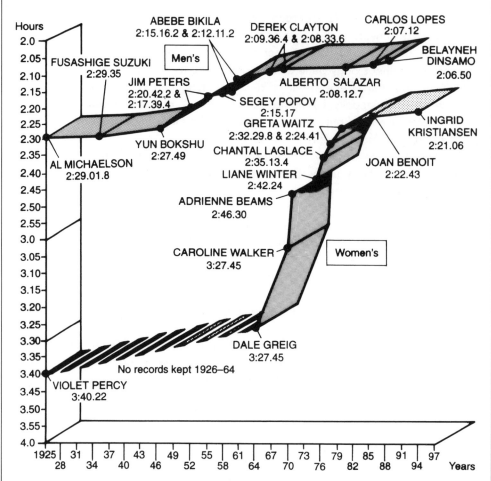

* The year before Violet Percy's first recorded women's marathon, Al Michaelson, of the USA, set the men's world best time with 2hrs 29mins 01.8 secs. Since then, the men's record has progressed evenly, the only exceptions being 1952–54, when Britain's Jim Peters lowered the time four times for a total of almost 7 minutes, and 1967–69, when the Australian Derek Clayton sliced 2mins 23.6 off the record, then reduced it by a further 1min 2.8secs. It took until 1981 before Alberto Salazar, of the USA, was able to improve this by less than 21 seconds. Ethiopian Belayneh Dinsamo's 2hr 6mins 50secs (set on a flat Rotterdam course) was rarely threatened, though Mexican Dionicio Ceron's 2hr 8mins 52secs in adverse London conditions in 1994 is acknowledged as a proximate achievement.

* Official records of women's times began in 1964 and, over the next 20 years, the world record was broken on average every year by over 3mins 57secs, compared with an average increment of 66 seconds for men. After Norway's Ingrid Kristiansen's 2hr 21min 6secs in 1985, Joan Benoit, of the USA, ran 2hrs 21min 21secs, but it was not for a further nine years that another woman broke 2:22 and, even then, Germany's Uta Pippig's 2hrs 21mins 45secs was assisted by a drop of 152 yards in the course. Significantly, Kristiansen's time was set when women and men started together; subsequently, television required women to start 30 minutes before men, effectively removing the head-to-head challenge that had proved vital to Kristiansen.

The graph does not show every marathon record: only representative runs.

It is misleading comparing performances in male and female events which have developed separately. Tennis has for long been open to at least those women of resources sufficient to afford it. Only in the most playful mixed doubles have they been allowed to confront male adversaries. One-off exhibitions between the likes of an aged Bobby Riggs and Billie-Jean King (and, before her, Margaret Court) have produced inconclusive results after matches that owed more to pantomime than competitive sport. The question we asked of marathons stands with tennis: how would Monica Seles fare in a head-to-head with Michael Stich had women been playing competitively against men for the past 60 or 50 years? Again, the skeptic might argue that the results would be basically the same, the support this time coming from the copious amount of evidence on the physical differences between the sexes – that is, differences which do not refer to social or cultural influences.

No sweat

Not all physical differences between men and women have a bearing on sporting performance, so interest is here confined to those areas that may affect a person's ability to compete on equal terms. The areas are the skeletal and cardiovascular systems and body composition. Typically, women are shorter, with narrower shoulders, shorter limbs, a wider pelvis, and leg bones that are less bowed than men's. So, compared to males, women have a lighter body frame to carry, a lower center of gravity, slightly less leg rotation (because of the pelvis) and shorter arm movements when running, and a marginally greater proneness to knee injury because of the less-bowed lower leg bones (although this may possibly be because girls are not encouraged to exercise as much as young boys so their bones do not grow as strong and dense in maturity).

Generally, untrained women carry a greater percentage of body fat than untrained men (22 percent to 14 percent); they have less bone and less muscle. A female will have a greater concentration of subcutaneous adipose tissue, particularly in her buttocks, which are relatively inactive metabolically (making it hard to "burn off" the fat, but helpful for buoyancy). In swimming this is an advantage, especially in distance or open-water events, where the insulating effects of fat are needed against cold water. Importantly, the smaller proportion of muscle in relation to body fat gives a lower ratio of strength to weight than in men, but this ratio is significantly changed by resistance training. Training can also minimize differences in muscle strength as women power-lifters demonstrate. Untrained women can be as much as 50 percent less efficient than men, though at peak a woman's lifting strength can be within 5 percent of a trained man's.

Here is a key to equalizing: research shows that women's strength responds to training in much the same way as does men's. After training, when fitness levels are equalized, there are more differences in performance ability within sexes than between them. Women gain strength without corresponding muscle bulk. They have less muscle and bone to drive, so don't suffer from having smaller heart and respiratory volumes (which affect the amount of oxygen used).

During distance events, males sweat sooner and more profusely than females in response to increases in body temperature. This apparent advantage is balanced by a woman's ability to adjust her sweat rate more efficiently. Both sexes acclimatize to work or exercise in heat, but females do so without increasing sweat rates: before a woman sweats her body temperature will have to be two or three degrees higher than the equivalent male's. Because she has more active sweat glands than the male, her sweat is more evenly distributed over the body for maximal cooling by evaporation, thus compensating for the smaller body surface. This is why women seem to go red while men pour with sweat.

As we've seen, myths about the detrimental effects of strenuous exercise on a woman's fertility reigned for many years but eventually died away. It's no longer believed that during menstruation women lose the all-important hemoglobin that combines with oxygen and travels to muscle. Women have reached peak performance during all phases of their menstrual cycle. There is no conclusive evidence to suggest that menstrual function affects sporting performance.

The point to remember when charting the physical differences between the sexes that may influence sporting performance is that there is also an equally important reverse effect: performance causes very serious physical changes that tend to compensate more than adequately for any disadvantage a female may have in terms of muscular strength or oxygen uptake. The body is extremely susceptible to change, even transformation in certain contexts.

For example, strenuous physical training can boost levels of growth hormone in children, perhaps enhancing their growth; increases in the hormones prolactin (which regulates breast development and milk production) and androgens (the male sex hormone) may be promoted by strict training and specific diets. At a more obvious level, we know athletes develop stronger bones and larger hearts after prolonged training and muscles obviously grow as a response to demands made on them. As evidence, witness the many 8-year-old children in Darjeeling who regularly carry about 3 tons of bricks on their heads in the course of a day. Women in various parts of East Africa perform similar tasks. Making habitual demands on the body from an early age can induce physical changes in both men and women. The idea that biology is destiny in sport is nonsense. Exceptionally strong Australian power-lifter Gael Martin has done her very best to show that, though she has been known to augment her efforts with anabolic steroids.

There is, of course, the tried-and-trusted argument that, no matter how hard a woman may train or supplement her regime, she will forever be handicapped by her breasts; not just because they burden her with extra weight to carry but because they're vulnerable to damage. Boxing's governing organizations have led a brigade of other sports which won't allow women competitors. But amateur boxing in particular equips fighters with headguards, and all boxing, as well as many other sports, permits the use of protective cups worn about the genitals. In taekwondo, where punching is confined to the upper body target area, women wear body pads which seem to provide adequate protection. There seems no reason to suppose that these would be any less effective in other combat sports. And there is interest from women in the West, as the number of active female kickboxers indicates.

The picture that emerges in the West is one in which women have not excelled in sports. Yet this is not because they are physically ill-equipped but because (1) they haven't been encouraged to compete, and (2) when they have been allowed to compete they have done so against themselves and not against trained men.

Some countries, especially the former German Democratic Republic and Russia, have shown what can happen when women are assisted in their development in a partially integrated program that starts during school years. From the mid-1950s, women progressively made up more of official Soviet and GDR international teams (about 40 percent immediately before the dissolution of the Soviet Union), the trend, according to James Riordan, being consistent with the general treatment of women. "The Soviet authorities have used sport as a vehicle for that type of women's emancipation officially desired in the USSR," he wrote in his book *Soviet Sport* (1980: 142). It's still interesting to note that women's participation in soccer and wrestling is disapproved of in Russia in particular, on the grounds that they are open to "commercialization" and may be turned into "strength-and-beauty" contests.

If Riordan's point about "emancipation" might be borrowed, we might suggest that women's involvement in sport in the West reflects their "officially desired" position. They've been shut out of sport in a way that mirrors their shutting-out of society. Since the sea-change of the late 1960s and 1970s, when legislation technically outlawed discrimination on the basis of sex, women have made much more of an impact in sports not traditionally associated with Western women. Tessa Sanderson of Britain and Tina Lilak of Finland perhaps exemplify this with their successes in the javelin. Despite sex discrimination, equal pay, equal opportunities laws, and Title IX, the general attitude Western societies have toward women is ambiguous.

Title IX

Part of the USA's educational amendments, 1972 Title IX reads: "No person in the United States shall on the basis of sex, be excluded from participation in, be denied the benefits of or be subjected to discrimination under any education program or activity receiving Federal financial assistance." Educational institutions were made to accommodate females within their sports budgets At first, this was unpopular among the male-dominated sports officials of schools, colleges, and universities. In 1979, three women athletes from the University of Alaska sued their state for failing to comply with Title IX in providing better funding equipment and publicity compared to the male basketball team. This set in train more actions, so that by the end of 1979 62 colleges and universities were under investigation by the Office for Civil Rights. The resistance to offering equal opportunity to women has continued to the present day.

Whether this is because of the timeless, iron-clad oppression of patriarchy or the more time-limited but equally iron-clad system of capitalism is open to debate. Either way, there is substantial evidence for both theories, all of which adds up to the fact that women have been subordinated and encouraged to play out their lives as private auxiliaries rather than public prime movers. Most of the women who have penetrated sport at the higher levels haven't exactly defied this publicly.

In the 1980s, Florence Griffith Joyner cut the image of a glitzy, shock-haired glamor queen, equally at ease modeling running gear or camiknickers. Gabriela Sabatini's dark latin good looks attracted a following of young males; and Katrin Krabbe's legs were always a talking point. The young nubile plaything has been a durable winner, as Mary-Lou Retton and, more recently, Jennifer Capriati have shown. These are more typical than the nonstereotype women who occasionally succeed. Most of the others who don't fit the mold are regarded as anomalies, the most famous being Martina Navratilova who was known to favor the company of other females.

Like it or not, women who succeed in sport do not always succeed in the popular imagination: where are the female Shaqs or Marinos? In recent years, only Nancy Kerrigan has generated enough interest to guarantee her a portfolio of endorsements and, in her case, a movie. For a while she was America's favorite covergirl. Had she been pear-shaped with carious teeth, scrubby hair and pimples, only skating fans would have ever heard of her. Her athletic ability on the ice alone would have quickly been overlooked. Well, not entirely: her conflict with arch-rival Tonya Harding would have guaranteed headlines. But the soft-focus treatment reserved for Kerrigan, in spite of her failure to gain an Olympic gold medal, indicates that her physical appearance was uppermost in the minds of those who bombarded her with contracts.

Sportswomen who have been helped to stardom by men – and there is no other way of achieving such a status – have either had to be so extraordinarily good at their sport that they couldn't be ignored (like the indomitable Navratilova) or quite good and possessed of looks that men found appealing. All of which leads us to conclude that having the right body (right = how men define "right") is essential to success beyond sports. But there is an interesting exception to this rule as we will soon discover.

Ripped women

Some early advocates of physical exercise for women, like Madame Bergman Osterberg, insisted it was necessary for healthy growth in the more general sense. Most others simply dismissed the idea as nonsense. Assumptions about the character, potential and role of women's bodies were integral to women's position in society. Subordination in the political and social sense was based on control over the body and its functions, particularly reproductive functions. If women were to be controlled effectively – and this was thought desirable – then their bodies need also to be controlled. In other words, male control of women has been predicated on control of the female body.

Historically, men have been able to disempower and subordinate women, use their labor, influence their thought and secure their co-operation in unequal relations because of the power they have held over women's bodies. At a conscious level, this has manifested itself in a physical control: actually coercing women into performing duties deemed appropriate to their sex. But there are subtler methods, such as initiating pressures on women to conform to a perfect body shape. These two examples might seem only tenuously related, but they both express the male imperative to exert some measure of control over the female form. The ultimate triumph has been in securing the consent of women themselves in experiencing their bodies in the ways designated by men.

Throughout the nineteenth century there was a symmetry in how men conceived of women's bodies and how women themselves experienced them. Men scoffed at the idea of women being able to participate in sports in a meaningful way because of the inadequacy of their bodies. And, as Hargreaves points out, "Many women believed in their own inferiority and hence supplied further 'proof' of the 'rational' validity of the belief" (1994: 48). In a way, then, not only had women to convince men of their physical

Madame Bergman Osterberg

Author of an influential pamphlet published in the 1887, which advocated the use of a Swedish system of gymnastics for young working-class women who had no access to apparatus or facilities, Osterberg taught the method to classes of over a hundred at a time drawing crowds in the streets of London. The method was seen as symbolizing social control: its instructors were upper-middle-class women who demanded absolute obedience from their classes and the movements were precise and mechanical – far from the aerobics movements of today, though the essential idea of instructing large classes was the same.

and, for that matter, mental ability to compete in the most exacting circumstances but also needed to convince themselves that their bodies were not simply ornaments for the delectation of men – objects of what was later to be called the "male gaze." But have they? The unsatisfactory answer is: yes and no.

Think for a moment about the ways in which men have sought to repress women. The ancient Chinese practice of footbinding was ostensibly to prevent women developing large and therefore (in Chinese males' eyes) ugly feet: small feet were the epitome of beauty in Chinese culture. It also effectively confined them either to the boudoir away from the gaze of men other than husbands. As feet were generally first bound when the woman was 7 years old, she would be hobbled The custom was abolished by imperial decree in 1902; it had lasted for more than a thousand years.

As cultures define physically appropriate shapes for women, so women have been obliged to conform. Witness the neck brace used by Ndebe women, or the plates that are wedged between the lower lips and the mandible of Ubangis in Equatorial Africa. Neither practice has the practical utility of footbinding, which restricted women's physical mobility so that it was virtually impossible to escape servitude. In these cases, women voluntarily mutilate their bodies for the pleasure of men.

Cliteroidectomy is widely practiced in many parts of the Middle East and in the North and sub-Saharan desert. About 74 million women have currently undergone this procedure, which involves excising part or all of the clitoris. The catalog of infections, complications and long-term effects of this mutilation is immense. It reminds us of how far men will go to reaffirm the subjugation of women through the control not only of their reproductive functions, but of their ability to experience sexual pleasure (in one form of cliteroidectomy, the clitoris is excised, as is the labia minor, before the sides of the vulva are sewn together with catgut, to be ritually opened with a dagger on the eve of the woman's wedding). The process is defended as an integral part of some sections of Islamic faith, but, as Linda Lindsey writes, "Regardless of how it is justified, it is a grim reminder of the subjugation of women" (1990: 104).

What we must ask ourselves is: are these kinds of gory activities so different from the things women do to themselves even today? Victorian women and their daughters self-destructively squeezed themselves into whalebone-lined corsets that were so tight that they stopped blood circulation and distorted the spine. Now, women have swapped this contraption for lipo-suction (vacuuming fatty tissue from the epidermis), rhinoplasty (slicing open the nose and filing down gristle) and all sorts of cosmetic surgery designed to bring women's bodies into alignment with men's expectations (silicone breast implants being a supreme example; the American Federal food and Drugs Administration severely restricted these after the damaging effects of them became known).

Then we still have to reckon with the less invasive, but no less disabling attempts women make to meet with men's approval. By defining ideal shapes in ways that please them, men actually force women into near-starvation diets or, worse still, chronic eating disorders like anorexia nervosa and bulimia. The burgeoning popularity of aerobic classes and their progeny, step classes, boxercise, etc., are related to changes in how men define the perfect shape. The 1950s Monroe model looks podgy by comparison with the busty but slimmer supermodels of today. Women remain willing to connive with men: they are still prepared to risk their health to chase what Naomi Wolf calls *The Beauty Myth*. But, the myth is "not about women at all," argues Wolf. "It is about men's institutions and institutional power" (1991: 10, 13).

In their book *Becoming Feminine*, Leslie Roman and others remind us that: "We must not begin by conceiving of women as manipulated by mass media or subject passively to male power . . . when we speak of 'femininity'" (1988: 39). Femininity, they argue, is more a matter of self-creation, not just imposition. This allows for a conception of femininity, or, perhaps, more accurately *femininities*, that is not fixed but always in the process of redefinition. No one is suggesting that there is an equally weighted balance of power with men and women trading ideas on how the body should look. Men have had their own way in most areas of society and this is no exception. But, where the female body is concerned, they have had either to resort to coercion (foot-binding, cliteroidectomies) or secure the complicity of women themselves.

Like many other women, competitive body-builders feel pressures to conform to an ideal shape defined by men. But in their case the body shape has been defined by men *for* men. In body-building, the ideal is a classic v-shape: broad shoulders on taut torso that tapers to a narrow waist. Arm and

---

Anorexia nervosa

From the Greek *an*, not, *orexis*, appetite, sometimes called "slimmers' disease," this is a mental illness in which the sufferers, often young female athletes, go to such great lengths to lose bodyweight that they deprive themselves of basic nutrition and sometimes die. Its impact on sports was first recognized in 1980 when Gillian Sinclair, Britain's junior ice skating champion unexpectedly retired at the age of 15 and entered the Institute of Psychiatry for treatment. Since then, many female sports performers, especially gymnasts, have been prone to the sickness. According to the American Anorexia and Bulimia Association, 1 million American women develop eating disorders every year, a staggering 150,000 women dying of anorexia alone every year. The related illness, bulimia, is also a product of a culture that emphasizes the value of slim over fat bodies and involves inducing vomiting after eating. For more, see *Helping Athletes with Eating Disorders* by Ron Thompson and Roberta Sherman (1993).

---

leg muscle groups should be long, tendons short. There should be absolutely no smooth curves similar to those associated with women; a visible separation between muscles is essential. Instead, fat-to-muscle ratio must be low: whereas most women, as we noted earlier, have about 22 percent body fat, body-builders should have less than 6 percent for competitions. The body must look, in the body-building vernacular, *ripped*.

Watching a female body-building competition on television, you can sense the thought bubble above every male viewer's head: "Thinks ... a woman with a body like that is *unnatural*." As any reader of this book knows, there is nothing more unnatural about this than there is about Arnold's body. Women's bodies, as we have seen, respond to training in much the same way as men's. In fact, there is no such thing as a natural body state: our bodies inevitably reflect the way we use them, what we do to them, how we nourish them and even how we think about them; and all these are heavily affected by the culture of which we are part. Women body-builders just happen to parts of a culture in which they are seen as odd. Actually, they would be regarded as odd in practically any culture, apart from that of Scythia, home of the fabulous female warriors known as Amazons.

Female body-builders self-consciously reject the perfect shape as defined by men. This is bad enough for many, but it gets worse. They are invading territory traditionally claimed, prospected and occupied exclusively by men. In the early 1980s, the women's contests were seen as enjoyable

Female body-building

As a sport, female body-building began in 1979, a product largely of Doris Barrilleaux who was formerly a physique photography model. Barrilleaux started the Superior Physique Association which set down competition rules for female body-building contests. In 1980 she was asked to head a national American Federation of Women Body-builders. In a relatively short period of time the sport has grown to international proportions and today rivals the men's competitions in terms of exposure and prize monies.

divertissements between the rounds of the men's competitions. The contestants were fit, toned, but still discernibly "feminine." No threat. Then a new player changed everything.

Maybe it was because Bev Francis came from Australia that no one had heard of her. She had been picking up prizes from Down Under for several years before Americans realized that this was a woman who not only challenged traditional conceptions of femininity, but crushed them like an aluminum beer can in her mighty fist. Square of shoulder and jaw, Francis became the first female body-building icon. She made no concessions to male-defined femininity. Her symmetrical, finely cut, vascularized muscles were the product of a program that dispensed with all but the minimum body fat; meaning that the adipose tissue that surrounds the aveolar glands was dramatically decreased, leaving Francis with a hard, relatively flat chest.

The women's sport never fully recovered: Francis was a phenomenon; her accomplishments with her body were such a quantum beyond anyone else's that judges of major competitions were thrown into confusion. The criteria in evaluating women were always ambiguous and a redefinition in 1984 that included the term "feminine physique" did not help. Francis became a perennial runner-up, despite her obvious superiority. Carla Dunlap and Cory Everson, Francis's rivals in many competitions, were lighter, less defined and, by popular consent, more physically attractive to men. One suspects that their edge over Francis was based more on this than anything else. Part of the instruction to judges in assessing women was to penalize women whose bodies "resembled the massive musculature of the male physique." This disadvantaged Francis.

The instruction was removed in 1993, too late for Francis, though her presence was no doubt instrumental in the rule change. Just seeing what Francis had achieved inspired a new generation of female body-builders to resculpt themselves in a way that demolished old ideas about femininity. The bigger and harder shape became the norm: and women competitors were judged on virtually the same criteria as men (though, even today, there are resistant judges who still believe traces of more traditional femininity should be evident). Confusion over judging is understandable in a sport so overwhelmingly dominated not just by men but by hunks. The ultimate male preserve was no more. Today, it is possible for a woman champion, like Lenda Murray, to make as much money from appearances and endorsements as her male counterparts; this is perhaps the final indignity for many men.

One is tempted to discern in female body-builders a protofeminist impulse: here is a group of women encroaching on male turf, knowing full well that their "look" defies traditional ideas of femininity and probably repulses a great many men, even those who habitually lift free weights. The admiration they seek is of others in the gym, not glaring men. Most women chase or at least acknowledge the "beauty myth," while body-builders just laugh at it. A similar conclusion is reached by Alan Mansfield and Barbara McGinn: "Because muscularity has been coded as a fundamentally masculine attribute, its adoption by women has offered a threat and a challenge to notions of both the feminine AND the masculine" (1993: 65).

Their programs are unsparing: diets are meticulously controlled, and training sessions are typically twice per day. It is an all-or-nothing sport, so women have to have the discipline of mind as well as body. It would be interesting to interpret the whole movement over the past several years as an attempt by women to reclaim the body, to restore a control that has traditionally been denied them.

I confess this was my idea when Amy Shepper and I conducted a research project in Tampa, Florida, and Birmingham, England, in the early 1990s. As is often the case, the empirical evidence gathered from a series of interviews with female body-builders didn't quite bear this out. Most of the women interviewed gladly compartmentalize their lives into two. In their body-building roles they are austere, resolute and aggressive toward men who make sarcastic remarks about their sexuality. Yet, once out of the gym and into the home, they become dutiful homekeepers, cooking, washing and cleaning. What's more, they see no contradiction in this, defying male expectations in one sense, obediently conforming to them in another. Gaining control over one's body, it seems, does not imply gaining control of one's life. This tells us something about the pervasiveness of male hegemony: a woman can release herself in one very important sphere, while at the same time retaining attachments, identifications and dependencies in another.

Women, like black people, have never managed entirely to shrug off their stereotypes: each group is in the process of redefining itself in a way that suggests they are much more capable than popular images have given them credit for. But old ideas die hard. Blacks in sport have unwittingly contributed to the stereotype of a brawny and physically adept specimen but with little "upstairs." They've grasped the only opportunity they were offered for escaping deprivation and, in the process, have become so brilliant that their prowess appears natural.

Women's experience has been one of denial: they simply haven't been allowed to enter sports, again on the basis of a mistaken belief in their natural predisposition. Because of this, the encouragement, facilities, and, importantly, competition available to males from an early age hasn't been extended to them. In the very few areas where the gates have been recently opened – the marathon being the obvious example – women's progress has been extraordinary. Given open competition, women could achieve parity with men in virtually all events, apart from those very few that require the rawest of muscle power. The vast majority of events need fineness of judgement, quickness of reaction, balance, and anticipation; women have no disadvantages in these respects. Their only disadvantage is what men believe about them.

Biology has not held women back in sport any more than it has propelled blacks, male or female, to sporting excellence. Sexual and racial discrimination has been responsible for both trends. On the one hand, sexual discrimination has indirectly persuaded women that their proper place is at home where they can care for children and present no effective challenge to male dominance. On the other hand, racial discrimination has had a more direct effect on blacks and has worked to keep them pressed into subservience, offering them as a way out only the opportunity to entertain white audiences. The experience in sport of both groups has been shaped by these powerful social forces much more than putative biological ones.

FURTHER READING

Sport and the Physical Emancipation of English Women, 1870–1914 by Kathleen McCrone (Routledge, 1988) looks at the entry of women into sport during the Victorian period. It was a crucial time in the development of sport and also one in which myths about women abounded. At public schools, the new sports with rules and time-scales were meant to instill character and decisiveness fitting for future purveyors of the Empire. Women were not seen as purveyors.

Power at Play by Michael Messner (Beacon Press, 1992) emphasizes the "hegemonic masculinity" that has acted as a central dynamic to contemporary sports. This is complemented by *Sport, Men and the Gender Order* edited by Michael Messner and Donald Sabo (Human Kinetics, 1990) which draws together contributions from a variety of sources to attempt "a critical feminist reappraisal of sport." It suggests ways in which the hegemonic position of men in sport could be exposed and challenged.

Women in Sport edited by Greta L. Cohen (Sage, 1993) is a solid collection with contributions from economists, psychologists, historians and other disciplines, all organized around the theme suggested by the title. The chapters range from "Understanding nutrition" to "Women with disabilities." The editor's own chapter examines the role of the media in impacting women's developments in sports.

Women and Sport: Interdisciplinary perspectives edited by D. M. Costa and Sharon Guthrie (Human Kinetics, 1994) is split into three sections: (1) Historical and cultural foundations of women's sport; (2) Biomedical considerations; (3) Psychosocial dimensions. This may profitably be read in conjunction with Women, Sport and Culture, a collection of pieces from various writers, edited by Susan Birrell and Cheryl Cole (Human Kinetics, 1994).

ASSIGNMENT

It is 1880 and the scenario imagined at the start of this chapter is unfolding. Reconstruct the history of any three sports (you choose) plotting the progress of women and men to the present day. Remember: women are able to compete freely in open competition with men and sports authorities do not recognize separate gender-based events. Extrapolate creatively from known evidence.

Chapter eight

Champs or cheats?
Drug use and attempts
to contain it

Making it by taking it

Amid the memories of the 1994 soccer World Cup tournament in the USA, one will remain. Not the record-breaking five goals scored by Russian striker Oleg Salenko against Cameroon. Nor the astounding murder of Colombia's Andres Escobar, shot dead in a Medelin bar after conceding an own goal that hastened his country's exit from the competition. The story that will remain in the memory will be that of Diego Maradona, captain of Argentina and the third soccer player in history to be ejected from a major tournament for taking banned drugs – in his case a cocktail of five substances including ephedrine. Similar drugs used in over-the-counter remedies were taken in 1974 by Ernest Jean-Joseph, of Haiti, and in 1978 by Scotland player, Willie Johnston. The players claimed they had suffered from asthma and hayfever. Maradona claimed innocence, though it was widely known that he had experienced weight problems; ephedrine is used in weight-reducing medicants.

Like Ben Johnson, who was sent home from the 1988 Seoul summer Olympics and stripped of both his gold medal and 100 meters world record, Maradona was immediately transformed from one of the world's greatest athletes to the world's biggest cheat, his cleats all but replaced by cloven

hooves by a mass media intent on demonizing him as they do all sports performers found taking drugs.

Contemporary sport has taken on a Manichaean character in which good coexists with evil; the evil is represented increasingly by the spread of the use of drugs among athletes eager to improve their performance and willing to risk all manner of chemical side-effects, or even direct effects in the attempt to build muscle, steady the hand, flush out body fluid, speed up the metabolism, or spark more aggression. There are drugs available that can assist in all these, but woe for any athlete caught taking them.

Johnson was the thirty-first competitor to be disqualified for drug use since the International Olympic Committee (IOC) instituted full-scale testing in 1972. Johnson's stature in world sport ensured that his case would make news everywhere and that he as an individual would carry the sins of everybody. As well as his medal and record, he instantly lost at least $2 million in performance-related product endorsements.

Maradona and Johnson were exceptional in that traces of banned substances were discovered in their urine samples. Both were roundly shamed because of it. The vast majority of the athletes tested daily at the World Cup and Olympic games yielded negative results. But the suspicion was, and is, that Maradona and Johnson were quite ordinary in another respect: they were simply two of countless others who systematically use drugs to enhance performance and who either come off them early enough to escape detection, or mask their presence with an additional drug, such as probenecid (sometimes used to treat gout), though this too was banned in 1988.

In 1987, the year before Johnson's dismissal, IOC tests brought to light 521 infringements using anabolic steroids, 37 of them involving the use of stanozolol; but this almost certainly conceals the true extent of drug use among athletes. David Jenkins, former Olympic silver medallist and convicted trader in steroids, guessed that as many as 50 percent of active track and field athletes had used drugs at some time. This contrasts with the "official" estimates of about one in ten. The discrepancy suggests a "dark figure," the true proportions of which are destined to remain unknown. The two cases have commanded more space and air time than other comparable cases, but scandals of lesser proportions have affected American football (stimulant use) and, to a much lesser extent, boxing (stimulants and narcotic analgesics; diuretics use is overlooked). Weightlifters and body-builders compete in sports in which steroids confer obvious advantages.

It's quite probable that drug use in sport dates back to ancient times. Greeks are said to have used hallucinogenic extracts from mushrooms to aid their performance. Chemically active derivatives of plants have had many applications. The opium extract morphine has been used extensively for the relief of pain, colchicine from the autumn crocus is a well-known treatment for

---

Dubin inquiry
This was the official inquiry headed by Charles Dubin set up following Ben Johnson's positive test at the 1988 summer Olympics. Among its conclusions was the fact that there was a conspiracy of silence among athletes, coaches and physicians. Dr Jamie Astaphan, Johnson's physician, referred to "the brotherhood of the needle." Dr Robert Kerr of San Gabriel, California, testified that he had prescribed anabolic steroids to approximately 20 medalists at the 1984 summer Olympics. The inquiry identified drug use in sports on a grand scale previously only suspected.

---

gout, and the heart drug digitalis comes from foxglove. There are countless other examples in history and, today, natural derivatives are quite commonly used to treat ailments and often to enhance performance; the Asian root ginseng is thought to have all manner of beneficial properties. Natural stimulants to alter body functions have been used extensively, particularly as a prelude to fighting.

In sports, we know little of the systematic application of stimulants, though after 1879 when six-day cycle races began in Europe, riders favored ether and caffeine to delay the onset of fatigue sensations. Sprint cyclists used nitroglycerine, a chemical later used in conjunction with heroin, cocaine, strychnine, and others to make "speedballs" which were given to race horses before races in the 1930s. The highly poisonous stimulant strychnine was also used by the winner of the 1904 Olympic marathon.

Cycling perhaps more than any other sport drew world attention in the 1960s to both the extent of drug taking in sport and its perils when two competitors actually died after taking doses of amphetamines. Knut Jensen collapsed and died at the 1960 Olympics after taking nonicol, a blood dilatory, and, seven years later, Tommy Simpson died during the Tour de France. In the same decade, stories escaped from American baseball and football clubs that told of the extensive use of amphetamines and narcotic analgesics. Paul Hoch, in *Rip Off the Big Game*, drew together a number of accounts from the 1960s to conclude "that the biggest drug dealers in the sports world are none other than team trainers" (1972: 122).

Coaches were administering amphetamines to pep players up, and analgesics to help them play painlessly while carrying injuries before a game *and* "tranquilized to get their eyeballs back in their head – to even get a night's sleep" after. Hoch cites two players who filed law suits against their clubs for administering drugs "deceptively and without consent" (1972: 123), and which eventually proved detrimental to their health. Various exposés led to a

California state legislative subcommittee on drug abuse and alcoholism to extend the tight regulations governing drug use in horse-racing to human sport. The movie *North Dallas Forty* graphically shows football players trotting onto the field as virtual zombies after taking copious amounts of dope.

The drugs we now tend to associate with sport are anabolic steroids and cocaine. Sketchy evidence suggests that some NFL players were experimenting in the 1960s. Jack Scott in *The Athletic Revolution* (1971) reported that over a quarter of one college team had used steroids. In the same book, Scott covered the 1968 Olympics, at which competitors talked freely – not about the morality of taking drugs but of the practicality: which drugs were most effective? While estimates about the extent of steroid use are always hopelessly flawed, it's at least suggestive that less than twenty years after Scott's information, an article in *Sports Illustrated* stated that NFL steroid users accounted for between 40 and 90 percent of all players (13 May 1983). The Players' Association rejected this. In 1984, Robert Goldman, the director of sports medicine research at the Chicago Osteopathic Medicine Center, attributed the death of six sports performers to steroid use. In Britain, body-builder Keith Singh died with liver tumors after a period of using steroids. In 1987, the IOC recorded 521 cases which tested positive for steroid use; and this was 16 years after the International Amateur Athletic Federation (IAAF) had introduced antidrug legislation.

Anabolic steroids

From the Greek *ana*, meaning "up" and *bole*, "throw," anabolism is the constructive metabolism of complex substances for body tissues (i.e. body-building). Steroids are compounds whose molecules contain rings of carbon and hydrogen atoms. They influence cells by causing special proteins to be synthesized. So, an anabolic steroid is a compound considered to be responsible for the particular synthesis that causes the construction of muscle mass. The idea behind using an anabolic steroid is to mirror the chemical action of the male hormone testosterone in the body and facilitate muscle growth.

While anabolic steroids have specific functions and are confined mainly to sports, cocaine is used recreationally by a variety of groups. In the 1980s, its status as a yuppie drug enhanced its appeal. Tales of cocaine use by football, baseball, and basketball players are legion. Richard Lapchick (1986) referred to an "epidemic in American sport" and highlighted some of the sports stars who were either in gaol or fighting addictions. Seven New England Patriots were identified as having a "serious drug problem" on the day following their appearance in the 1986 Super Bowl.

In the same year, a pro footballer and a college basketball player died from cocaine poisoning, 57 top senior collegiate prospects for the NFL draft tested positively, 21 major league baseball players were penalized and Michael Ray Richardson was banned by the National Basketball Association after his *fourth* failed test for cocaine. Many world-class boxers, including Hector Camacho and Gilberto Roman (former holders of world titles) were penalized in the 1980s. Atlanta Falcons' Dave Croudip was a victim of a cocaine over-dose. In 1995, LA Rams' Darryl Henley was implicated in running a cocaine ring. The Arsenal soccer player Paul Merson was suspended and ordered to do community service after declaring his habitual use of cocaine for recreational purposes in 1995.

Trying to quantify the amount of drug use in sport is as futile as trying to assess the extent of drug taking in society generally: the truth will never be known. Yet there is enough illustrative evidence, anecdotes, insider accounts and publicized cases to infer that drug use in sport has been growing steadily since the 1940s, and more rapidly since the crucial decade of the 1960s when drug use generally became widespread. Questions arise out of this. What are the drugs and what are they supposed to do? Why are more and more sports performers prepared to use them? How do governing bodies react to drug use and, most importantly, is the reaction appropriate?

Cocaine

A derivative of the South American shrub *Erythroxylon coca*, this drug's striking effects on the CNS have made it appealing to many sports performers. The first site of action is the cortex and the effects of the stimulant can manifest themselves as exhilaration, euphoria, or laughter. There is some evidence that cocaine increases perceptual awareness and thinking abilities. It also reduces fatigue sensations. In low doses, there is no impairment in body movement co-ordination to offset the increase in activity levels. Higher doses may lead to excessive stimula-tion of the lower brain centers, prompting convulsive movements. Long-term effects are severely detrimental. Used topically, cocaine can work as a local anesthetic. Contrary to popular belief, it has little in common with opiates such as heroin or morphine and is not physically addictive in the same way as these, though it often leads to a powerful psychological dependence.

Banned substances

David Matza, the writer on crime and deviance, once reasoned that by banning something you immediately make it more attractive than it would otherwise be (1969). If this is the case, then sports have been enhancing the appeal of an awful lot of substances that might have been otherwise ignored. The IOC's banned list includes 4,000 substances which are grouped into five categories of drugs. They are anabolic steroids, stimulants, narcotic analgesics, beta-blockers, and diuretics. I will deal with them in that order, before moving to an examination of blood doping and its high-tech equivalent, growth hormones and procedures for detecting substances in sports performers.

In 1889, Charles Brown-Sequard devised a rejuvenating therapy for body and mind: the 72-year-old French physiologist had claimed he had increased his physical strength, improved his intellectual energy, relieved his constipation and even lengthened the arc of his urine by injecting himself with an extract derived from the testes of dogs and guinea-pigs. His discovery triggered a series of experiments that led to synthesis of testosterone, the primary male hormone produced in the testes, in 1935. Since then, synthetic testosterone has been attributed with almost magical qualities and become the most controversial drug in sports. For this reason, it's worth detailing its history.

There is nothing new about the concept of ingesting animals' sexual organs and secretions: Egyptians accorded medicinal powers to the testes; Johannes Mesue, AD 777–857, prescribed a kind of testicular extract as an aphrodisiac; the *Pharmacopoea Wirtenbergica*, a compendium of remedies published in 1754 in Germany, refers to horse testicles and the penises of marine animals. These and several other examples are given by John Hoberman and Charles Yesalis, whose *Scientific American* article on the subject is essential reading for students of the history of performance-enhancing drugs (1995).

In 1896, an Austrian physiologist and future Nobel Prize winner, Oskar Zoth, published a paper which concluded that extracts from bulls' testes, when injected in athletes, led to improvements in muscular strength and the "neuromuscular apparatus." Here was the first official recognition of the significance of hormonal substances for sports performers. Zoth anticipated the objection that a placebo effect may have accounted for the change in his sample of athletes and denied it. Around the same time, other scientists were excited by the prospect of finding the active ingredient in the male sex organ and specifying its effects.

Clinical applications were many. In 1916, two Philadelphia doctors transplanted a human testicle into a patient who was suffering from sexual dysfunctions, starting a spate of similar transplants, the most audacious being a mass removal of the testes of recently executed inmates for transplanting

> **Testosterone**
> From *testis + o + sterol + one*, this is a steroid androgen formed in the testes. The basic function of testosterone is to control the natural production of sperm cells and this, in turn, affects the male's masculine appearance. A feedback control system is at work involving the hypothalamus; this secretes a hormone called LHR which stimulates the pituitary gland to secrete luteinizing hormone (LH) and this, in turn, stimulates the testes to produce the testosterone. A high concentration of testosterone inhibits the secretion of LHR by the hypothalamus which causes a drop in the level of testosterone, triggering the hypothalamus to release more LHR, LH, and ultimately testosterone in a smoothly regulated system.

into patients suffering from impotence. The commercial potential of this wasn't lost on the large pharmaceutical corporations which initiated research programs to isolate the active hormone and synthesize it. By 1939, clinical trials in humans were underway, employing injections of testosterone propionate. Early synthetic testosterone was used with some success by women suffering from a variety of complaints, the intention being to alter a female's hormonal balance. One of the problems was that the testosterone virilized the patients: they took on male secondary features, like facial hair and enlarged larynx.

The book that prompted the awareness that testosterone might have direct application in sport was *The Male Hormone*, written by Paul de Kruif and published in 1945: it recorded research into the impact of testosterone on the endurance of men for muscular work. Inspired by this, a group of West Coast body-builders began using testosterone preparations in the 1940s and 1950s and, as rumors of this circulated in the sports world, other strength-reliant performers, like field-eventers and football players started using the substance. Other sports weren't slow to realize the importance of testosterone and, through the 1960s, it was commonplace for cyclists, skiers and an assortment of other athletes to use the substance. So widespread was the use of synthetic derivatives of testosterone, anabolic steroids, that, in the 1970s, governing bodies of sports declared them illegal and began testing.

In 1988, the Johnson case thrust steroid use into the headlines and helped establish a place for the substance alongside crack cocaine and ecstacy as great destructive drugs of our time. Neglected was another story. From the 1940s androgens have been used to treat wasting conditions associated with chronic debilitating illnesses and trauma, burns, surgery and radiation therapy.

Anabolic steroids' efficacy in accelerating red blood cell production made it first choice therapy for a variety of anemias (having too little hemoglobin) before bone marrow transplants and other treatments arrived. Between the 1930s and the mid-1980s, psychiatrists prescribed anabolic steroids for the treatment of depression and psychoses. Most recently, steroids have been used to arrest the muscle wasting that occurs during the progression of HIV infection and Aids.

Hoberman and Yesalis predict that testosterone treatment will be commercially exploited as an aging population grows. It is currently in use for strengthening older bodies, rejuvenating an ailing libido and improving a declining memory. "Implicit cultural acceptance of mass male hormone therapy seems evident in the fact that over the past several years the lay press has broadcast and printed numerous reports on the potential benefits of both testosterone and estrogen therapy for the aging population," conclude Hoberman and Yesalis (1995: 65). In the kind of narcissistic, youth-adoring culture we have today, old age is increasingly regarded as a "problem" worthy of medical attention.

In sports, no one doubts the efficacy of anabolic steroids: they *do* work. Precisely what makes them work, we still don't know. There is, for instance, a school of thought that argues that the critical component in the equation is our belief that they will enhance our performance. If, for some reason, we stopped believing in them, then maybe anabolic steroids would not yield the results they apparently do. At present, so much money is spent on testing for drugs that there is little left for ascertaining exactly what they do to sports performers. If self-belief is the single most important factor, it may be that a placebo is at work. (For a fuller discussion of the purported effects of anabolic steroids, see Yesalis 1993.)

While anabolic steroids are the most widely used drug in track and field events – an estimated 1 million regular users in the USA alone – stimulants are the second most common and probably the most popular in sport as a whole. Amphetamine use has been widespread for at least three decades. The basic effect of stimulants is to get messages to a complex pathway of neurons in the brainstem called the arousal system, or reticular activating system (RAS). This system is ultimately responsible for maintaining consciousness and determining our state of awareness. So, if the RAS bombards the cerebral cortex with stimuli, we feel very alert and able to think clearly. Amphetamines are thought to cause chemical neurotransmitters, such as dopamine, to increase, so enhancing the flow of nervous impulses in the RAS and stimulating the entire CNS. The sympathetic nervous system is stimulated, speeding up heart rate, raising blood pressure, and dilating pupils. In sports terms, the performer is fired up and resistant to the sensation of fatigue, particularly the muscular pain associated with lactic acid.

Placebo

From the Latin *placere*, to please, this is a pharmacologically inert substance given to patients usually to humor them rather than effect any cure. Yet the substance often works as effectively (if not more so) as an active substance because the patient believes it will. The substance is called a placebo and its result is known as the *placebo effect*. This has many applications outside the clinical setting. Weightlifters have been told they were receiving an anabolic steroid while, in fact, only some of them received it – the others were given a placebo. Both groups improved leg presses, the first group by 135 lbs, the other (receiving the placebo) by 132 lbs. The sheer expectation of benefit seems to have been the crucial factor. A similar process can work in reverse. For example, subjects may be given active drugs together with information that they will have no effect: consequently the drugs may not have any effect. In other words, the direct effect of drugs alone may not be any more powerful than the administrator's or experimenter's suggestions along.

One problem facing users active in sport who need nutrition for the release of energy is that amphetamines depress appetites. They used to be prescribed to dieters, though less so nowadays because dieters became dependent on the drug. This came about because the body quickly develops a tolerance, probably through the readiness of the liver to break down the drug rapidly. An obvious temptation is to increase the dose to achieve the same effect. So with increased use of the drug, the user becomes dependent. Weight loss and dependence are the more obvious side effects; others include irritability (probably due to irregular sleep) and even a tendency toward paranoia. Cyclists Jensen and Simpson demonstrated that the effects can be terminal.

There is another class of stimulants called sympathomimetic amine drugs, such as ephedrine, which, as the name suggests, acts not on the brain but directly on the nerves affecting the organs. (This produces effects in the sympathetic part of the autonomic nervous system: it speeds up the action of the heart, and constricts the arteries and increases lung inflation.) Ephedrine is used commonly as a decongestant and is often prescribed for asthma sufferers.

At the 1988 Olympics a pentathlete, Alexander Watson of Australia, was disqualified for having an excessive level of caffeine in his system. To have reached such a level he would have needed to have drunk 40 regular-sized cups of coffee; other methods include the use of a suppository or the chewing of small nuts of caffeine.

Narcotic analgesics are used in all walks of life, but especially in sports where injuries are commonplace and a tolerance to pain is essential. Soccer and US football are examples of games involving the "walking wounded". Derivatives of the opium poppy were probably used by ancient Mesopotamians around 3000 BC; they left instructions for use on wax tablets. There are now methods of producing such derivatives synthetically. Opium, heroin, codeine, and morphine, along with the newer "designer" drugs, are all classified as narcotics which relieve pain and depress the CNS, producing a state of stupor. Reflexes slow down, the skeleton is relaxed, and tension is reduced. The negative effects are much the same as those of amphetamines, with the additional one of specific neurons becoming dependent on the drug and so providing a basis for addiction.

The immediate effects of stimulants or narcotic analgesics would be of little or no service to sports performers who rely on fineness of judgement, sensitivity of touch, acuity of sight, and steadiness of hand. Success in sports like darts, archery, snooker, shooting, or show jumping is based on calmness and an imperviousness to "pressure." The Canadian snooker player Bill Werbeniuk was famed for his customary ten pints of beer to help him relax before a game. His CNS would become duller and tensions presumably disappeared. How he managed to co-ordinate hand and eye movements, stay awake, or even just stay upright is a mystery. Alcohol has serious drawbacks, which include nausea and impaired judgement, not to mention liver damage and a variety of dependency related problems.

Werbeniuk

While Vancouver-based professional snooker player Bill Werbeniuk was known for his consumption of large quantities of lager, he was also a habitual user of Inderal, a beta-blocker which helped counteract the effects of an hereditary nervous disorder. After criticism from the British Minister for Sport, the World Professional Billiards and Snooker Association (WPBSA) reviewed its drugs policy and included Inderal on its list of banned substances. Unable to find an alternative, Werbeniuk admitted to the WPBSA that he intended to continue using the drug and was eventually banned from tournaments.

Beta-blockers are a newer alternative. Originally used by patients with irregular heartbeats, these relieve anxiety by controlling the release of adrenaline and by lowering the heart rate; they are used by edgy showbusiness performers – and horses. In November 1994, a racehorse, Mobile Messenger, tested positive for propranolol, a beta-blocker, after winning a race at Southwell, England. The effect of the drug on the horse would have been similar to that on a human: to slow down the heart rate and thereby alleviate stress.

Weightlifters and other sports performers who compete in categories based on body weight have to calibrate their diet and preparation carefully. A couple of pounds, even ounces, over the limit can destroy months of conditioning if the performer is made to take off the excess at the weigh-in. Jumping rope, saunas, and other methods of instant weight reduction can be debilitating and may drain cerebral fluid that cushions the brain against the wall of the cranium. Competitors in weight-controlled sports always check-weigh during the days preceding an event and, should their weight seem excessive, may take diuretics. These substances – widely used therapeutically for reducing fluid levels – excite the kidneys to produce more urea and, basically, speed up a perfectly natural waste disposal process.

Diuretics are found in alcoholic drinks and coffee (in the caffeine), which explains why a visit to the toilet is necessary shortly after imbibing any of these liquids. Diuretics inhibit the secretion of the antidiuretic hormone which serves as a chemical messenger, carrying information form the pituitary gland at the base of the brain to parts of the kidneys, making them more permeable and allowing water to be reabsorbed into the body (thus conserving fluid). Hormones, of course, are carried in the blood. If the messages don't get through, the kidneys move the water out of the body. Continued use of diuretics can damage the kidneys. In recent years, the suspicion has grown that competitors have not only been using diuretics to reduce weight but also to flush out other substances, in particular the above-mentioned drugs. It follows that competitors found to have diuretics in their urine immediately have their motives questioned. Kerrith Brown of Great Britain lost his Olympic bronze medal for judo despite pleading that the diuretic furosemide, found in his urine was introduced into his system by a medical officer who gave him an anti-inflammatory substance containing the chemical to reduce a knee swelling.

Another athlete to be disqualified, though at an earlier Olympics, was Martti Vainio who lost his silver medal for the 10,000 meters at Los Angeles after steroid traces were discovered in his urine. The Finn had been careful enough to cease using the drug well before competition to escape detection, but had blundered by having himself injected with blood that had been removed from his body early in 1984 when training at altitude. In Chapter 3, we noted the importance of protein molecule hemoglobin, which is found in red blood cells. It has a remarkable ability to form loose associations with oxygen. As most oxygen in the blood is combined with hemoglobin rather than simply dissolved in plasma, the more hemoglobin present in a red blood cell, the more oxygen it can transport to the muscles. Obviously then, performers can benefit from having a plentiful supply of oxygen to react with glucose and release energy stored in food. The advantage of training at altitude, where the oxygen in the atmosphere is scarce, is that the body naturally compensates by producing more hemoglobin.

The performer descends to sea-level carrying with him or her a plentiful supply of hemoglobin in the blood, which gradually readjusts (over a period of weeks). Each day spent at lower altitudes diminishes the benefit of altitude training: proliferation of hemoglobin ceases in the presence of available atmospheric oxygen. One way to "capture" the benefits is to remove a quantity of highly oxygenated blood during intense altitude training, store it, and re-introduce it into the circulatory system immediately prior to competition, which is what Vainio and probably many others did. He neglected to take account of the fact that he had been on steroids during the time spent at altitude and that the stored blood contained evidence of this.

The "doping" in this process doesn't refer to the administration of drugs but to the more correct use of the term, pertaining to a thick liquid used as a food or lubricant. There is, however, a synthetic drug that can achieve much the same effect. Erythropreotin (EPO) facilitates the production of extra red blood cells, which absorb oxygen, and leaves the user with no tell-tale needle tracks. As EPO does not show up in urinalysis, inspection is possibly only by blood tests, before and after competition, to take red blood cell counts. As well as being more convenient than a transfusion, EPO has the advantage of being undetectable in competitors who object to invasive techniques on religious or ethical grounds. "Blood doping" or "blood boosting" and EPO, in a sense, copy the body's natural processes and, at the moment, their long-term effects seem to be broadly the same as those of living at high altitudes.

Another, more controversial, method of mimicking nature is by extracting the naturally occurring growth hormone somatotropin, which is produced and released by the pituitary gland, as discussed in Chapter 3. This hormone controls the human rate of growth by regulating the amount of nutrients taken into the body's cells and by stimulating protein synthesis. Over-production of the hormone may cause a child to grow to giant proportions (a condition referred to as gigantism), whereas too little can lead to dwarfism. The growth hormone also affects fat and carbohydrate metabolism in adults, promoting a mobilization of fat which becomes available for use as fuel, and sparing the utilization of protein. The potential of this mechanism for promoting growth has not been lost on field athletes, weightlifters, body-builders, and others requiring muscle build.

Illicit markets in growth hormone extracted from foetuses have been uncovered, though a synthetically manufactured version, somatonorm, may make this redundant. Eventually, skeletal and muscular abnormalities may result. These outward physical signs are some of the few reliable ways of determining whether performers have been taking the hormone, in either form, or whether they have an abnormally high level. Nor would pure EPO be detectable through existing techniques. This has led some to believe that drug users can always stay one step ahead of those wishing to identify them: the line between what is "natural" and "unnatural" for the human body is not so clear-cut as testers would like and science finds ways of replicating nature.

Others believe that drug-testing methods are keeping pace and hold up the Maradona and Johnson cases as examples of how not even the elite can escape detection, given a vigilant team of toxicologists and a sophisticated laboratory. The system at Seoul was a costly state-of-the-art set-up and easily the most effective drug detection center to date. Before moving on, we should briefly take note of its apparatus and methods.

Hewlett-Packard, the multinational computer specialists, charged the IOC $3 million (£1.9 million) to set up the scientific testing equipment at the Korean Advanced Institute of Science and Technology. The system of gas chromatography and mass spectroscopy could, according to its makers, "detect concentrations [of banned substances] as low as one part per billion; roughly the equivalent to detecting traces from a teaspoonful of sugar after it has been dissolved in an Olympic swimming pool." A further claim was that it could check a compound found in urine against 70,000 held in a computer's database in "less than a minute."

The entire testing process has four phases. (1) Within an hour of the finish of an event, two samples of a performer's urine are taken, one is tested for acidity and specific gravity so that testers can get a broad indication of any illegal compounds. (2) The sample is then split into smaller batches to test for certain classes of drugs, such as anabolic steroids, stimulants, etc. Testers make the urine alkaline and mix it with solvents, like ether, causing any drugs to dissolve into the solvent layer, which is more easily analyzed than urine itself. (3) This solvent is then passed through a tube (up to 25 meters long) of gas (or liquid chromatogram) and the molecules of the solvent separate and pass through at different rates, depending on their size and other properties (such as whether they are more likely to adhere to the material of the tube itself). More than 200 drugs are searched for in this period, which lasts about 15 minutes. (4) Any drugs found are then analyzed with a mass spectrometer, which bombards them with high-energy ions, or electrons, creating unique chemical fingerprints, which can be rapidly checked against the database. Should any banned substances show up, the second sample is tested in the presence of the performer. (Another method is radioimmunoassay, in which antibodies to known substances are used like keys that will only fit one lock; the lock is the banned substance which is found by the key that fits it.)

Encouraged by the Seoul experience, the IOC stated its intention to implement all-year-round testing and, while it is by far the most stringent sports body, others have followed its example. Efforts to stamp out drugs are obviously related to the degree of drug use in sport and, as I indicated earlier, there seems to have been a fairly sharp increase over the past twenty to thirty years. The reasons for that increase are to be found in cultural changes, as we will see next.

Bodies under control

Sport is a human enterprise, as are the many sciences and technologies that have assisted or augmented it. Readers of this book may be engaged in a scientific endeavor to explore the application of academic study to sport. Some explorations, especially in the field of medicine, have yielded striking results. Injuries are better tended, pains are anesthetized and recoveries are accelerated. Nutrition has aided both training and performance. Psychology has helped to strengthen commitment and develop beneficial attitudes. Biomechanics has identified more efficient methods of locomotion.

Pharmacology's specific contribution is more ambiguous. Sports performers can legally benefit from some drugs, for example some painkillers, but not from others, such as those that add speed and power to an athlete's performance. Despite this ambiguity, many sports competitors seem willing to assist their performances by using both prescribed and proscribed drugs. Changes over the past fifty years have ensured that drugs are now part of sport. To authorities, many sports have drug problems; to competitors, drugs are simply available for use should they be required. The first point to remember when trying to uncover the reasons for the apparent rise in drug use is that sport is not a solitary endeavor. Romantic visions of lone trainers are rife, of course, but, in practice, the pursuit of excellence in sport is a team effort. And, over the decades, teams have grown larger and have been augmented with a widening network of "back-ups," including medical personnel and the whole range of technologies they employ.

The scientifically designed and assisted preparation of Balboa's Russian opponent in *Rocky IV* was a fiction that strayed only marginally from fact. High-tech training equipment, monitoring systems, and specialized personnel all combine to assist a competitor and, ultimately, improve performance. In the process, the individual's body practically becomes the property of scientists. Drugs are but one element in an elaborate technology of control, which has led to the hysterical view that modern sport is contested by scientists more than actual performers.

As we saw in Chapter 4, the historical trend that Norbert Elias calls the civilizing process has fostered a dual approach to the human being in which the physical body is subordinated to the rational mind. Scientific advances have made it possible to reshape the body in accordance with the mind's imperatives. We find in works of literature diverse treatments of much the same theme. Shelley's *Frankenstein* and Stevenson's *Dr Jekyll and Mr Hyde* show attempts by scientists either to reconstruct or remold humans, in both cases with hideous, unanticipated consequences. Many found the Press sisters, Irene and Tamara, rather hideous products of Soviet sports science. They dominated their events (hurdling and pentathlon; shot and discus, respectively) in the 1960s and retired – fortuitously, perhaps – before sex testing was introduced in 1962. But their appearances were freakishly muscular; their flat chests and heavy jaws had the hallmarks of steroid users. Mutterings suggested the sisters' bodies had undergone fundamental chromosomal changes during their preparations.

All sports demand changes in the body and bodily processes. Even though physical input varies from sport to sport, all involve some degree of mastery over technique and this by extension means adjusting the body, whether it be adding strength or sensitivity to touch. The higher the level of achievement, the higher the level of bodily control required. Every activity demands physical control; sport demands an exaggerated level of control that only discipline and surveillance will achieve. Control over the body has always been integral to sport. Yet recently, the degree of control technically possible has been raised considerably by the whole panoply of sport-related science. The implicit claims made by such movie series as *Robocop* and *Universal Soldier* may not be as wild as they at first seem.

The civilizing process itself implicates individuals in some form of control over their bodies. Elias focuses mainly on the restraint in using physical violence, but notes the simultaneous trend for people to subdue spontaneous bodily functions and control their physical being. Sport, in this sense, is regarded as a cathartic release from the stressful tensions generated by the trend toward control. But, of course, sporting activity has also been controlled externally by governing organizations and internally by individual participants who needed to transform and canalize "their drives and feelings" as Elias puts it, rather than remain in the "grip" of their impulses. Success of any kind in a competitive activity means conforming and this, in turn, means internal disciplining – control. So, control over the functioning and even appearance of the human body has been important to all societies where, as Elias puts it, "fairly high civilizing standards are safeguarded."

In the late twentieth century the body is open for big business. Health foods, fitness clubs, sports goods, diets, rowing machines; all these and many more money-spinning goods and services cater for people eager to reproportion their bodies according to socially desirable standards. Consider also some of the traumatic experiences to which bodies are subject, such as Aids, smoking, pollution, rape, and child abuse. These form layers of a rich soil, or, as John Hargreaves would have it, "the compost in which moral panic flourishes and on which the forces of law and order thrive" (1987: 141).

Not only have we been encouraged to take control over our bodies; we have become acutely aware of the power at our disposal for doing so. Drugs are one such source of power. We can alter the most basic of bodily functions, like eating, sleeping, and defecating with the appropriate drugs. Pain can be removed, rest can be restored, even moods can be heightened or depressed depending on the "need." Nothing is more rational than the desire to have consummate mastery over the body. Only a short step away is the irrational, of course, and dependence surrenders mastery to the drug itself, taking away responsibility, and eventually resolve, from the user and subverting the control once held over the body.

Sports performers are meant to stop short of the irrational. Success is contingent on organizing physical and mental facilities in accordance with structured rules and imperatives, so control over the body is absolutely necessary. Careful use of artifacts to attain such a control has been generously endorsed in sport, but drugs have acquired a notoriety that has not affected exercise equipment, from stop watches to multigyms, esoteric diets based on everything from vitamins to recycled urine and monitoring that can produce elaborate physical and psychological profiles.

What were once take-them-or-leave-them facilities became essential equipment for some sports. It seems quite illogical to suggest that drugs would be ignored in a world awash with devices to keep the body under control. Medications to alleviate pain or accelerate healing processes became parts of performers' baggage to be carried in kitbags. Many experimented with the alleged benefits of hypnotherapy, autogenics and other positive-thinking techniques. Vitamin, phosphate, and cortisone (steroid) injections became commonplace. Sedatives calmed nerves.

Set in a wider context, trends in sport reflect what goes on in life generally. The past twenty-odd years have witnessed the rise of new spirits. Young people have welcomed the use of stimulants, hallucinogens, and all manner of narcotics to alter behavior and perception. But recent generations have edged toward drug dependence: tranquillizers have led a seemingly endless list of prescriptives to counter the stress-inducing effects of modern life. The "drug culture" is world-wide and transgenerational, embracing those who wish to open new doors to perception, those who merely want to make it to the next day, and many more besides. Whether they like it or not, sports performers are part of a universal culture in which drugs of one form or another play an important role.

The science-assisted effort to pursue athletic excellence and the enveloping swirl of drug dependence: take the two together and one has a compelling mixture. Sport, if only because of its competitive nature, has urged its competitors to exploit the gifts of science, and our habits as a population have been transformed by the availability of drugs. Some might wish to add a further factor to this combination – an exaggeration of the importance of winning. As Michael Messner writes in his study *Power at Play*: "Many [competitors], because of the 'win at all costs' values of the sportsworld and the instrumental relationships they have with their own bodies, tend to feel that the short-term efficiency or confidence that is gained through drug use will outweigh any possible problems that might ensue from the drug" (1992: 78).

Commercialism is the malefactor here; as sport has slid further from the Corinthian ideal, its passage lubricated by business interests, so the joy of competing for its own sake has been superseded by an unprincipled win-at-all-costs approach; winning is what matters in modern sports. Exactly *how* one wins is largely irrelevant. Few people would doubt that victory in any sport is the single most important motive for competing.

Whether this is anything new or just a continuation of old traditions is open to question. Those to whom the cherishing and upholding of ideals are so important often ignore the fact that sport, by definition, is competitive and competition is meaningless unless some individual or group is actually doing their level best to win. Commercialization has certainly increased the tangible rewards for winning. Olympic winners of ten years ago went home with a gold medal; today they take with them a portfolio of contracts worth six-figure sums. A victorious world championship boxer can look forward to a purse worth dozens of millions of dollars while his vanquished opponent may be relegated straight to low-budget promotions.

It was but a few years ago that pool and darts were down-to-earth sports enjoyed by those who liked a drink at the local bar; now, for today's players, a major professional title means a substantial premium on their earnings. Clearly, there is more at stake nowadays in terms of both material gains and status. And this has fostered more aggressive competitors, prepared to train more and even risk more to realize their ambitions. If science can help the realization, then common sense dictates that sports performers use it; if drugs can assist, one can be sure many competitors will give only a sideways glance to moral warnings reading "just say no."

Sport is too profound, too serious, and too lucrative for simplistic slogans. The crucial edge which drugs can provide may be the difference between a fortune and ignominy. Competition has come to occupy such a central place, not only in sport but in society, that it would be a virtual betrayal of sporting ideals to neglect the potential of drugs in maximizing performance. Three trends together help explain why sports performers have been prepared to use drugs: advances in science; growth of drug culture; and intensification of competitiveness. But equally important as changes in actual use are the changes in reactions to drugs and, more pertinently, the reasons for the changes.

Law and drugs

Many of the drugs used by sports performers are available, often without prescription, in EC countries and the USA. But, in 1989, an amendment to the British Misuse of Drugs Act 1971 made the illegal possession of anabolic steroids a criminal offence. This was the first time that sport's own rules for banning the use of drugs were given the force of law, making sport's own sanctions (e.g. bans) largely irrelevant. Possession of drugs, which if used excessively can promote cancers, carried a maximum of a fine and a two-year gaol sentence. Producers, importers, and suppliers faced unlimited fines and gaol sentences of up to five years.

By accident or choice?

The reasons why the IOC and other governing bodies of sport are prepared to go to quite extraordinary lengths in their efforts to solve the supposed drug problem may be self-evident to many. But we will evaluate each reason on its own merits, beginning with the most obvious.

Drugs are not fair. They confer artificially induced advantages on the user; and competing with such advantages is tantamount to cheating. Fairness is a rather troublesome concept to define, but we can assume, with Peter McIntosh, who wrote the book *Fair Play*, that: "Fairness is related to justice" and "breaking the rules with intent to avoid the penalties" as a definition of cheating is too simple (1980: 2, 182). He favors the definition of Gunther Lüschen who believes that the "principle of chance beyond differences in skill and strategy are violated" when the conditions agreed upon for winning a contest "are changed in favor of one side" (1976: 67). Drugs change the conditions for winning. But, then again, so do many other things.

Take the example of blood doping for which athletes may draw penalties, including bans. In a strict sense, this is cheating. But, how about athletes born in Kenya or Ethiopia, both several hundred feet above sea-level? Such athletes may be fortunate enough to be brought up in an atmosphere that encourages hemoglobin production in the body and they may find the transition to sea-level really quite comfortable as a result. Witness as evidence the dominance of Kenyan middle- and long-distance runners over the past twenty years. Equipped with naturally conferred advantages, Kenyans capitalized on the track and cross-country circuits, leaving weary European and American athletes in their wake.

Another accident of birth meant that the 5-year-old Boris Becker was given every available coaching and equipment facility to help him develop his tennis skills. His parents, being wealthy, could afford to indulge their child and, as things turned out, their money was a shrewd investment for Becker became the youngest-ever Wimbledon champion and, in so doing, unlocked a multimillion dollar treasure chest. Let's imagine that tennis produced its equivalent of world boxing champion, Riddick Bowe, an archetypal ghetto child from Brooklyn, who had the added disadvantage of being black. Were this imaginary figure to play Becker, would it be a fair match? When they came face-to-face in matchup, the conditions may appear fair, but one would hardly say they were "fair" in a deeper sense. One player has benefited from *social* advantages in a similar way to Kenyan runners, who have benefited *naturally* from being born at high altitudes. It would be a naïve person indeed who believed all is fair in sport and that background, whether social or natural, is irrelevant to eventual success or failure.

Drugs are taken by choice. There is a difference between the advantages bestowed by social background or place of origin and those that are enjoyed by the taker of drugs. Sports performers can, as the slogan goes, "say 'no' to drugs" in much the same way as many say "yes." Swallowing tablets or allowing oneself to be injected are voluntary activities over which individuals have a high degree of control; one presumes – and only *presumes* – that they realize the potential costs as well as benefits and they exercise volition when doing or agreeing to the action. Obviously, the same performers have no say in where they were born or the state of their parents' bank account. By contrast, using drugs involves procuring an advantage quite voluntarily.

Yet there is more to this: first, because there are many other forms of advantage that are actively sought out and, second, because some are better placed than others either to seek out or eschew them. Were you a Briton following home Dominic Kirui in a 5,000-meter race, you might wish you were born in Kenya. Impossible, of course, so you might think about going to high altitudes and engaging in a spot of blood doping. Quite possible, but illegal. Another possibility is just to train in some part of the world high enough to give you some advantage, or at least to neutralize Kirui's advantage. Perfectly possible and legal. The probable result is an advantage quite legitimately obtained through voluntary effort. But an advantage is gained all the same.

Not that everyone is able to exercise choice in such matters: a dedication to competition, a determination to win, and an unflinching resolve to withstand pain are needed and these qualities are easier to come by if the alternative is a one-way ticket back to the ghetto. If your alternatives look unpromisingly bleak, then choices can be rather illusory. Ben Johnson was born in Jamaica and migrated to Canada in 1980 at the age of 19, his ambition being the same as any migrant – namely, to improve his material life. Lacking education, but possessing naturally quick reflexes (which couldn't be changed) and fast ground speed (which could), he made the best of what he had, so that, within four years, he was in the Canadian Olympic team. Sport is full of stories like Johnson's: bad news – poor origins, little education, few occupational prospects: good news – physical potential and the opportunity to realize it. There's no realistic choice, here. Countless young people with some form of sporting prowess when faced with the once-and-for-all decision of whether or not to sink their entire efforts in the one area in which they just might achieve success don't want to contemplate the alternatives. Given the chance, they'll go for it. And this means maximizing every possible advantage in an intensely competitive world. It's doubtful whether any athlete with a similarly deprived childhood would have any compunction about gaining an edge by any means. The choices they have are often too stark to need much mulling over.

Asking whether choice was exercised in trying to determine whether cheating took place is not adequate. Even if we were to dismiss the claims of a performer (who tested positive for a given drug) that his or her drink was spiked (or similar), the question of whether that person *freely* exercised choice remains. Returning to Becker, let's suppose he was found guilty of something untoward; it's feasible to argue that his choice was less restricted than a Turkish migrant worker's son in Germany whose one chance for some material success is through sport. All this isn't intended to exonerate those from deprived backgrounds who have sought an advantage through "foul" means rather than "fair." It merely casts doubts on the hard-and-fast distinction between fair play and cheating. If we want to sustain the distinction, we have to ignore the manifold advantages or disadvantages that derive from a person's physical and social background and which are beyond his or her power to change. We can attempt to get round this by isolating the element of choice and defining cheating only when a person has consciously and deliberately taken some action to gain advantage. This works up to a point if we cast aside doubts about the circumstances in which the decision was made. Again, backgrounds are important in influencing the decision. So the pedestal on which sport stands when it tries to display itself as a model of fair play is not quite as secure as it might at first seem. Not only are advantages dispensed virtually at birth, but they operate either to limit or liberate a person's ability to make choices.

Drugs are harmful to health. Imagine a new drug is introduced. It has great recreational value, giving pleasure to the consumer; its other alleged benefits include a calming effect on the user and a tendency to curb the appetites of those who want to control their weight. A wide range of sports performers spy advantages: the drug steadies the nerves of those who wish to remain relaxed under pressure and helps others unwind after stressful competition. But it contains a chemical that is extremely addictive, another that is carcinogenic, it also causes heart disease, bronchial complaints and a number of related physical problems. Conservatively, it accounts for about half a million deaths a year in the USA and Britain. In contrast, the doses of the anabolic steroid taken by Ben Johnson in the 1988 Olympics was allegedly lower than what the World Health Organization subsequently found safe to administer as a male contraceptive. In fact, many of the substances banned from sport and condemned as harmful to health are condoned, and even prescribed in other circumstances, prompting the thought that the banned drugs may not be so dangerous as some of the legal ones

Sport's central philosophical point seems to be that, whatever people's backgrounds, if they are given the chance to gain advantages over others, they may fairly do so as long as they stop short of knowingly using chemical substances (at least *some* chemical substances). Most drugs used to enable or assist performance rather than gain advantage by enhancement are acceptable. So it was perfectly possible for British runner Peter Elliott to earn his 800 meters silver medal while being treated with a painkilling drug to alleviate a groin strain, while ten other competitors at the same Olympics were disqualified, two for using the diuretic pseudofurosemide (which may have been used to conceal anabolic steroids).

Some might counter the argument that supports this by saying that the ability to achieve anything at all in sport is limited by the body's natural early warning system – pain – and interfering with this is artificial and unnatural. "But unlikely to cause any long-term damage in the user of certain painkillers" might be the riposte. To which the answer might be that there are other types of conditioning that do not include drugs, but which are detrimental to a performer's health. A good example of this might be the former gymnast, Olga Korbut, who in her early teens was a lovable urchin who charmed the world's TV viewers by her spellbinding displays, but who in her twenties was haggard and arthritic. The effect on health of a great many banned drugs is negligible by comparison.

Controlled dieting, hypnotherapy, and psyching techniques, as well as many more practices used by competitors may yet prove to have long-term consequences. And there is a growing school of thought that supports the view that the quantity and intensity of training needed in today's highly competitive sports may depress natural immunity systems, exposing performers to infection. Sports clubs themselves acknowledge that players in need of surgery will often postpone operations in order to compete in key games. They do so with the full consent if not encouragement – and perhaps, in some cases, at the request – of coaches or managers, who are surely aware of the probability of exacerbating a condition by delaying corrective treatment

This has led some observers to believe that the use of drugs is no better or worse than some other aids to performance. They are certainly no worse than many of the drugs commonly available outside the world of sport. Most sports frown on smoking and drinking too, though some, like motor racing and cricket, have been grateful for sponsorship from tobacco companies. Others, like English soccer, have openly embraced breweries, at the same time committing itself to clamping down on drugs, both performance-enhancing and recreational. Alcohol kills about 100,000 people a year, probably more if alcohol-related road deaths are included. The positive effects of alcohol in oxidizing blood, making it less sticky, are outweighed by the physical and social consequences of its excessive use.

Even everyday drugs such as aspirin and antihistamine, which we presume to be innocuous, are not completely without potentially harmful consequences. Caffeine found in coffee and tea is mildly harmful, but who, apart from governing bodies in sports, would dream of banning its general use? The argument that some drugs are more harmful than others has an *Animal Farm* logic to it and, as such, is fraught with inconsistencies. Even if some drugs were found to be dangerous (and steroids in particular are thought to be responsible for cancers and deaths) it would be something of an intrusion into the lives of responsible individuals to tell them not to take them.

Medical bodies are not averse to doing this as the campaigns or, more properly, the crusades of the British and American Medical Associations against boxing have shown. Prolonged involvement in boxing exposes the boxer to the risk of brain damage and many other less severe injuries, is the claim of the anti-boxing lobbyists. So boxers have to be protected, if necessary from themselves, in exactly the same way as any other sports competitors contemplating actions that may result in harm to their health. The effect on health of many banned drugs is small compared to that of boxing. But to make boxing illegal because of this presumes that all the young and physically healthy young men (and a few women in some parts of the world) are oblivious to the hazards of the sport when they enter. It assumes they are not rational, deliberating agents with some grasp of the implications of boxing – a grasp sufficient for them to do a cost–benefit calculation and weigh up the probable rewards against the probable losses.

Were information about the long-term consequences of boxing or drug use concealed, then the "protector" would have a very strong case. But the results of scientific tests are available and to assume that competitors are so witless as to know nothing of this is insulting and patronizing. If young people with a chance to capitalize on the sporting potential are informed of the dangers involved in their decision to pursue a line of action, then it is difficult to support a case for prohibiting this, at least in societies not prone to totalitarianism. Boxers may well judge the brain damage they risk in their sport preferable to the different kind of "brain damage" they will almost certainly sustain in a repetitive industrial job over a 40-year period, or in an unbearably long spell out of work. Other sports performers with few prospects outside sport may evaluate their own positions similarly and, when the Mephistophelian bargain presents itself, the decision of whether or not to box should be theirs. Unless, of course, one believes that superordinate moral agents should guide our thoughts and behavior.

But the crudity and patronage of one argument doesn't license disingenuousness in the attack on it; which means that we should acknowledge that sports performers of whatever level do not reach decisions unaided. We have noted previously that all manner of influence bear on an individual's decision and, quite apart from those deriving from background, we have to isolate coaches and trainers. Bearing in mind the case of American football in the 1960s when coaches were assuming virtual medical status in dispensing drugs, we should remind ourselves of the important roles still played by these people in all sports. We must also realize that sport is populated by many "Dr Feelgoods" who are only too happy to boost performance without necessarily informing the competitor of all the possible implications. It's quite probable that many competitors are doing things, taking things, even thinking things that may jeopardize their health. But do they know it? Perhaps sports authorities might attempt to satisfy themselves formally that all competitors in sports which do hold dangers are totally aware of them and comfortable about their involvement. This would remove the educational task from coaches and trainers and shift the onus onto governing organizations.

Drugs *are* harmful to health – as are many other things. Sports authorities quite properly communicate this, though the distinctions that are often made between harmful substances and activities and apparently innocuous ones are frequently arbitrary and difficult to support with compelling evidence. Further, the assumptions carried by governing bodies in their efforts to regulate the use of drugs can be seen in some lights as demeaning, suggesting that performers themselves are incapable of making assessments and decisions unassisted.

Sports performers are role models for the young. It follows that if athletes are known and seen to use drugs of any kind, then young people may be encouraged to follow. There is adequate evidence to support this and, while the substances which competitors use to enhance performance are often different to the ones that cause long-term distress at street-level, the very act of using drugs may work as a powerful example. But the argument can't be confined to sports: many rock musicians as well as writers and artists use drugs for relief or stimulus. Rock stars arguably wield more influence over young acolytes than the sports elite. The shaming of a sports performer found to have used drugs and the nullifying of his or her performance is a deterrent or a warning to the young: "Do this and you will suffer the same fate." But Pearl Jam isn't disgraced and the band's albums wouldn't be taken from the charts if it were discovered that they recorded them while using coke. No one considers asking Pavarotti for a urine sample after one of his concerts. The music of Charlie Parker, a heroin addict, the acting of Cary Grant, who used LSD, the writing of Dylan Thomas, an alcoholic, all have not been obliterated; nor has the idolatry afforded them.

Sports performers are different in the sense that they operate in and therefore symbolize a sphere where all is meant to be wholesome and pure. But this puts competitors under sometimes intolerable pressure to keep their haloes straight and maintain the pretence of being saints. Clearly, they are not, nor, given the competitive nature of sport, will they ever be. Gone are the days portrayed in *Chariots of Fire* when winners were heroes to be glorified and losers were "good sports" for competing. Nowadays, hard cash has spoiled the purity. A yearning for money has introduced a limitless capacity for compromise and previously "amateur" or "shamateur" sports organizations, including the IOC, have led the way by embracing commercialism rather than spurning it. Competitors too are creatures of a competitive world and probably more preoccupied with struggling to win than with keeping a clean image.

Drugs are not natural. Clifton Perry, in an interesting article "Blood doping and athletic competition" argues the case for and against blood doping, which facilitates sporting performance through the introduction of a natural material that is indigenous to the body – blood. He offers the distinction between "performance enhancers" that do not cause lasting changes to the body of the user and "capacity enhancers" that do have long-term effects. This means that anabolic steroids are ruled out – not on the grounds that they are capacity enhancers but because they have deleterious effects (there is evidence that they elevate enzyme levels in the liver). But does this mean that blood doping should be allowed as it enhances capacities without deleterious consequences? Perry says no. His reason is based on the body's response to coming off the enhancer. "There is a difference between the loss of performance output through the loss of a mere performance enhancer and the loss of a capacity through inactivity" (1983: 43). After coming off an enhancer, the body returns to homeostasis: "There is nothing the athlete can do by way of performance to retain the former level of performance. This is not the case when a performer simply stops training" (1983: 42). Perry is also concerned about the implications of blood doping. It could lead to the use of "artificial blood" or other people's; or even the supplement Fluosol-DA, which increases the oxygen-carrying capacity of blood.

It's a provocative argument in favor of banning blood doping, but significantly Perry en route to his conclusion dismisses one of the staple reasons for banning performance-enhancing substances. There are many things that are allowed in sports that are deemed acceptable, but which are artificial: if we ran only on natural surfaces performance would be diminished, as they would be if we stripped any sport down to its "natural" basics: archery without sights, sprint cycling without the banked track of a velodrome, etc. Sports utilize any number of devices that don't actually make *us* faster or better, but certainly enhance performance. Pole-vaulters are not better vaulters when they use a particular type of pole, but they achieve better performances.

These don't just facilitate the exploitation of the body: they supplement it for specific periods of time. We have accepted world record times without dismissing them as due in large part to the wearing of lightweight, air-inflated spikes on fast synthetic surfaces. When pressed, we would have to agree that the same times couldn't have been achieved in flats on cinders. Blood doping, one might argue, is actually only the reintroduction of our own blood into our systems, albeit by means of transfusion and, in this sense, is more natural than some of the other devices that are commonplace in sports.

We might anticipate that a standard reply to this would be that blood doping and other banned methods of enhancing performance involve the ingestion of substances. This is true; but it doesn't make them any more or less natural. No one accuses a 300-lb defensive lineman or an Olympic heavy-weight weightlifter of being unnatural. Yet, they have achieved the bodies they have through a combination of resistance training and high carbohydrate diets. The activities – or lack thereof – we perform affect our bodies, as do the physical environments in which we live and the cultural definitions we try to live up to (or reject). Biochemical changes are affected by virtually everything we do. There is no natural body state: just living means changing our bodies.

These then are the main reasons why governing bodies have sought to eliminate drugs from sports and discredit those found using them. Yet the opposing school of thought has advanced its argument quite simply on two grounds. The first ground is practical and involves recognizing that drugs are part of sports and whatever attempts are made to extirpate them, ways and means will be found. In a decade's time, it is possible that there will be no way of preventing competitors from taking drugs which does not involve prison-like supervision in training as well as competition: inspection, invigilation, regulation, and punishment would become features of sport.

Argument	Evidence	Counter
Drugs are not fair.	Some evidence that drugs can supplement, assist or compensate in athletic performance.	(a) Historically, other performance supplementing devices, like spikes, have been seen as unfair; (b) Circumstances of birth may confer advantages.
Drugs are taken by choice.	Usually on advice of peers.	Often, alternative is lack of success at the highest level.
Drugs are harmful to health.	Some have known harmful effects; others do not.	(a) Some sports activities are dangerous. (b) Many legal drugs are more harmful than banned substances.
Sports performers are role models.	Young people do try to emulate sports stars.	Rock stars, movie actors, etc. are also role models.
Drugs are not natural.	Many drugs are synthetic versions of natural products.	There is no natural body state. Training elicits considerable biochemical changes.

The second ground is a moral one and involves bringing into the debate the people who are least frequently consulted – the performers. Peter Corrigan, a sports journalist with the British newspaper *The Independent on Sunday*, writing on the positive test of 1988 Tour de France winner, Pedro Delgado, observed that none of the other 180 competitors had protested at Delgado's infringement or showed any disinclination to continue to race with him. Corrigan argued that the demands of the race itself were so great that drugs were essential and that cyclists should be allowed to make up their own minds on whether or not to use them. This harks back to my previous point about the appropriate assumptions organizations hold about performers.

Were they to be seen as able, reasoning, and aware humans equipped with up-to-date information on drugs, then it's possible that we could safely leave the big decisions to them, as Corrigan suggested.

It's quite possible that many would object to drugs, but it is also possible that many would object to those elite performers who can afford to employ a staff of doctors and nutritionists and use only permitted drugs. It's possible that some might object to the use of blatant pacemakers in track events, for they are only of service to specific athletes. Maybe they wouldn't see steroid-pumped sprinters as mere projectiles fueled by drugs, but as athletes so utterly committed to pursuing excellence that they are prepared to rip apart the limits of their own frame to run faster than others. It would be useful to know what competitors thought. This is not an argument designed to satisfy purists, but it is certainly a cogent one and one wonders why sports organizations, in particular the IOC, haven't paused to consider it. Instead they have gone headlong down the road of regulation and punishment, spending millions of dollars on test centers all over the world in a campaign that borders on the obsessive. In the process, the mystique of drugs is enlarged, convincing sports performers that drugs do enhance performance, when in fact they only may.

Reynolds case
In 1992, Harry "Butch" Reynolds, the American world's 400-meter record holder, was awarded $26 million (about £16 million) damages after the IAAF had banned him for two years for failing a drugs test in 1990. Reynolds was reinstated. A US court of appeal later overturned the award, ruling that the Ohio judge who had made the original decision had no jurisdiction over the IAAF. Despite this, the IAAF took the precaution of having competitors sign a declaration that effectively prevents them from seeking legal redress through the courts.

Anomalies are multiplying. The Butch Reynolds case should have sent out a warning to sports bodies, but the tests just get more stringent and even headache remedies and an assortment of over-the-counter products are banned. British sprinter Solomon Wariso found himself banned after taking a commercial substance bought in a drug store. Many medically prescribed chemicals have been added to the banned list, making competition difficult if not impossible for those who suffer from asthma and other conditions. Britain's Diane Modahl insisted she had taken nothing despite two positive tests that indicated the presence of anabolic steroids in her system.

If others follow Modahl's example and pursue their cases, the day may not be far away when one of the major governing bodies is embarrassed by the courts. A world-class sprinter, contracted to run for, say, $200,000 may awake feeling stuffy and inhale a decongestant to ease his or her breathing. On arrival at the stadium, the athlete may declare this and be told that he or she can't race. Feeling deprived of earning a living, he or she may feel sufficiently aggrieved to claim restraint of trade or similar. Sports are busily revising their rules to prevent competitors repeating Reynolds' actions and appealing to law, but their jurisdiction may be tested.

Why then has sport committed inordinate amounts of money to the control of drugs? We have considered the more conventional and predictable reasons for the hard line against drugs. We have also exposed some of the ambiguities and even contradictions in these. Against these reasons there is what seems a practical and morally sound case for legitimizing drugs in sport. It seems insufficient to argue that sport benefits from purging itself of drugs; this may be so in an ideal world, but in reality the concept is vague and unspecific. Exactly who or what in sport benefits?

Were we to approach the question cynically, we might cast eyes outside sport and isolate beneficiaries who have no formal position on drugs in sport, but stand to profit very handsomely from the current attack on drugs. The companies supplying the equipment used for testing clearly have vested interests in the attempts of the IOC and other organizations. They have the technology without which those attempts are worthless. For the campaign on drugs to be in any degree successful, detective technologies will have to keep pace with ingenious chemists. This is an expensive business. The 1988 laboratory cost the IOC $3 million from Hewlett-Packard. Future centers are to cost more. Drug testing in sport is set to become a virtual industry in itself. The cost of drug testing represents a multimillion dollars outflow from sport into private industry. Clearly, someone is profiting. Perhaps it is sport if it can successfully instigate a return to its glorious past. This is unlikely. But while it tries, big business will stand by and applaud its stance, pausing only to prepare its next colossal invoice.

This is but one facet of an alliance between sport and business that has developed over the past several decades. Many nowadays go further than calling it an alliance: sport has become big business, they would argue. Next, we'll consider the argument.

FURTHER READING

Drugs, Sport and Politics by Robert Voy (Human Kinetics, 1991) is a power-fully argued text which gives a reliable indication of how widespread drug use is in sports today; the author was the Chief Medical Officer for the United States Olympic Committee and is therefore committed to the eradication of drug use. "Sports administrators have to decide they want drugs out of sport, and they have to back their words with action," he writes. Apart from the moralizing, the text is full of interesting features.

Philosophic Inquiry in Sport edited by William Morgan and Klaus Meier (Human Kinetics, 1988) has a section "Drugs and sport" that contains five searching (previously published) articles, all of which probe the moral issues underlying drugs policies. Every argument has the kind of bite missing from most standard textbook discussions of drugs in sport. Very valuable reading.

Anabolic Steroids in Sport and Exercise edited by Charles Yesalis (Human Kinetics, 1993) is an interesting package of contributions looking at the ergogenic properties (i.e. how efficiently they work) of anabolic steroids and the problems entailed in testing procedures.

The Government and Politics of Sport by Barrie Houlihan (Routledge, 1991) looks at the broader picture, noting that sports governing organiza-tions' response to the use of drugs cannot be seen in isolation from other processes that affect sports.

ASSIGNMENT

Imagine you are a researcher for a television documentary on drugs in sport. You have five telephone calls to make. Whom do you call? What are the first three questions you ask each? What answers do you get?

The Great Debates III
Should boxing be banned?

Both the American and British Medical Associations have called for a ban on professional boxing similar to the one operated in some Scandinavian countries.

Those who want boxing BANNED argue:	*Those who want boxing to CONTINUE argue:*
• It is the only sport where the object is to inflict as much physical damage on opponents as possible.	• Combat is one of the oldest forms of competition and a ban would only force boxing to go underground.
• The chances of long-term brain damage are disproportionately high compared to other sports in which head collisions are inevitable.	• The actual deaths in boxing are statistically far below those in air sports, motor sports and running.
• Young people are aware of the rewards but not sufficiently aware of the risks to their health.	• Boxing attracts working-class youths and a ban would be a form of class discrimination, denying them a means of earning money.
• There are too many deaths as a direct result of boxing.	• Preventing people from boxing would be an infringement of basic rights to make decisions about one's own life.

Chapter nine

Strictly business
Commercialism and
sports

Vanishing amateurs

We've always been paying for sports in one way or another. It's just that we're paying disproportionately more than ever before. It's not difficult to see why when you consider how much people stand to gain. Not only performers, who often earn more money in a month than the cost of an average family's house, but the tv networks who have efficiently exploited a market of viewers with disposable incomes and advertisers who want them to dispose some of that income on beer, cars and clothes. Sponsorship is also an integral part of sport: many major sports events, including the Olympic games have sponsors willing to spend millions to have their name or just logo attached to something as pure and wholesome as sports. Then, there are the promoters, governing bodies, paraphernalia manufacturers and so on. The business surrounding sports is very much bigger than what goes on in the ring, on the field, on the boards, or on the ice; and that has dismayed many fans.

"It's not sport any more: it's business!" they cry. The argument's premise is a popular one and, basically, it is that nothing is sacred. Well, nothing that can be profitably used to turn a penny, anyway. Sport has much utility in this respect. Being made into a business, according to this argument, doesn't

173

simply mean that commercial profits have been derived from sport. It means that filthy lucre has actually corrupted the ideals that were once integral. Moral qualities and principles associated with justice and fair play have been slaughtered on the altar of market forces. Now sport is bought and sold rather like any other service or commodity, but most like entertainment – showbusiness.

Part of this argument is undeniably true. Sports, or at least large numbers of them, have become the prey of commercial interests and these have transformed sheer competitive activity into high-yield business. Whether this has corrupted the central values of sports or merely taken sports in a new direction is open to question. Defenders of commercial interests would insist that they are only part of an inexorable movement. People enjoy watching and appreciating a contest and, in some circumstances, are willing to pay to do so. The trend has been that they are prepared to pay more and more. And where there is a demand and a raw supply there is rarely a shortage of enterprising people with ideas on how to connect the two – and appropriate a surplus. In this chapter, I will chronicle this trend and, in the next, I will pay special attention to the crucial part played by television in transforming sports.

Business
An habitual activity in which commercial considerations take priority; this term embraces trades, professions, and virtually any field interested in financial return rather than artistry or aesthetic principles.

All sports that are watchable have potential for commercial exploitation. An after-dinner game of snooker played in private with no pecuniary motive would not have this potential. Nor would one-to-one basketball matchup in the privacy of a school gym. Make the snooker players Stephen Hendry and Jimmy White and transport them to London's Wembley Arena, or the ball players David Robinson and Scottie Pippen and pitch them together in New York's Madison Square Garden and they become spectator sports. If contests can draw crowds they qualify as spectator sports. This doesn't make them implicitly corrupt, of course: those who rue the commercialization of sport might insist that it's perfectly possible to have mass spectator sports, but without the taint of money. Proponents of this view hark back to the golden days of amateurism when sport was for, as the name implies, love (from the Latin *amatorious*, "pertaining to love"). Fondness for the activity itself or the satisfaction drawn from winning were the motivating principles, though competition was, or should have been, regarded as more important than achievement.

Nowadays, "amateur" is virtually a pejorative word implying unskilful and lack of refinement – the opposite of professional. In the eighteenth and nineteenth centuries, the reverse held sway. The amateur was the elevated symbol of all that was good in sport, while the professional was despised as someone who prostituted athletic exercises as a means of livelihood. "Sports had as their ideal aim the production of pleasure," write Eric Dunning and Kenneth Sheard, "an immediate emotional state rather than some ulterior end, whether of a material or other kind" (1979: 153–4). It was regarded as "unsportsmanlike" and "ungentlemanly" to show elation in victory and disappointment in defeat. British public schools and universities were the wellsprings of the amateur ethos and there was concern at the prospect of the "dignified" ball games practiced at Rugby, Harrow, and elsewhere being copied by "lower classes" whose opportunities and desire to win amounted to a defilement.

"Subsidized" players who were reimbursed for work time lost when playing, or who accepted straight payment for their services, were a particularly threatening development in rugby because amateurs could not devote so much time to their game as professionals and so would be hard-pressed to maintain their superiority. There was also the suspicion that dangling a carrot in front of players would encourage them not only to play harder and forget the joy of it all, but to raise the level of competence through training. This was unfair in the eyes of the amateur: it produced a competitive advantage for those who committed themselves to improvement. Sport was meant to be about enjoyment, whereas "to train for sport and take it too seriously was," as Dunning and Sheard observe "tantamount to transforming it into work and, hence, to destroying its essence" (1979: 148).

Alarming as it seemed to members of an English upper class reared on a conception of sports unspoiled by the intrusions of the working class, professional sports grew steadily, so that by the second half of the nineteenth century, cricket, ball games, prize-fighting, and pedestrianism (the equivalent of competitive walking) were able to subsidize competitors for their efforts. Some sporting clubs, specifically golf and cricket clubs, were able to employ coaches, while other sports could pay expenses simply because they were popular enough to attract paying spectators. This actually caused the amateur gentlemen to confound the professional trend with even greater fervor. Mass gatherings of working-class spectators, some of them strongly partisan, posed what was seen as a threat to public order, so much so that such assemblies were outlawed in certain circumstances, as we have seen.

Spectators didn't benefit from sport in the same way as participants; quite the contrary, they suffered by degenerating into an excitable amoral mass. The gentlemen amateurs reaction to spectator sports presents us with a metaphor for changes that were occurring in society generally: the industrial working class was getting organized and showing signs of cohesion and solidarity in the face of employers clearly troubled by the prospect of having their absolute authority challenged from below. Class antagonism or sheer prejudice manifested itself in several notable incidents, all designed to cocoon the exclusive elite of gentlemen from others. As well as the landowning aristocracy, gentlemen would have included *nouveaux riches* merchants, physicians, solicitors, MPs, and others with prestige rather than inherited wealth.

Audience effects

The very presence of one onlooker can affect a sports performer. This observation has provided the premise for a series of experiments designed to explain the exact psychological processes behind the relationship. Some theories indicate that drive-like motivational effects due to the presence of others facilitate enhanced muscular performance, though at the expense of skill. Zajonc (1965) proposed that the mere presence of another individual was sufficient condition for arousing a biologically based innate drive. It was an influential idea, but too simplistic for more recent researchers; who have highlighted situational factors (summarized by Wankel 1982). One of the more interesting findings in recent research on this subject contradicts the common-sense view that champions, or ex-champions, who have experienced stressful and distracting championship events with their mass audiences, have an advantage over challengers who are not used to the "big occasion" and are unfamiliar with performing in front of large audiences and so may be overawed. What research there is on this subject points to the opposite conclusion: having the experience of stress in front of an audience confers no advantage and lacking an awareness of this may give the inexperienced performers an edge.

In 1846 at Lancaster, in the north-west of England, there was a dispute following a Manchester crew's victory in the Borough Cup rowing competition. Two of the crew, a cabinet maker and a bricklayer, were not, it was alleged, acceptable entrants on the grounds that "they were not known as men of any property." The debate continued until, in 1853, when the category of "gentlemen amateur" was distinguished from the pure amateur, for the

Lancaster Rowing Club's purposes. Other clubs followed suit stipulating that those who worked as mechanics, artisans, or laborers would not be eligible for competition as their employment, being physical in nature, equipped them with advantages.

This may have seemed a subterfuge to members of the working class, but it was perpetuated by the Amateur Athletic Association which, in 1866, officially defined an amateur as a person who had either never competed (1) in open competition; (2) for prize money; (3) for admission money; (4) with professionals; (5) never taught or assisted in the pursuit of athletics exercises as a means of a livelihood; or (6) was not a mechanic, artisan, or laborer. Condition (6) was removed in 1880, but the intent of this typical pronouncement was clear: to exclude working-class competitors by seeming to respond to the evils of professionalism. Redrawing the boundaries around amateurs effectively secured sport as an upper- and middle-class stronghold. But this was not so in all sports.

By the mid-1880s, rugby and soccer had become so popular in England, especially in the North and the Midlands, that spectators, particularly those in the industrial cities, would pay to watch *en masse* thus making money available to induce good players to appear regularly. The Rugby Union was intractable in its opposition and by 1895 had effectively forced the formation of a professional union, which in 1922 became the Rugby League. Soccer prevaricated, but by 1885 had agreed to strictly controlled professionalism, with maximum wage and transfer stipulations. From this point, we see soccer becoming increasingly organized so as to offer entertainment to spectators not fulfilment to players. About the same time, in the USA, baseball was beginning to realize its commercial potential. Veterans of the Civil War, 1861–5, had become used to watching competitive games while at military camp and, at the conclusion of the war, wanted more. So popular was baseball that in 1868 the Cincinnati Red Stockings started to charge admission fees; in the following year it professionalized its playing staff by paying salaries. By 1876, enough teams had duplicated the process to form the National League, the first major organized sports league in the USA. Twenty-four years on and it had a rival, the American League. In 1903 the two leagues got together to create the World Series.

As leagues sprung up on both sides of the Atlantic, so success grew in importance; competitions multiplied. Spectators watch winners so clubs encouraged winning; competing for itself was fine, but began to appear slightly anachronistic by the 1920s. Some sports, such as athletics and tennis, held out staunchly, refusing to permit those who had earned money from playing a sport into the major events. Boxing, for long a pursuit of professionals at some level, whether in fairground shows or street fighting, evolved two coexisting organizations with amateurs often proceeding to professional ranks in their early twenties. In other sports, amateurs played with and against pros, though, as the example of English cricket demonstrates, they would not necessarily "mix" and were provided with separate changing facilities. As hostility to professional players gradually dissipated, cricket desegregated, though some sports, Rugby Union included, continued their elitist policies.

Exactly the same tensions were felt in the States. Prosperous "gentlemen" of New York, concerned over the rise of professionalism, helped organize the National Association of Amateur Athletes of America in 1868; this became the Amateur Athletic Association in 1888. Intercollegiate sports, which gained in currency during the 1880s, were very much amateur affairs and looked disdainfully at the professional goings-on of baseball. As soccer had emerged as a predominantly upper-class sport which was appropriated by the working class, so American football began life as a derivative of rugby played by the sons of the wealthy. At the turn of the century, working-class interest in football started to rise and the game extended beyond the boundaries of the university campuses. As with soccer, football was played by factory teams, two of the earliest coming from the Green Bay Packing Company and the Decatur Stanleys Starch Company, who later became the Packers and the Bears.

Tennis adamantly refused to allow professionals into its prestigious competitions until 1968 when it became "open." From that point, players like Rod Laver, who had previously changed to the status of pro, reintegrated with amateurs whom they dominated so overwhelmingly that amateurism vanished from top levels over the next several years. Athletics for long buried its head in spite of widespread knowledge of "shamateurism" with performers accepting generous gifts and exaggerated expenses for their services.

When the modern Olympic games were introduced in 1896, many other sports had already professionalized, though it was not until 1983, that the International Amateur Athletics Federation took a new approach, recognizing that competitors were being paid, but insisting that their monies should go directly via a subvention to a trust fund and dispensed later to cover "expenses." Prior to this, athletes who were either discovered to have accepted payment, or publicly transferred to a sport where professionalism was recognized were forbidden from track and field competition; though in the USA, strictures were often relaxed to reinstate such athletes as Dwight Stones and Renaldo Nehemiah, who, like many others before him, signed to play pro football. (He returned to hurdling after track and field had gone "open".)

Track and field athletics and some other sports, like soccer, now allow participation between professionals and those who, in official terms at least, wish to preserve amateur status, so that there is no compromise involved when ex-Soviet football teams play Western sides in European Cup competitions or Cuban athletes compete against pros in, for instance, the Pan-American games. The integration doesn't extend to boxing, and top Russian and Cuban boxers have not been permitted to fight pros unless they relinquish amateur status. Occasionally this happens: Kostya Tszyu and Sergei Arbachakov, both Russians, and other ex-Soviets competed successfully as pros after amateur careers. The most celebrated refusal to do so was that of Teofilio Stevenson, Cuba's fourtimes heavyweight gold medalist, who resisted multimillion dollar offers to fight American professionals. It would be inaccurate to label Soviet sports as amateur, in the original sense at least. There is a pronounced emphasis on winning and the rewards of success are tangible. The state-assisted programs enable performers to devote themselves to preparation with meticulous attention paid to every facet of training. It would be no contradiction to describe the approach as totally "professional," business-like, thorough, and disciplined.

Even Rugby Union, which once witnessed the professionalization of sport from a position of supreme detachment, has been known to condone some clubs' efforts in attracting players by offering employment packages – in other words, "jobs for the boys," the idea being that a player signed for a club on the understanding that the club arranged suitably undemanding but well-paid work. In 1988 the English club, Bath, introduced the concept of a track and field-style trust fund system in which players would receive a lump sum at the end of their playing careers. Field hockey too is poised to follow suit.

There are few current examples of amateurism left in today's sport. Gentlemanly pastimes and the noble spirits that guided them have ceded place to an industry with products, producers, and buyers and this has transformed the structure and, in some cases, the content of modern sport. A corruption of a misty ideal it may be, but the trend is undeniable and quite unstoppable. Sport has changed in nature over the past century; it hasn't so much been infiltrated by business, but rather, it *is* business.

Promoters and owners

No one is officially credited with being the first sports promoter, but we can assume that, in some dark and distant age, an enterprising witness to a contest noticed a crowd react excitedly to the sight of competition and thought, "Lo! the gathered masses act as if 'twas them joined in battle!" Inspired by this, the first promoter would have brought the same or similar contestants together and drawn the same crowd but this time charging a fee for watching – the assumption being that the pleasure taken in just observing the spectacle was worth a small amount. So the sports business started.

James Figg improved on the basic idea when he opened his "Amphi-theatre" in 1743. As we saw previously, Figg attracted large crowds to watch his combat events, which were arranged on a regular basis and supplied him with a successful business. His concept was adopted from that of the ancient Romans, except that his motive was merely to extract a profit from the enterprise. His patrons' motives were probably mixed: to identify with and support their favorite, to extract vicarious pleasure from watching, to wager, or just to meet other members of the "fancy" (as patrons of prize-fighting were collectively known). This reflects much the same mixture of impulses of fans today.

Early promoters (though not called by that name) would have been less interested in why spectators attended than with their actual presence, though the positive correlation between high-caliber performers and large crowds would not have been lost on them. Figg's natural successors were the prize-fight organizers of America in the 1800s. Some states, like Massachusetts, outlawed prize-fighting and this prompted the organizers to stage illicit con-tests "behind locked doors" with a small but paying crowd. Jeffrey Sammons, in his history of American boxing, *Beyond the Ring*, writes that the first unofficial world heavyweight championship between Paddy Ryan and Joe Goss, in 1880, was "fought in virtual secrecy at Colliers, West Virginia. Organizers chose the tiny Brooks County town for its proximity to the Ohio and Pennsylvania state lines: if raided by hostile law officers, participants and followers could scatter across the border to escape arrest" (Sammons 1988: 6).

In the same period, an Irish migrant named Richard Kyle Fox was scratching a living by writing about events such as oyster-opening and one-legged dancing and, occasionally, promoting the events which he could then cover for his newspaper. In 1881 he had a chance encounter with John L. Sullivan, a prize-fighter, who, so folklore has it, spurned Fox's offer to promote him. Sullivan went on to become the most famous boxer of his day and Fox's determination either to secure his services or ruin him drove him to the position of American sport's first major promoter, offering either purses (fixed sums) or percentages of gate receipts to fighters. By the mid-1890s, top pugilists fought for what were then enormous purses of thousands of dollars. Sullivan is known to have charged in the region of $25,000 per championship fight.

The legalization of prize-fighting in New York in 1920 opened up new commercial possibilities. Sammons notes that, in 1922 alone, gate receipts in New York State totalled $5 million (in those days, about £1.5 million), a sum that prompted some to contend that boxing was "an industry, financed by banks, and licensed and supervised by state laws and officials just as banking and insurance" (quoted in Sammons 1988: 66). If this was so, then boxing was a prototype for other sports. Opportunistic entrepreneurs were key agents in the process of establishing the sport along business lines. Unquestionably, the most visionary was George "Tex" Rickard, who promoted all but one heavyweight title fight that resulted in a new champion from the reign of Jack Johnson to that of Gene Tunney and whose elaborate publicity stunts and gargantuan promotions (regularly attracting over 100,000 spectators, with receipts of nearly $1.9 million for one fight in 1926) established him as *the* sports promoter of his era and, probably, of any other. Allegations that many of Rickard's contests were not only run as but actually were showbusiness events complete with scripts and stage directions were commonplace. But the controversy only added to his infamy and he was able to exploit the growing mass enthusiasm for "live" sport, which featured not only contestants but also a sense of occasion – an atmosphere that drew together the working class and the plutocracy, the anonymous and the famous.

Massed audiences for sports events were not confined to boxing. For the English FA Cup Final in 1923, 200,000 people were squeezed into Wembley Stadium. By this time soccer had become totally professional, top clubs having charged admission since the 1870s – around the same time that race track events began imposing entrance fees. Rugby League football, which had split from Rugby Union in 1895, was committed to taking gate money and made no pretence to uphold the ideal of the unpaid gentleman of its amateur counterpart, which refused to turn rugby into a spectator-oriented sport.

American fans too showed a penchant for ball games, their favorite at the turn of the century being baseball. The game had eclipsed cricket as the sport of the wealthy, and the fact that an admission was charged at the games of teams from the National League, founded in 1876, ensured that it was beyond the reach of the poor. But the rival American Association halved admissions and even enhanced its appeal by selling cheap beer at the ball parks. The sport was well-patronized by Irish and Italian fans. By the 1920s and 1930s, baseball had developed into America's "national game," attracting five-figure crowds. In the midst of economic depression, star players like Babe Ruth were able to command staggering sums of $80,000 p.a. They were able to do so not because gate receipts were soaring, but because entrepreneurs had seen the commercial possibilities of having their products identified with a formidably popular sport. For example, in 1934, Henry Ford paid $100,000 for the rights to the World Series. The sport's most prestigious event effectively became a vehicle for advertising Ford's automobiles. Gillette and major brewers followed suit, setting in motion a trend that was to continue to the present day, as we will see later in this chapter.

Unlike British ball clubs, which are mostly run by an elected committee, the chair of which has executive, but not autocratic, power, baseball and football clubs in the United States are invariably under the control of an individual. A handful of British soccer clubs, such as Blackburn Rovers and Wolverhampton Wanderers, moved toward an American system with a single powerful individual taking control. The owner's influence is extensive; to have control of a ball club is to be able to make decisions on every facet of the operations. So owners have played a pivotal part in commercializing sport. As they are established in business before moving into sport, owners, according to Jonathan Brower's research, have been "neither accustomed to nor comfortable with losing money in business ventures" (1976: 15).

Not surprisingly, they have established and run sports organizations as if they were any other business, with a criterion of success in the form of a winning season (when wins outnumber defeats) being added to that of profit. While they're run on broadly similar lines, British clubs, particularly soccer clubs, have less success in yielding a profit, if only because they outstrip demand with supply, with a nine-month season featuring 92 league clubs in at least three consecutive competitions. But, while buying into a British football team may not seem a sound business investment, as Jay J. Coakley points out, "To be an owner or part owner of a sport or a banker of a large sporting event is likely to enhance personal prestige more dramatically than any other form of business investment" (1978: 212–13). Whatever the motives of promoters, owners, chairs, or any other entrepreneur in sport, their impact has been to transform sport into a unique commercial enterprise. Why unique? Because sport may have veered toward, but has never become, pure entertainment. Its packaging is nowadays indistinguishable, but sport's abiding appeal has lain in its essential unpredictability. The outcome of competition is never known, at least, nearly never. During the 1950s, organized crime had such a stranglehold on American boxing that the outcome of a great many title fights was prescribed. Promoters of sports events, and owners or chairs of clubs, are integral parts of a modern landscape filled with sponsors, agents, and hard-boiled marketing executives, all seeking to manipulate competitive sport to their own requirements. The early efforts of Rickard and others were to lay sport bare to the unyielding Mammon of market forces.

But they, and the others who improved on their ideas, have not been simple conveyers of public demand. They have, in some cases, originated the demand, shaped it, managed it, occasionally destroyed it, and, even more occasionally, been stung by it – as the abortive North American soccer league of the 1970s demonstrates. Market forces being what they are, it's unlikely that sports would have secured the interest of the aspiring entrepreneurs, like Don King, who have dragged competition toward something resembling showbiz without assistance from the mass media. As things transpired, they did have such assistance and the media have implemented changes that have taken the commercial possibilities of sport into realms that would have been considered pure fantasy by any one of the 120,757 people who watched Dempsey and Tunney fight it out in Philadelphia in 1926.

A trend in North America has been for entire corporations to own, co-own or be affiliated in some way with sports clubs in a thinly disguised attempt to promote their own products, or secure favorable contracts. So, the Toronto Blue Jays become something of a vehicle for Labatts beer. The Turner Broadcasting System (TBS) is owned by Ted Turner, who also has interests in the Atlanta Braves

Exploitation?

Are we being exploited by sports? Look at it this way: television fans may sit in the comfort of their own homes, taking in the "live" tv coverage of a SuperSonics basketball game at the Seattle Coliseum and enjoying every second of it. The cost is a minuscule fraction of the cable/satellite subscription, or – if you wanted to push it – the mild discomfort of having to sit through the commercials that interrupt the action. The viewer may or may not buy an airline ticket for Alaska Airways, or rent a video from Blockbuster and may use a different phone company to GTE, but whoever does will probably have to pay a few extra pence for their products as a result of the money these and other companies pour into sports. No matter where the camera pans in the Coliseum, our eyes fall on a logo of some description.

Jacob Weisman describes the scene: "The scoreboard is a whirl of computer-generated graphics, advertising such products as Isuzu Motors, Miller beer, Oberto Sausage, Elephant Car Wash, Taco Bell ... In all, sixty-five different product lines ... The Sonics dance team, brought to you courtesy of Nestlé crunch, performs original dance numbers' (1993: 164). Weisman goes on to list all the commercial products that are in some way represented at the game. Intrigued by Weisman's article, I noted every brand name that flashed across the screen during the BBC's coverage of the 1995 world indoor track and field championships at Barcelona: Carlsberg, Coca-Cola, Fuji Film, Mita copiers, Mercedes-Benz, Schweiz, TDK, Visa (hoardings); Adidas, Mizuno, Nike, Reebok, ViewFrom (on vests); Snickers (on numbers); Olivetti, Seiko; (on screen graphics). (Officially, the BBC does not show commercials.) It's unlikely that the room in which you're now sitting does not contain at least one item made by these companies.

There certainly will be something connected with the corporations who bought into The Olympic Movement (TOP): Visa, Brother, Philips, Federal Express, Kodak, and Times Inc. Such companies do not donate money to sport out of the goodness of their hearts. They do it to increase their share of the world market and so make more profit. The mechanism is quite simple: the telecast of the games and the attendant previews and post-mortems give sponsors a potential vehicle for promoting their product, not in an intrusive way, but by association, by linking their logo with an event as pristine and pure as sport.

The Olympics, that most ancient and wholesome of sports, provides a good example. Since 1976 and the financial débâcle of the Montreal summer games, the Olympics, like most other sports, have grown increasingly dependent on outside money. ABC paid 45 percent of the cost of staging the 1984 games in Los Angeles. NBC contributed marginally less than the South Korean government to Seoul. Compared to these, sponsors provide only a little more than 5 percent of the costs. The IOC's Juan Samaranch has made it clear that, under his presidency, the Olympics will try to extricate itself financially from governments and become economically independent. It can do so only by uniting with the media.

Prior to Seoul, Samaranch had a problem, for the IOC had no power to license its five-rings symbol on a world-wide basis as, under Rule 53 of the Olympic Charter, exclusive rights to use all Olympic names and symbols is held by individual member countries, who may do so only in their own territory. Basically, the problem was solved by buying the rights from 150 member countries over 18 months. Negotiations were smoothed by the involvement of Horst Dassler who had interests in a sports marketing group called ISL and in Adidas, the sportswear manufacturers which held contracts with many IOC member countries. ISL worked the oracle with most members, then approached 44 commercial companies with project TOP.

The lure was the chance of exposure in 167 markets, though the Olympic rings logo could be used commercially only in the 150 countries which had sold out. So, for example, Belgium refused and a company like Kodak, which incorporated the rings in special packages, had to create alternative packaging for the Belgian market, omitting the rings and the instant recognition they carried. The question of whether the exercise was cost effective to the sponsors is presumably answered. The biggest sponsor paid $14 million (almost £9 million), which takes quite a lot of justifying in terms of increased sales. In a slightly different sense, the Olympic games themselves, are being sold and the indications are that bigger pieces of the games will be sold than the 5 percent at Seoul.

The IOC is able to sell the games in this way because of television's continuing interest – something that it cannot necessarily rely on, as we will see in the following chapter. Take away the international coverage and sponsors will take away their millions. Similar principles operate in other major sports that can offer comparable market penetration through mass media. Soccer's World Cup finals offer another vehicle for potential advertisers to reach international markets. Advertising boards surrounding the pitches have FIFA's approval and are sold off in meters to commercial organizations eager to have their product name or logo form a backdrop to the players who stampede across the world's tv screens every four years. The same mode is employed at domestic levels with major sponsors enhancing their exposure by having players' shirts bear their logo. The more often the players appear on tv, the more valuable the sponsorship grows. For example, Sanderson Electronics appliances can enjoy 90 virtually uninterrupted minutes of exposure every time a Sheffield Wednesday game is screened; a photograph of the game appearing in a newspaper is also valuable.

The concept of associating a commercial product with a sports phenomenon with which it has no natural connection is not a particularly new one. "The first sponsor of sport was probably a Roman patrician currying favor with his Emperor by underwriting a day of blood-letting at the Colosseum," writes Neil Wilson in *The Sports Business*. "Since he was seeking a return on his investment, he was being no more philanthropic than any of today's commercial sponsors" (1988: 157). Wilson goes on to quote one-time British sports minister, Denis Howell: "Sponsorship is the support of sport, sports event, sports organization or competitor by an outside body or person for the mutual benefit of both parties" (1988: 157).

There are isolated examples of commercial companies financing events and tours in the late nineteenth century, but the significant factor in alerting commerce to the possibilities of exposure via sport was, of course, the mass media. In the USA, commercial companies had realized the potential of radio in the 1930s, Buick in particular paying the then astronomical amount of $27,500 for the radio rights to the second Dempsey–Tunney encounter. Parts of the media, specifically the press, sponsored athletics, billiards, and snooker in Britain between the wars. Newspapers had a clear and fairly direct interest in events, which they would cover extensively and hope to boost circulation as a result. Companies such as Dunlop and Penfold supplied golf equipment and were ideally suited as sponsors for the sport.

After the war and the burgeoning of television, all manner of sponsors sought to help raise the market profile by associating themselves with sporting events. Breweries were particularly eager to have their beverages associated with sport and the macho tendencies it implied. Pabst Riband was actively involved in the United States and, in Britain, Whitbreads sponsored a horse-racing cup in 1957. The events were televised. The Gillette razor company was an interested party on both sides of the Atlantic. The beginning of its sponsorship of one-day cricket in 1963 also marked the beginning of an era, for since then, as Tony Mason observes, "sports sponsorship has become an industry in itself. In the last fifteen years or so, in particular, its growth has been phenomenal" (1988: 4). In 1971, the British Sports Council calculated that the sponsorship of sport was worth only £2.5 million. By 1982, this figure had grown to £84.7 million. This rose to £200 million in 1988, with more than 2,000 companies involved. The figures for the USA are $1.4 billion spent by 3,400 companies.

THE TRUE VALUE OF SPONSORS

THE JORDAN GRAND PRIX TEAM'S ACCOUNTS

Debit	$ millions	Credit	$ millions
Testing *including hire of circuit and* *test team accommodation*	3.2	Sponsorship *from 32 companies, including* *Goodyear, Marlboro, Pepsi* *and Pizza Hut*	24.8
Cars and spares	4.8	Prize money (est.)	2.1
Wages and administration (70 staff)	3.6		
Research and development	1.6	*Plus* Peugeot provide engines worth $6.4m and Total provide fuel and oil worth $0.8m	
Transport and travel	1.6		
Drivers	1.6		
Tires	0.8		
Factory and offices	0.8		
Hotels	0.56		
TOTAL	18.56	TOTAL	26.88

26.88m (£16.8m)
−18.56m (£11.6m)
_____

$8.32m (£5.2m)

There are 32 companies sponsoring the Jordan Formula One racing team, three paying about 10 percent of the budget in return for prime advertising spots on the cars. Peugeot supplies between 15 and 20 engines per year, each costing about $160,000 and Total contributes approximately 16,500 gallons of gasoline. As the balance sheet shows, the income from prize money alone accounts for less than 8 percent of the total input.

The money is dispensed in a variety of ways, by using logos, as in the Olympics, or by advertising on hoardings, as soccer's World Cup. Product endorsement is another way: individual sports performers are contracted to declare publicly their approval of a product or service. Middlesex cricketer, Denis Compton, became known as the "Brylcreem Boy" after his endorsement of the hair preparation in the late 1940s. More recently, Dan Marino has endorsed gloves, Gary Lineker (the former soccer player) potato chips and Michael Jordan, well, just about everything. This can result in a clash of interests if individual players endorse particular products. The endorsement lacks some plausibility if, say, an English soccer player's shirt is emblazoned with JVC while the individual player endorses Sony, as is occasionally the case. Perhaps the most embarrassing situation of this kind was when the Carling beer company (makers of "Black Label") closed a deal with the English Football Association to sponsor its major league. Hence it became known as the "Carling Premiership." Someone overlooked the fact that four clubs playing in the Premiership were actually sponsored by rival brewers, such as Carlsberg and Newcastle.

If this tends to diminish the purity of some sports, they still stand unsullied when compared to motor racing, a big-budget sport which has consumed the billions of commercial sponsors as voraciously as it has fuel. Motor sport has long since seen the end of days when a willing enthusiast with a few thousand dollars or pounds would buy an off-the-peg car and race it with the assistance of a few mechanics and courtesy oil and tires.

In 1985, the French car company, Renault, pulled out of the sport because of the punishing costs; it had dropped $1.6 billion in 1984 and estimated that $80–100 million would be needed over the next four years from sponsorship. Honda's engine development program for the Frank Williams's racing team cost $21 million. For such sums, the car companies have their vehicles displayed on every meet of the Grand Prix circuit, all 16 of which are televised internationally. They also gain the prestige associated with winning, a feat they include in their direct advertising. The car firm has to share space with any number of other companies, the logos of which are plastered over every square millimeter of the car's bodywork and the driver's uniform. (Most drivers take 30 percent of prize monies, as well as expenses and a retainer; the late Ayrton Senna's retainer from the Lotus team was $5.4 million back in 1988.) In motor racing, the chief sponsors virtually own the sport and sublet pieces of the cars to affiliates. For instance, in 1987 Canon bought the rights to prefix its name to Williams's Honda team and adorned the sides and rear wings in its colors, red and white. The cockpit and engine cover were sprayed yellow for ICI, the front wing and plates being sublet to products as diverse as aftershaves and tires.

Logo
An abbreviation of logotype (from the Greek *logo* for word), this was largely advertising jargon 20 years ago, but has come into popular use in recent years. It describes an unbroken strip of type, lettering, badge or insignia used by organizations to promote their corporate identities in advertising and publicity material. Now, it is difficult to find a sports performer or team which does not bear at least one and, more usually, many logos. An NFL team's uniform, for example, has only a sportswear logo plus the NFL's. A pro cyclist's, on the other hand, will carry the team sponsor and six or seven others. Logos have been especially important in licensing sports-related products. Sports governing bodies strictly control the use of logos by manufacturers and will seek redress from any company using, for instance the "W" of Wimbledon or the silhouette of the basketball player of the NBA, without permission. The growth of the sports logo is, in many ways, a symbol of the commericalization of sports.

Potential sponsors were initially scared off by the Football Association's prohibitive price for the rights to the prestigious FA Cup, but Littlewood's eventually found the millions. It's unlikely that any major British sports competition will avoid having its name prefixed or appended with that of a commercial product over the next decade. In the United States, the situation is different, with the cardinal leagues operating franchise deals, which means that, for a fee, they authorize commercial companies to manufacture and sell goods bearing their name, or logo, within a particular area. Official NFL jackets, coffee mugs, even underpants are commonplace. It obviates the problem of having brand names appearing on telecasts for which tv companies have paid huge fees and need to recoup funds through advertising. Miller beer may find it uncomfortable to have its ads appearing in the breaks of a game in the "Budweiser League," for instance.

Beer companies have been consistent sponsors of sport. While sports organizations may have reservations about being identified with an alcoholic product that has no health benefits, apart from working as a vasodilator, breweries have targeted energetic and healthy pursuits. So there has been an accommodation of sorts, though some individual soccer clubs have refused brewers' sponsorship, pointing out that they can't credibly argue that alcohol is a contributory factor in crowd disorders if they actively promote it. Despite this, beer and sport have learned to live with each other. The advances of cigarettes, on the other hand, have been spurned, though not until quite recently. Tobacco clearly undermines the personal health and fitness that sport allegedly represents. Yet in the 1940s, the links between cigarettes and such conditions as heart disease and lung cancer weren't realized and sports personalities gladly had their pictures on cards distributed within cigarette packets.

Like other sponsors, tobacco companies, including Gallaghers and Philip Morris, were tempted by the possibility of mass exposure through television, especially after British tv banned the direct advertising of cigarettes. Sport, which occupied up to 20 percent of a network's output, seemed an ideal way of having a cigarette's name and crest shown to millions throughout the year. John Player made incursions into various sports, most notably cricket with its Sunday John Player League. The Virginia Slims women's tennis circuit in the USA was also fashioned to meet the requirements of the tobacco company as much as the sport. Tobacco companies started their now considerable interest in motor racing in 1968 when Imperial Tobacco created the Gold Leaf team. Marlboro followed, signalling a strong trend for cigarettes to maintain their presence on television through racing cars flashing their logo across screens, or drivers wearing overalls with the appropriate appliqué, or even the words of a commentator announcing the "Marlboro team." The Philip Morris organization leads the way by spending a reputed $85 million (£53 million) on sports, an amount sufficient perhaps for individual sports to rearrange formats, timetables, and presentations to suit sponsors' requirements. As well as motor racing, the main beneficiaries of tobacco firms sponsorship have been tennis, cricket, golf, show jumping, and snooker.

Every time a tobacco-sponsored event is televised, it represents a negation of tv's ban on advertising. It is also, arguably, a more cost-effective method of gaining exposure for tobacco firms. While none of them reveals the actual benefit it derives, it's instructive to know the estimates of the car makers Volvo. They sponsored an international tennis Grand Prix tournament in 1986 for $3 million (then about £1.6 million) and reckoned it was worth six times that amount in exposure. Television, in the same year, tightened up its restrictions on tobacco displays on hoardings at televised events: it began covering them, just as it had taped over players' badges at certain events. It has also promised to phase out the televising of tobacco-sponsored sport. This won't shut cigarettes out of sport; it will simply divert interest to sports attracting large numbers of spectators, but which do not receive tv coverage.

Sponsorship, many will argue, is not only desirable to sport, it is as essential as spectators. Perhaps neither was essential at some stage in history, but, with Allen Guttmann, I would agree that sport as we understand it is *spectator* sport and this can be traced back to the ancient Greeks and beyond (as Guttmann does in his book *Sports Spectators*). Where sport can engage spectators' attentions there is scope for commercialism of some degree. The fact that the structure and administration of contemporary sport bears a close resemblance to that of most other business enterprises suggests how closely the development of sport has shadowed business. Industrialism and urbanism, which made possible the large concentrations of people from which mass spectators were drawn, were components of large-scale changes in Western society in the nineteenth century. Guided by the Protestant work ethic, the spirit of capitalism contributed to the creation of a unique culture in which profit-making enterprises were the rational response to market pressures. The mandate of capitalism was to organize resources so as to maximize the chances of exploiting the market to the full. Simple as the mandate seems, it was responsible for transformations not only of the environment, but of the mentality. People began to sense that they could control markets instead of being at their mercy.

Commercial sport was born from such an observation. The concept of staging sport and controlling the numbers of people wanting to watch may not have been totally original, but when combined with the principles of the business enterprise it produced a type of sport that paralleled other capitalist ventures. Promoters and organizers adopted approaches similar to other entrepreneurs. Professional sport may have been a rogue when amateurs dominated, but its powerful simplicity made it an unstoppable force against which amateurism was ultimately no match.

The kinds of audiences major sports events attract today are measured in dozens of millions rather than the thousands of earlier years. The reason, of course, is simple: television. This piece of technology has revolutionized the commercial possibilities of sport by opening out the potential market for those who want to sell products and by making sports themselves into products. Television is arguably the single most important factor affecting sports today and, for this reason, we need to spend some time examining its deepening liaison with sports and the effects of this. Next.

FURTHER READING

The Name of the Game: The business of sports by Jerry Gorman and Kirk Calhoun (John Wiley, 1994) peels away any pretence that contemporary sports are anything but, as the title suggests, business.

"Big-buck basketball: Acolytes in the temple of Nike" by Jacob Weisman in *Sport in Contemporary Society: An anthology* edited by D. S. Eitzen (St Martin's Press, 1993) exposes the extent of the NBA's relationships with various shoe, chocolate, beer, car, and clothes manufacturers, airline and telephone companies, video retailers , restaurants . . . the list goes on.

Sociology of Sport by John Phillips (Allyn & Bacon, 1993) estimates that "5 percent of the American economy is somehow related to sports." This book is one of a number of texts that have chapters or sections on the business aspects of sports. Among the many others are *The Sociology of Sport: An introduction* by Conrad Vogler and Stephen Schwarz (Prentice-Hall, 1993) and *Sociology of North American Sport 5th edn*, by D. S. Eitzen and G. H. Sage (Brown & Benchmark, 1993).

Pay Up and Play the Game by Wray Vamplew (Cambridge University Press, 1989) focuses on British sport between 1875 and 1914 and shows an odd and irregular pattern in which some sports (like soccer) become fully commercialized, while others (like cricket) strove only to break even. To illustrate the different approaches to commercialism, Vamplew quotes from Wisden, which virtually scorned the doubling of Warwickshire's gates in 1911 (when that county won the cricket county championship): "Such sudden enthusiasm suggests rather too much the spirit of Association Football."

Another sport that underwent commercialization is baseball and Andrew Zimbalist's *Baseball and Billions* (Basic Books, 1992) is a brilliant exposition of the process, made up of incorporated enterprises whose major purpose is the accumulation of profits.

ASSIGNMENT

You are appointed head of marketing services at a world-wide credit card company, not unlike American Express. For years, your brand has marketed itself on class and privilege. Despite competition from other credit cards, the cachet your company has enjoyed has kept it among the market leaders. Recently, however, your exclusivity has become dated. Even your advertising slogans, such as "never be without it," and "that will do adequately" have become the target of comedians' jokes. Market share has declined sharply. After studying the spending and lifestyle habits of each of your 1 million cardholders your research department has concluded that there is a growing interest in sports among them. Design a series of initiatives that will exploit the sports connection and report the result.

Chapter ten

A match made in heaven
Why sports and television are inseparable

McSports

The year is 2005 and you're a sports fan. Today is a big day: the World Super Bowl Sunday. This year it's between the Tokyo Samurai, appearing in their first Super Bowl, and Las Vegas Buccaneers. The Bucs are going for their third championship this century; their fortunes really turned around after they were sold again in 1999 and the new owners moved the franchise for a second time. The National Football League is much bigger than it was ten years ago when it was strictly a US affair. The incursions into the US of the Canadian Football League weren't a problem until the CFL secured a contract with the TNT cable network in 1998, and within a season the ratings were encouraging enough for them to extend the franchise even further into the States. The NFL retaliated and, with one eye on the revitalized World Football League, globalized the game, integrating European and Japanese teams into the league.

You will watch the game on your 8 × 6 foot high definition screen which sits at the center of a bank of 16 screens, all linked to an international communications infrastructure that covers the world. All screens are loaded with games you have ordered. When there's a touchdown in a game on one of the peripheral screens, you say "Five" or whatever screen it's on and your voice-activated remote downloads the game onto the center screen, backtracks ten seconds and shows the td. You can order a replay of the action or "Slow-mo," "Reverse angle" and so on. You also have a choice of camera. The old helmet cam, which was first tested in the World League, is still in use, but now every player has one, so you can name the number of the player and get his perspective. Other sports have made full use of this facility. Soccer fans love the one referees wear in their caps (they resisted wearing headgear at first, but the tv companies insisted): they can view the action as he or she sees it. Baseball catchers and cricket wicketkeepers wear them as well. But the cameras they stuck in the nose of a football was a terrible failure; it made you giddy. One of the recent innovations is a new command enabling you to "Tighten" or "Widen" the scope of the camera shot. This lets you get a close-up of anybody, or a panoramic vista of the whole field.

On a typical day, you pay $65 (£40) for five sports events of your choice, which is not bad considering the cheapest seat at most stadia is $80 (£50). The games are fed through optical fibers known as the electronic pipeline, run by SportServer in conjunction with the world's sports governing bodies. This means you can view virtually watch any sports event in the world. Of course, you have to pay for them. There was a furore about this when the concept of pay-per-view (ppv) was introduced in the 1990s. The first ppv was in the 1980s. People have got used to paying to watch their boxing, but football was different. At first, it was just the post-season games, but now it's the whole season, which now includes 22 games in a regular season.

When the major US and British terrestrial tv networks dropped sports completely in 2000, the major organizations, like the NFL, NBA and NHL decided to set up their own communications systems and charge per event. Some years before, England's Football Association had deepened its involvement with the BSkyB satellite network and charged fans by the game. We've all been weaned off the idea of getting sports for free. It's amusing to talk to your parents sometimes when they reminisce about the old days when they were able to watch sports on tv for nothing. They were probably amused by *their* parents who could remember the days when their was no tv at all; if you didn't go to the game, you didn't see it. Now, attendances have slipped right down. Who wants to brave the elements when you can see more games, from more angles, with informed commentary and analysis in the comfort of your own home?

Is this how we'll be watching sports in the near future? Technologically, everything in the scenario is already possible; the hard part is persuading the public to part with their hard-earned. NBC thought it could do it, but got its fingers burnt in 1992 when it offered 24-hour coverage of the 1992 summer Olympics from Barcelona to those prepared to pay $125 (£78) for a 15-day package, or $19.95 (£12.50) for a single day at a time. The meager number of viewers and the resulting losses didn't inspire confidence. But it is all part of a steady process of weaning viewers off the "free" sports they have become used to over the past four decades.

If ever there was a marriage made in heaven it was between television and sports. The commercial success of each was almost directly attributable to the other. From the 1940s to the present sports have grown in proportion to tv. Not only have they grown in scale and popularity, but they have become modified into virtual theater. And television's efforts at dragging sports toward the popular entertainment end of the market have paid off in terms of record-breaking viewing ratings. High-profile sports events draw audiences comparable with televisual phenomena, like the last ever show of *Cheers*, the moon landing or the "Who killed JR?" episode of *Dallas*.

But, as we will learn later in this chapter, sports have paid a price, too high a price for some who believe that sports have become what we might call "McDonaldized." I steal this term from George Ritzer, who has written a provocative essay entitled *The McDonaldization of Society* in which he argues that almost every aspect of the world today bears resemblance to the famous fast-food chain. McDonald's restaurants are known for their quick, efficient, no-frills approach to food: uniform packaging, standardized methods of service, controlled entry and exit points; everything organized in terms of a model. We order our food from a limited menu and get it over the counter within seconds. "It's quick, easy and efficient," Ritzer quotes a supporter (1993: 108). So is watching television.

Grand, sprawling, majestic sports, like cricket and golf, no less than the cramped, frenetic basketball, have been McDonaldized, primarily through their contact with television, but also just to stay popular with new generations of fans who demand instant gratification. Not that sports have objected too much to tv's intrusions: more usually, they take the money and run. When tv takes an interest in sports it ceases to be a Corinthian activity and becomes a product, something which, as the word implies, can be manufactured in large quantities, packaged and sold.

In the past, some sports have resisted television's advances, at least for a while. Other sports have actively courted television, believing it to be their only salvation from obscurity. Others have just been dropped on: like Sumo, which gained a cult status after being shown regularly on Britain's Channel 4, or tree-sawing competitions in Hopkinton, New Hampshire, which American networks have developed into something approximating a sport. Still others have been created anew, like ESPN's Extreme Games, which included bungee jumping, skateboarding and kite skiing. Virtually any event that has the "the thrill of victory, the agony of defeat," to use ABC's slogan, qualifies as sport as far as tv is concerned.

Almost any sport draws tv viewers. As Gary Whannel argues, "if sport gains a lot of airtime ... it will almost by definition get a large mixed audience" (1992: 196). Exposure is a "major determinant": just filling the screen with sports guarantees an audience; as long as the audience does not feel it's having to pay for it. Television has, in the past, found a way of giving this impression, disguising the real cost of televising sports, yet events in recent years may presage the end of this.

Pay per view (ppv)

A system through which viewers can pay for specific events, including sports events, to be cabled or beamed to their television sets or to public meeting places, such as bars. The first ppv event was in 1980 when the Sugar Ray Leonard–Roberto Duran fight drew 170,000 customers who paid $15 (£10) each. Rock concerts and operas followed sporadically, until the advent of TVKO, an agency owned by Time Warner, which also owned HBO. TVKO struggled to establish itself as an alternative, more selective way of viewing until 1991 when it sold the Evander Holyfield–George Foreman fight to 1.45 million homes at $34.93 (£22). The Mike Tyson – Peter McNeeley fight in 1995 was an even greater success, going into 1.52 million households and grossing $63 million (£42 million) in the USA alone ($96 million world-wide). By comparison, less than a tenth of this number chose to buy a Guns 'n' Roses concert for $24.95 (£15.60) in 1992 and just 34,000 homes took a Pavarotti concert in 1991. NBC's 1992 "Olympic Triplecast," a 15-day event was the biggest disaster to date: out of a potential 20 million homes equipped with the receiving equipment only 165,000 took the whole deal, with 35,000 taking single days.

Let there be television . . .

CBS, the US broadcasting group, spent $1.1 billion £700) million) for the exclusive rights to show the jewels of major league baseball for a four-year period starting 1990. The cost was about 25 percent more than the previous contract for the games, shared by ABC and NBC. The high price, coming after NBC had bid a comparatively paltry $400 million (£250 million) for the 1992 summer Olympic games, showed the lengths to which networks will go to wrench prestige programming from competitors, including the expanding cable systems.

The irony of this deal was that advertisers, who are American tv's principal source of revenue, would be unlikely even to cover the outlay, as interest in baseball declined from about 1978, and this was reflected in viewing figures. But, in a business where a few rating points (the measurement of viewing audiences) means hundreds of millions of dollars in advertising revenue, CBS was prepared to absorb losses – estimated at the end of the contract to be *$450 million (£281 million)* – in the expectation that it could use the World Series to include October promotions for its prime-time shows in its crucial autumn schedule, from which ratings are extrapolated. CBS effectively wanted to use the sport as an instrument for generating interest in its future programs. Not that baseball cared: the deal meant that each team would start the 1990 season with about $10 million (£6.25 million) in its coffers before a single ticket had been sold.

The contract reveals the extent of television's virtually symbiotic relationship with sport. tv uses sport to boost its viewing figures and sport uses tv as an irreplaceable means of income. Most major sports today could simply not exist without the prop of tv. It would be unthinkable to stage a Super Bowl or a World Cup Final without tv coverage. Quite apart from the outrage among consumers who now expect transmission as a right, the medium would lose out on valuable prestige as well as income.

Both television and sports have seen the mileage in a relationship that had its beginnings in the early nineteenth century when the news-sheet *Bell's Life in London* (founded 1822) found its circulation rising as it included more sports reports. It held a monopoly until 1865 when the *Sporting Life* issued what was to prove a successful challenge, with the result that *Bell's* eventually folded. The success of the *Sporting Life*, with its quick and detailed reporting and varied advertising, prompted newspapers to include sports sections. The US equivalent, *The American Farmer*, first appeared in 1819 and was followed by many others, including *The Spirit of the Times* (founded 1831). "It was the press who first elevated a minority of sportsmen and women into national celebrities, whose names and faces were recognized by people uninterested in sport; performers whose mere presence on the pitch would tempt people to the event; the exceptional performer," writes Tony Mason on the beginnings of what we now call the "superstar" whose fame relies as much on the media as on performance (1988: 50). Nationally recognized individuals were, and are, good news for newspapers and over the decades sports celebrities have been created by the media for matters quite unrelated to their technical capacities. The case of Eddie "The Eagle" Edwards, an inept ski jumper at the 1988 winter Olympics, proves the point – he made headlines around the world by being a gawky, but amiable, loser.

There was a clear symmetry of interests between those with an interest in exploiting the mass spectatorship potential of sport and those who could sell newspapers with stories about sport. Reporting in the press had the useful effect of raising public awareness, so enlarging the spectator market which had emerged by the 1920s. But radio didn't have such an advantage for promoters and organizers. It would relay information on any event, but any advantage it held in terms of boosting interest might be outweighed by its immediacy; that is, listeners might prefer to listen to "live" firsthand accounts of events instead of physically attending. Big events such as the England–Wales Rugby Union internationals, the Oxford–Cambridge boat race and Wimbledon were all reported "live" in 1927 and by the mid-1930s the BBC had started its now standard magazine format, Saturday afternoon coverage.

Despite the possible drawbacks of radio, it did have one big factor in its favor: it paid – and sometimes very well. In 1935, the radio rights to the Joe Louis–Max Baer world heavyweight title fight drew a then record $27,500 (then about £9,000). What's more, the gate was 88,000, so fears that "live" coverage would hurt the gate were unfounded. By this time, radio coverage was commonplace and, as this involved issues of proprietorship and copyright, it gave rise to an economic relationship between the mass media and sports organizers. It was a relationship that was to broaden with the coming of television.

Filmed news of sports events occupied a segment of newsreels shown in cinemas even before radio transmissions, but the films were at least a week after the event and couldn't compare with the excitement of a "live" radio broadcast. In the United States, a ban from 1912 on showing fight films was under pressure from 1927 after an exhibition of the Tunney–Dempsey rematch. In 1939 Senate passed a bill to permit the transfer of boxing films from state to state, in spite of strong disapproval from the Women's Christian Temperance Union. By this time, a new medium had crept into the homes of a select few.

In 1937, a few hundred Londoners were the first to *see* the first outside broadcast coverage of British sport, when 25 minutes of a men's single match was televised from Wimbledon. It was strictly an experimental service from the BBC which had improved on an earlier, unsatisfactory, attempt by CBS to broadcast a fight by "sight and sound." The main technical shortcoming of televising events was that cameras were fixed and were fitted with lenses that made the performers appear as tiny figures. Boxing, whose action takes part in a small, finite territory seemed reasonably suitable for the new medium and, in 1939, BBC and NBC both broadcast fights, BBC being fortunate enough to capture the British lightweight title fight between Eric Boon and

Arthur Danahar, which is regarded as amongst the best-ever fights on British soil. In the same year, the BBC, still in its infancy, showed its first FA Cup Final and NBC telecast baseball, at first with one camera and, later, with two, which was a significant innovation as it permitted close-ups not even visible to audiences watching the game live.

Television was still only a futuristic luxury of the rich, with just 5,000 sets being sold in the USA in 1946. Within ten dramatic years, 75 percent of the country's households had a set. John Goldlust, in his book on sport and the media, argues that "The significance of sports for this phenomenal rate of penetration should not be underestimated" and that the televising of major events was "a key element in launching the television industry" (1988: 8).

Goldlust cites the transmission of the Melbourne Olympics in 1956 as a key event that greatly assisted the sale of television receivers. After this, the television industry of continental Europe and Latin America developed within the framework of either the BBC, which considered the televising of sport one of its statutory obligations in order to provide as many aspects as possible of the "national culture," or the American companies, which geared their schedules so as to maximize demand from advertisers. If manufacturers had products to sell and wanted exposure for their products, then placing commercials in the "natural breaks" of a high-profile event was rational and effective.

Even with a minute fraction of its potential audience, televised sports were attractive: as early as 1947, Ford and Gillette paid $65,000 (then about £20,000) for the rights to sponsor baseball's World Series on television, despite the fact that less than 12 percent of US households could receive it. Sports themselves were wary of tv, thinking its impact could only be detrimental. As if to illustrate the point, between 1948 and 1956, the Cleveland Indians baseball team won a World Series and a pennant, yet suffered a 67 percent drop in attendance. The Boston Braves' crowds plunged by 81 percent following their National League victory in 1948, immediately after which they signed a tv deal for the next three years. The situation needed drastic remedial action, so the owner Lou Perini moved the franchise to Milwaukee and banned television cameras, apart from the World Series winning games of 1957 and 1958.

The gates stayed healthy, prompting Perini to announce smugly: 'We have come to believe that tv can saturate the minds of the fans with baseball. We would very much like to guard against this." Perini relaxed his strictures after 1962 and eventually sold out to a group which wholeheartedly embraced television by relocating the club in Atlanta where a tv–radio guarantee of $1.25 million (then over £600,000) per year awaited.

Another sport whose gates were hit severely was college football. Between 1949 and 1953, attendance declined by almost 3 million. The

National Collegiate Athletic Association (NCAA) formed a special television committee and instituted rigid rules for limiting the number of telecasts. Even then, it took the years before gates rose to their 1949 levels.

Television feasted on boxing, which it left as a carcass in 1964 after 18 years of the kind of saturation Perini had feared for baseball. In some areas of the States, boxing was on every night of the week, with promoters eagerly accepting television monies to augment profits. Gradually, the tv fees *became* the profits: live audiences dwindled. As TV was interested only in "name" fighters, the bigger promoters who had the champions under contract were able to capitalize, while the smaller promoters went to the wall. In the period 1952–9 alone, 250 of the country's 300 small boxing clubs shut down. At the height of its power in 1955, boxing was watched by 8.5 million homes, about one-third of the available viewing audience in those days. By 1959, boxing commanded only 10.6 percent – which sounds much more impressive now than it did then when the market was uncluttered by cable channels. NBC was the first to cut boxing from its schedules in 1960. The other networks followed suit. But the sport and the medium had merely obeyed the logic of the market. Yet the signs were clear: many sports were being tempted by a cozy and highly profitable relationship; but, in doing so they were exposing themselves completely to television and risking becoming totally and possibly ruinously dependent on the networks.

Apart from boxing, North American television's sporting energy in the 1950s came from wrestling and roller derby. From a production viewpoint, these were perfect sports for the technically naïve tv companies of the day, CBS and NBC. All that was needed was a fixed orthicon camera trained on a small finite area of action, insulated from natural weather conditions. The two networks enjoyed a relatively peaceful coexistence, carving up the major sporting events between them. ABC's entrance changed all that. Not having access to the big sports, ABC decided to feature minority sports and activities that were barely sports at all and treat them in such dramatic ways that even those with no interest in sports would be converted.

Rodeos, demolition derbies and even the bizarre fireman's bucket-filling championships were all fair game for ABC's cameras, which wouldn't just document what happened but would take the viewer to where it happened. Cameras would venture to the tops of cliffs, peer over the edge, then draw back to view a diver hurtling into the seas below, where another camera joined him or her in the water. Sports were drama. Inspired by the iconoclastic philosophies of Roone Arledge, ABC vandalized the established traditions and made an overt appeal to younger audiences which were not bound by the fidelities of their parents. Women viewers were wooed, as they were demographically attractive to advertisers: research showed that women make decisions about household purchases.

ABC's approach was unashamedly populist, projecting personalities, highlighting unusual characteristics about them and reducing almost any competitive activity to its most basic elements. Frog jumping contests were not out of place in ABC's sports panoply. Gillette, one of television's biggest sports sponsors hooked up with ABC with a Friday night boxing series and, encouraged by the response, fed in more money, which enabled ABC to capture NCAA football in the 1960–1 season. This was the first of many coups, the biggest being the American Football League, a second-rate rival to the NFL, but one which, given the ABC treatment, rose in popularity. So much so that, in 1966, the two merged to produce the NFL as we know it today. One significant innovation in American football was the introduction of the television time-out in 1958. This allowed stoppages specifically for tv companies to screen commercials.

In the same year as the NFL–AFL merger, BBC television in Britain screened soccer's World Cup staged in England. It was a prestigious tournament and the BBC beamed its pictures all over the world. It was at this event that the advantage of the camera over the naked eye was fully appreciated. In the championship game, the English team's third goal arrived gift-wrapped for television. The ball thundered against the underside of the West German team's crossbar, appearing momentarily to bounce over the goal line before rebounding into the field of play. If the *whole* ball had crossed (not just broken as in American football) the plane of the goal line, then it was a goal. The referee said "yes," the Germans said "no." The cameras slowed down the action, freeze-framed it, reversed the angle; and it could still not prove conclusively whether or not the ball had crossed the line. The arguments raged and the footage rolled and rolled.

In Britain, the BBC has enjoyed an almost unrivalled position of leadership in sports. Unlike the USA, which has seen a preponderance of cable channels all keen to capture sports, Britain has had open competition since 1992 when the subscription channel owned by Rupert Murdoch, BSkyB, negotiated a £304 million (then equivalent of $575 million) deal for exclusive "live" coverage of the English Premiership. The BBC had to settle for tape-delay highlights, while the commercial stations got nothing. ITV, the main commercial station (the BBC is funded by a government license paid for by all tv owners), vied for a period in the 1960s, often following ABC's example in manufacturing events such as WWF-style wrestling. Its policy in recent years has been to target only four main sports: boxing, rugby, track and field and soccer other than Premiership games.

It is no coincidence that tv networks on both sides of the Atlantic have fought fiercely for the right to screen sports. Historically, the pairing of television and sports has been a dream match: sports, though once suspicious of the impact on attendance, has gratefully accepted the largess from television,

> **Monday-night football**
>
> This has become something of an institution since its inception in the 1970s. ABC's innovation was an attempt to broaden the appeal of football by incorporating elements of drama and popular entertainment into its coverage. Unusual camera angles, personality close-ups, half-time interviews: these were all used to distinguish ABC's football from that of the other networks. It quickly commanded a one-third share of the viewing audience. ABC paid the NFL $8.5 million per year for 13 games and claimed this back by charging advertisers $65,000 per minute during the game. By the end of 1979, it was regularly the eighth most watched program in the USA, enabling ABC to charge $110,000 for a 30-second commercial slot. A British soccer version of this was inaugurated in the 1990s after BSkyB's £304 million ($575 million) deal with the Football Association. Part of the arrangement specified a "live" game every Monday evening.

which includes not just money but exposure to huge audiences. Television has found sports a relatively cheap production number compared to drama or comedy; and its viewing figures are consistently high enough to attract advertisers. Those advertisers have not only poured their money into tv's coffers, but have actually paid to attach their name to sports' championships. Witness, in the USA, the Virginia Slims Tournament, the Lipton's Championship and the Nike Golf Tour, and, in Britain, the Carling Premiership and the Benson & Hedges Tournament. There are hundreds of others. Advertisements not only surround and punctuate the televised programs: they are embedded into the events themselves.

Is it worth it to the advertisers? Ask Macintosh which, in 1989, launched a new computer with a series of spots during the Super Bowl. The following day, $3.5 million-worth of said computer went over the counter. The sales figure increased to $155 million over the next 90 days. This kind of statistic gives whichever tv company is showing the Super Bowl chance to play with the following figures: charge $850,000 (£530,000) per 30-second slot, anticipating 56 units that yield a total of $45.9 million, a figure reduced to $40 million after ad agency commissions. This is a little more impressive than it sounds because the Super Bowl is an extraordinary event in drawing 120 million viewers to their tv sets and because the regular season before the play-offs can be a loss-maker. In the 1992–3 season, NBC lost $40 million in the games leading up to the Super Bowl and emerged with a profit of between $6–10 million derived from spots during the 150 minutes of pre- and post-game analysis plus commercial fees from NBC-owned stations. Few, if any, other sports events can have the potential to gross $46 million (£65 million) and counting in three hours, but the Super Bowl has become, as *New York Times* writer Richard Sandomir puts it, "like a luscious *crème brûlée* after a long dyspeptic dinner" (26 January 1993). Take away the dessert and all you have left is the kind of bellyache that may make certain sports – the expensive ones – less attractive in the future.

Earlier in this chapter, we noticed how CBS's baseball deal backfired dreadfully and that the network, along with others, started to whine about money. There may have been gamesmanship involved in this. In his *Baseball and Billions*, Andrew Zimbalist remarks: "The [CBS] network's sudden diffidence might arouse some suspicion about whether it is engaging in a public relations game in a bid for smaller contracts the next time round" (1992: 160). CBS raised a few eyebrows when it announced an estimated loss of $450 million (over £280 million) over the period of its contract. ESPN had to buy its way out of a $100 million baseball contract, complaining of punishing $36 million losses.

Having scrutinized the figures, Zimbalist predicts that a prudent sports executive should not expect as much television revenue in future. In 1993, with baseball's popularity waning and CBS licking its wounds, rival networks ABC and NBC actually joined forces to reach an agreement with Major League Baseball. For the first time, the sport did not receive an up-front television rights payment, but entered into a package venture with the tv companies for administering, marketing and selling the sport. The following year, disaster struck when the baseball players went on strike and the World Series was aborted.

Zimbalist's prognosis that the days of the megabuck tv deals would disappear seemed accurate. That is, until the Fox network seemed to defy commercial wisdom with its expensive acquisition of the AFC Eastern Division, which includes the Dallas, Washington and Giants franchises. Despite the familiar grumbles from tv companies that sports are pricing themselves out the market, there always seems at least one network prepared to cough up. Even if television did scale down its bids, the sports themselves would surely consider alternative outlets, ppv being the most obvious at the moment. The die may already be cast in Britain with the BBC relinquishing its once unrivalled supremacy in sports and ITV having to content itself with the left-overs from the cable/satellite channels.

Sports were once cheap production numbers that drew viewers to their screens in millions. Those days are gone: major sports in particular have realized their worth and play off bidders against each other. Only the minority sports desperate for exposure are willing to sell themselves cheap in the expectation that an increase in popularity will strengthen their bargaining position in the future. A major sport without TV coverage is almost a contradiction in terms. Sports and television have enjoyed a comfortable symbiotic relationship. However, television has changed the sports it has featured, not just in terms of their rules but their very character.

Made for television

As television improved its technology and techniques, it was able to combine documentary accuracy with a fast tension worthy of the most thrill-packed sports occasions. The high-gloss presentations had analyses of slow-motion replays and frozen moments, knowledgeable commentaries-cum-evaluations, and detailed close-ups that captured facial – and sometimes verbal – expressions that the attending fans could never pick up. Around the event, tv learned to edit events down to lean action and pad events with previews, postscripts, and all manner of factual information, all designed to make viewing from home a more enriching experience. In contrast to the swirl of tv coverage, attendance seemed quite pedestrian. The freshness and appeal of tv sport were undeniable and sport had no magic strong enough to resist it, as we have seen.

It would be mistaken to think that television reports sport. Its presence in sport is so invasive that it actually determines the organization and administration of certain sports. And it's for this reason that some analysts, like Goldlust, argue that tv nowadays has an "overpowering sporting autonomy" and that its calculated intervention in sport has been a "critical and possibly decisive factor" affecting the overall development of sport (1988: 164). He cites the crisis of cricket in the mid-1970s as an example. In 1976, one of Australia's major commercial broadcasting organizations, chaired by Kerry Packer, offered the Australian Cricket Board (ACB) a deal for the exclusive rights to screen Australian cricket for five years. The offer was refused, so Packer decided to run his own cricket tournament – called "World Series Cricket" – for which he secured the services of 35 international players. The "rebel" tournament was networked by Packer's own Nine channel, but in a way that was offensive to traditionalists. It wasn't simply that players were asked to wear brightly colored uniforms and play under floodlights with a yellow ball, but the monitoring techniques intruded so as to make each match both observable (eight different cameras were employed) and audible (microphones picked up players' often blasphemous comments as well as general sound effects). Its one-day format was, as Goldlust puts it, "unabashedly spectator oriented, geared towards providing entertainment, tight finishes, big hitting and aggressive play . . . ideally suited for television" (1988: 163).

BIG FIGHT – BIG EARNERS

Television company	Promoter	Boxer
In	*In*	*In*
750,000 ppv units @ $30 = $22.5m $2m foreign sales $2m sponsorships	$15m from tv $6m site fee $1.5m ticket receipts $1m merchandising	$6m ($4m for challenger) $900,000, 4% of ppv gross $500,000 share of merchandising
= $26.5m	**= $23.5m**	**= $7.4m**
Out	*Out*	*Out*
$15m to promoter $2m administration $2.5m commissions $2m production co	$12m to boxers (Inc. support bouts) $4m publicity $2m legal fees $500,000 sanctioning fee (to WBA or equivalent) $1.5 misc expenses	$1.25m training expenses $1.98m to manager @ 33% of gross purse $600,000 to trainer @ 10% of gross purse.
= $21.5m	**= $20m**	**= $3.83m**
Make $5m	*Make* $3.5m	*Make* $3.75m

- The site fee is paid to the promoter for staging the fight at, for example, the Mirage in Las Vegas, the casino owners estimating that the interest generated by a big promotion will draw gamblers, who will collectively lose more than the site fee.

- A manager may take up to 33 percent commission from a boxer's gross purse (25 percent in Britain) and a trainer usually 10 percent; payments to other aides are included in the training expenses in the above example. A big promoter, such as Don King, may also manage one of the main boxers, so that his make is even greater than represented here.

- Financially, the risk is taken by the tv company: if the promotion fails to sell through the ppv agency, the promoter and boxers are still guaranteed fixed fees (though some boxers occasionally prefer to negotiate a commission-only deal).

- The figures represent a typical world title promotion rather than a megabuck heavyweight extravaganza in which the main boxers might split anything up to $80m.

The cricket that Packer promoted was barely recognizable as the nineteenth-century pursuit of gentlemen, but people watched it. After a nervous first season, viewing figures and, interestingly, attendances rose, enabling the Nine network to attract more advertisers. While the established cricket organizations, including England's MCC, opposed the wanton commercialization, they capitulated after legal pressure from Packer, whose marketing subsidiary PBL Sports in 1979 secured a ten-year contract to organize the sponsorship of official cricket. Packer's attempt to capture exclusive broadcasting rights succeeded and he had virtually taken control of Australian cricket by the mid-1980s. Crowds continued to attend and, more importantly, more viewers watched tv cricket. The players themselves earned more money, the organizing bodies took a substantial fee for the rights and the network increased its advertising revenue by selling more commercial time in the traditionally quiet summer season. The arrangement satisfied all except those who wished to see cricket as having more than a faint resemblance to the game that was once played with a straight bat and stiff upper lip. To those traditionalists, cricket *à la* Packer was short, violent, and battered into distortion. To Packer and his patrons, including his sponsors, this was simply cricket moving with the times.

Television's interference in the organization of sport is not always so obvious. Some argued that the decision of boxing's three main governing bodies to reduce championship contests from the traditional 15 to 12 rounds was motivated not so much by safety reasons as by commercial demands. There was little conclusive evidence that the serious injuries associated with boxing were incurred in the final three rounds, but in the mid-1980s the World Boxing Council, World Boxing Association, and International Boxing Federation all changed their rules. Fifteen three-minute rounds, as well as 14 one-minute intervals, preamble and post-fight interviews amounted to an awkward 70–75 minutes. Twelve rounds yielded 47 minutes, as well as, say, 13 for padding, which fitted perfectly into a one-hour time slot.

The Association of Tennis Professionals (ATP) implemented changes in 1994 that were clearly motivated by television's needs. It reduced the time in preparing to serve by five seconds to 20 seconds, thus speeding up the game. It also allowed spectators to react freely and spontaneously and wander about during play instead of sitting still and gasping "oohs" and "aahs" as at Wimbledon. And, in the biggest concession, it allowed broadcasters to place microphones on the umpire's side of the court "so that conversations between players and officials may be heard."

The influence extends beyond the match itself and into the ambience: tv caught up with darts, a late nineteenth-century British pub parlour game, which was virtually tailor-made for the small screen in all but one respect. Potential advertisers and sponsors didn't like the look of the habitual smoking and drinking in the crowd. Tv approached the British Darts Organization, which instructed spectators and players to refrain from smoking and drinking in front of the cameras. Considering that the game's origins lie in pubs, the move was a major break with tradition.

Subscription television

Unlike terrestrial television and basic cable, subscription television operates on the principle that viewers will pay extra monthly fees for the privilege of watching movies and events that are unavailable on other tv stations. Home Box Office (HBO) is the leading subscription service in the world. It was founded in November 1972 when it broadcast a hockey game from Madison Square Garden, New York, to 365 subscribers. It now has more than 16 million subscribers across 50 American states and screens 24 hours a day (this is still a relatively small number compared to terrestrial network tv which reaches 90.4 million viewers). Beside being a major screener of international sports events, it has become actively involved in the promotion of events, particularly world title fights. In France, Canal Plus fulfills a similar function. In Britain, BSkyB is the foremost subscription channel.

In monetary terms, some sports have profited as a direct result of tv's quite recent involvement. Darts, for instance, took shape in 1896 in Lancashire and remained a pub activity until the 1980s when tv took an interest. In 1989, the sport's top earner, Eric Bristow, picked up the equivalent of $45,000 for one tournament alone and his yearly earnings are estimated at over 2 million. This has been made possible solely by television. The case of snooker runs parallel to that of darts: traditionally identified as a pastime for unemployed males, top players, like Stephen Hendry, earn millions. And, as players earn more, governing bodies take a larger slice. Not surprisingly, they rarely challenge publicly a system that has rewarded them well. Television, for its part, continues to exploit to the full the relationship with sport taking up to 20 percent of its total air time with sport in the USA, somewhat less in Britain, and not less than 5 percent in other parts of Europe.

But the penalty is often a heavy one and sports must be prepared to bend or change rules, allow intrusions into previously private domains, and generally jump when tv shouts "frog!" Rugby League, in 1996, dismantled a 100-year-old structure and switched to a summer schedule to comply with media entrepreneur Rupert Murdoch's plans for a Super League featuring

European and Australasian clubs and broadcast around the world by Murdoch's subscription networks. Commercial considerations come before those intrinsic to the sport itself.

Very occasionally, we find instances of sports that seem to have been plucked from their natural environs and reconstructed for tv without too much damage to their integrity. Ice skating seems to have survived intact, as does gymnastics which transferred to the small screen without modification. Television discovered the improbable epitome of ABC's "thrill and agony" slogan in the shape of Olga Korbut, who leapt euphorically at every triumph and dissolved into tears when setbacks threatened at the 1972 summer Olympics. Since then a miscellany of state-of-the-art technologies have framed the sport in new and interesting ways. Yet, gymnastics has kept its essence. It remains an exception: a sport independent of television and not an artifice.

This may be saddening for those who mourn the days when sport was really "sport," but, as Sut Jhally points out, "this seems to imply that before the influence of the media there was something that was pure sports" (1989: 80). Roone Arledge, who inspired ABC's sports coverage, has often defended his network's use of synthetic sports by reminding critics that sports were not delivered by God, with rules inscribed on tablets of stone. All sports are in some way artificial. Teams of firefighters competing over how many buckets of water they can carry from point A to point Z is no more or less of a pure sport than 11 men trying to move an inflated ball in the opposite direction to another 11 men. The comparison reminds us that television has not so much transformed sports as extended and reshaped them.

The change is not always so dramatic as many writers seem to think: over the past 50 years there has been a drip-by-drip titration, some sports gradually changing from one state to another. Sports, as we have seen in previous chapters, are evolving entities anyway. Rules, duration, start times, methods of evaluation, etc. have been changing since the mid-nineteenth century when loose-knit activities began to resemble what we now take to be sports. Television has imposed change rather than wait for it to happen. And the audience has responded.

Armchair quarterbacks

Sport in the raw is insufficient for the tv viewer: he or she wants it packaged and presented, just like any other commodity. After all, when viewers are asked to pay for the product, as increasingly seems to be the case, they want more than roving-eye-style presentation. In sports, the action doesn't speak for itself: it needs the direction and narration that produce drama. If you disagree, try hitting the mute button on your remote control next time you watch sports and see how long you can take it.

There is now a mature second generation of people reared on televised sports, the kind of people who prefer waiting for videos instead of going to the movies and playing computer games at home instead of playing ball in the park. Attendance at sports events must seem pretty one-dimensional to them. Some will insist the tension in the atmosphere of a packed stadium or arena can never be even remotely approximated by watching at home. Yet you can almost hear the groans: "Where are the captions and statistics?" "I missed that piece of action; how about a replay?" "I'd like to see that from a different angle, or slowed-down, or explained to me by an informed commentator."

Expectations and perceptions of sports have changed, as have patterns of viewing. Television has gently encouraged us to *read* sports differently: we may be watching the same piece of action as our grandparents, but we will not necessarily interpret it in the same way. We are also likely to watch more of it, if only because of the volume on the air, or through the cables. Television's facilities for replays allows us to relax our concentration. Missing a touchdown, a goal, a knockdown, a homer or a hole-in-one is not a disaster when we can see it reviewed again and again from different vantage points. This, plus the comments, summaries and statistics that accompany the action, encourages a certain detachment and predilection for analysis.

Today's sports-watcher sits like an argus, assimilating all manner of information, audial as well as visual. One hesitates before suggesting it, but the pre- and post-event features have all but supplanted the actual competition. Analyzing has become an integral part of televised sports and the better-informed viewer can cast a clinical eye on proceedings. The irony is: they can do so with less play-by-play concentration on the activity itself.

It's not only the sports that have changed: so have we. Our perceptions and expectations have altered considerably since the emergence of television as the paramount force in sports. And we have to admit it – television is *the* force in sports. It dictates when and where events take place, according to what rules and even what the competitors will wear – yet everything points to a change.

As far as television is concerned, sports may be becoming too expensive. Even cricket, a sport once known for its gentlemanly conduct, cut up tough in negotiating its best-ever deal with British television companies in 1995, immediately after which players pressed hard for increased salaries (a familiar sequence). In the golden years between the 1960s and 1980s, sports were as valuable a commodity as television executives could have imagined: relatively inexpensive (no salaries or heavy production costs) and very watchable, as the ratings bore out. Some sports were elevated to international stature as a result of television. It was a match made in heaven. Now, the relationship is much more conflict-torn and the possibility of a divorce looms.

Established television networks will probably seek a bigger interest in the cable/satellite systems. In Britain, Granada has a significant stake in BSkyB, ostensibly its competitor. In the US, all the networks have not only cable interests, but ppv links. As major sports find tv money harder to come by, they may buy into cable/satellite themselves or extend the kind of shared risk relationships. In England, the concept of a subscription channel solely or co-owned by the Football Association showing exclusively Premiership soccer would have sounded insane five years ago. Now, it seems a perfectly logical extension of present arrangements. A Pan-European league that controls and distributes its own games is probable by the end of the century. Whatever the future, we can anticipate much more interlocking between governing bodies and media groups in sports, rather than straightforward buying and selling of rights. The big sports will want more say in their own destinies. And this means, we, the consumers, the fans, the television-watching public, are going to have to pay more for our sports.

Since the 1940s, tv viewers have expected sports for no more than the nominal charge of a few pennies on the price of an advertised product, or the cost of a license in the British case. Sports have been as much a part of television's stock-in-trade as soaps, news and cop shows. But we have already seen some of the grander sports events either being lured away from the terrestrial networks by competing cable/satellite companies or passed over to the ppv services of the media giants themselves. For instance, NBC offered 24-hour coverage of the 1992 summer Olympics to those prepared to pay $125 for a 15-day package. The meager number of viewers and the resulting losses did not inspire confidence, but it was all part of the process of prying viewers away from the expectation of the "free" sports they had been getting for the previous half-century. The ppv route is already being explored by boxing, with promoters sharing some of the risks. It's likely that other major sports will pursue similar packages with media giants rather than just selling rights. In this way, viewers are made to pay for their sports directly. There again, in sports, nothing is for nothing. It never has been.

FURTHER READING

Games and Sets: The changing face of sport on television by Steven Barnett (British Film Institute, 1990) is one of a number of texts concerned with the crucial relationship analyzed in this chapter. Among the others are: *Sports for Sale: Television, money and the fans* by David Klatell and Norman Marcus (Oxford University Press, 1988); *Television and National Sport: The United*

States and Britain by Joan Chandler (University of Illinois Press, 1988); and *In its Own Image: How television has transformed sport* by Benjamin Rader (Collier-Macmillan, 1984).

Fields in Vision by Garry Whannel (Routledge 1992) focuses on the 30-year-old debate over the effects of television on sports, "some arguing that television has made sport, some that sport has been ruined, others merely content to bear witness to the unholy alliance." British in orientation, but with generic analysis.

Media, Sports and Society edited by Lawrence Wenner (Sage, 1989) draws together a variety of perspectives on the sometimes conflictual, but more often than not consensual relationship between sports and the mass media.

Baseball and Billions by Andrew Zimbalist (Basic Books, 1992) casts an economist's eye on America's "national pastime" to produce an original and thoughtful analysis. In his chapter on the media, Zimbalist predicts that, in future, sports teams may be induced to "opt for controlling their own programming and marketing."

ASSIGNMENT

Imagine the kind of futuristic scenario depicted at the start of this chapter – but with a difference. Major sports have come under the total control of the mass media. So much so that there is no need for "live" audiences and events are viewed only via the screen. When people refer to the spectators, they mean the people watching at home. What were once mass open-air sports, like football and baseball, are now played behind locked doors. Indoor sports are performed in studios. How realistic is this? Support your argument with evidence from current trends.

The Great Debates IV
Does television have too
much influence?

Television's influence on sport has been profound. Once it merely relayed pictures and sounds from sports; now, it can dictate when the games are played and according to what rules. Some say this is not a desirable state of affairs.

Those who say *NO* argue

- Television provides so much revenue that some sports would not have survived without it.

- Players' salaries are high because of television's interest.

- Television makes sports available to billions of viewers throughout the world and so increases the popularity of sports.

- The rule changes instigated by television have improved the entertainment value of sports.

Those who say *YES* argue

- Television has become more important to sports than the paying fans who attend games.

- Overpaid players have become greedy, as the baseball and hockey disputes illustrate.

- Fans have become armchair-bound, preferring to view the tv rather than attending actual games.

- Television can now control sports by insisting on changes in time of play and rules of play, etc.

Chapter eleven

Not for the faint-hearted Violence and the legal battleground

A ball game with a punch

It was an astonishing winter by any standards. In the three months leading to 9 April 1995, sports around the world were convulsed by a spate of violence that culminated in the killing of a soccer fan after a pitched battle between rival fans of London's Crystal Palace and Manchester United. Soccer, in fact, had been the forum for four violent episodes, including two deaths, the other being the stabbing to death of a fan of the Genoa club during a game against AC Milan. The Italian league called off a day's complete schedule as a token of respect.

Eric Cantona, the French soccer player, was ejected from a game and detoured into the crowd to attack a jeering fan. And, in a similar incident, Vernon Maxwell, of the NBA's Houston Rockets – a man whose volatile character was known to rival that of Cantona – set off in pursuit of a fan who had been verbally abusing him. "Mad Max" strode twelve rows into the stands to find his tormentor and punch him. Retribution was quick in both cases. Cantona was banned from playing by his club Manchester United for the remainder of the season and fined a club record of £20,000 (about $32,000, or about two weeks' salary); also Britain's Football

213

Association found him guilty of bringing the game into disrepute, extended his ban and fined him an additional £10,000. The NBA fined Maxwell $20,000 (£12,500) and suspended him for ten games, this equalling the highest fine in NBA history and being the second longest playing ban. In a separate incident, the NBA also fined Scottie Pippen for angrily hurling a chair across the court, though the chair did not hit anyone.

A disturbance in Dublin at a soccer game between The Irish Republic and England was abandoned after major crowd trouble, but, unlike some previous instances of soccer-related violence, without fatality. According to most accounts, it was precipitated by an organized group of neo-Nazi fans, known as Combat 18, operating out of mainland Britain with links to Northern Ireland Loyalist paramilitary groups. The Loyalist groups opposed the peace process intended to quell the violence that had sundered Northern Ireland and England for decades before. Before the game, English fans raised their arms in Nazi-style salutes at the national anthems. (It was, incidentally, the first time the British national anthem had been played in Dublin for 31 years.) Minutes after the Irish had scored, violence broke out in the crowd, then onto the playing field, forcing the referee to call off the game.

Combat 18

Formed in 1992 as an offshoot of the British National Party, Combat 18, or C18, was an extreme right-wing political organization, its name taken from the position in the alphabet of Adolph Hitler's initials, A = 1, H = 8. The 200-strong group, which was made up of cells attached to soccer clubs such as Chelsea and Aston Villa, opposed the British government's approach to the IRA in the search for peace and forged links with the similarly oppositional Ulster Loyalists. In October 1993, Combat 18 made its first impact at a game in Rotterdam, Holland: 50 members travelled from England specifically to provoke violence, though it was not until the Dublin uprising of 1995 that it achieved international notoriety. After the disorder, it transpired that C18 had liaised with several other "firms," as soccer gangs are called, to co-ordinate an elaborate plan designed to cause maximum disruption.

From 1990, the activities of British fans was monitored by a specially commissioned Football Intelligence Unit (FIU), which passed on information to police forces all over the world. This legally constituted unit's *raison d'être* was the identification of organized cells of fans, many having connections with racist movements. It was a sophisticated set-up, making use of undercover operatives and state-of-the-art surveillance equipment to further its aims. It may surprise North American readers to learn of an official organization affiliated to the National Criminal Intelligence Service whose sole purpose is to do to sports fans what the CIA does to potentially troublesome political regimes. But, soccer in Britain has attracted a following that supports its local teams with a near-worshipful devotion and a zeal that fully justifies the root word of "fan" – fanatic adj. [< L *fanaticus*, of a temple, hence enthusiasm, inspired < *fanum*, a temple] unreasonably enthusiastic; overly zealous (*Webster's Dictionary*). Or: *a. & n.* (Person) filled with excessive and mistaken enthusiasm, esp. in religion; hence ~AL *a.* (*Oxford English Dictionary*).

Football Intelligence Unit

This was set up in 1990 as an anti-hooligan squad to eliminate violence from English soccer and now operates as a specialist group within the National Criminal Intelligence Service (roughly the British equivalent of the FBI). The unit maintains a database of intelligence on individuals known or suspected of violence at soccer stadia and offers this information to overseas forces when the English team or clubs travel abroad to play. This information is gathered from a variety of sources, including "spotter" officers, who go undercover and accompany soccer fans to games.

According to a (very dubious) legend, the original sports fanatics were, appropriately enough, Anglo-Saxons, who, having defeated a Viking raiding party at Kingston upon Thames in the eighth century, celebrated their victory by playing a "ball" game with the head of the Viking chief. More certain is the fact that, in 1314, King Edward II banned football (all varieties): "Forasmuch as there is great noise in the city caused by hustling over large balls, from which many evils may arise, which God forbid, we command and forbid, on behalf of the King, on pain of imprisonment, such a game to be used in the city in future."

Frequent laws banning football followed the English game through the centuries, partly because of the violence that often erupted among its fans and partly because it was thought to distract young men from sports such as archery and boxing which, as we saw in Chapter 4, were useful for military duty. In 1514, the first published thesis on education in the English language described football, or at least its primitive equivalent, as "nothing but beastlie furie and extreme violence." Football, along with other forms of recreation, was banned under the Puritan regime of Oliver Cromwell in the seventeenth century, only to resurface again at the Restoration in 1660.

The term "hooligan" derives from an Irishman, Patrick Houlihan, who migrated to south-east London in the late nineteenth century and, by all accounts, enforced a reign of terror on the local pubs, many of which employed him as a bouncer. There's little evidence that Houlihan was even vaguely interested in ball sports, though ample to suggest he was a mean fighter and a bully to boot. An undistinguished and disagreeable character, Houlihan had the questionable honor of giving his name to a social problem that was to endure for the best part of a century after his death.

"Trouble at football match" like "Fight outside pub" is one of the oldest evening paper headlines: a ribbon of violence runs through the history of the sport itself. Early football violence normally took the form of trying to kill the referee. In 1921, a stadium in Bradford, Yorkshire, had to be closed for persistent violence. In the 1920s, fans of Arsenal and Tottenham Hotspur met in the streets of North London with knives and iron bars. Police baton charges on crowds were commonplace. One club took the view that a match should not be stopped unless the bottles being thrown were full rather than empty. In the 1930s, pitch invasions and attacks on players and the police were often the subject of public disapproval. The relative calm of 1945–60 was something similar to a blip.

Many of the early eruptions of violence were at meetings between local teams, "derby games," such as Rangers vs Celtic in Glasgow, and Everton vs Liverpool. The rivalry between fans in these cities was intensified by a Catholic vs Protestant edge, Celtic and Everton having Catholic ancestry. At a time when sectarian conflict in Northern Ireland was raging, the soccer "wars" seemed a logical, if perverse, counterpart. Anti-Semitism was thought to be behind the age-old conflict between North London fans of Arsenal and Tottenham Hotspur, the latter being traditionally a Jewish-owned club. But, then the violence, or "aggro" as it was called (short for aggravation), became, in the tabloid vernacular, mindless. Every Saturday, local stores boarded up their windows, pubs were demolished and hospitals filled up with casualties from the games. Every game of soccer carried with it the threat of open violence between fans, wherever it was played.

A new turn in the 1980s signalled a paramilitary tendency among many fans, who gave themselves names, organized their troops into divisions and orchestrated their attacks on rival fans. Among the more notorious was West Ham's Innercity Firm, which is credited with the innovation of leaving behind specially printed business cards at sites of their fights. Other firms were Arsenal's Gooners, Burnley's Suicide Squad and Chelsea's Headhunters. Soccer hooliganism reached its peak in the early 1980s.

Football

Football is a generic term covering the world's most popular team game, known variously as soccer, *voetbal*, *fussball* and other derivations; American football, sometimes called gridiron; rugby, which is divided into Rugby League and Rugby Union; and Gaelic football and Australian rules football, which differ only slightly in terms of rules. Accounts of its origins usually include primitive kicking games using the inflated or stuffed bladder of an animal. In the Middle Ages, adjacent English villages would incorporate a version of this into their festivals celebrating holy days. These were, as David Canter and his colleagues call them, melees rather than games with no rules: the object being to move the bladder by any available means to the boundaries of one of the villages. The inhabitants of villages in Chester in the English north became so fierce in their efforts to move the bladder that the event had to be abandoned (Canter *et al.* 1989). Lack of transportation and mobility meant that the games remained localized until the mid-nineteenth century when common sets of rules emerged and standards created. An unlikely but popular story that purports to explain the division into throwing and kicking games involves a certain William Webb Ellis, a pupil at Rugby school, who in 1823, became confused and picked up a ball in what was intended to be a kicking game. Legend has it that rugby was born that day and it was this game that had offspring in the form of American football, Australian rules and Gaelic football.

The government, in response, adopted a number of measures which led to decline in violence at games throughout Britain: it was not reluctant to step into the sports arena and implement what might seem draconian legal measures to halt a problem that many felt had roots far beyond the sports stadium. Alcohol was banned from all stadia in 1985. The 1986 Public Order Act made provision for the exclusion from games of those convicted of offences against the public order. The 1991 Football Offences Act and the introduction of surveillance cameras also reduced the incidence of criminal behavior at games.

None of these legal measures had too much impact on the behavior of fans travelling abroad, specifically to major European cities. Courts of law were empowered to prevent those convicted of hooliganism from travelling to games in countries outside England. But, this type of power was helpless to prevent the free travel of violence-seeking fans who had escaped prosecution.

In some ways, the British did the world a favor by creating, developing and refining a sport, then taking it to the rest of the world from Lima to Lahore. Years after it had exported the sport, it exported a grimmer cargo. During the 1980s, hooliganism was rife throughout Europe. British passions are hard to rival; but Italians come very close. So, when the top clubs of each country met on neutral territory to decide which was the top team in Europe, some form of fan conflict seemed inevitable. Few could have anticipated the scale of the disaster at the 1985 European Cup Final game between Liverpool and Juventus, of Turin, Italy, at the Heysel Stadium in Brussels, Belgium: 95 fans were crushed to death and 200 others injured in the worst tragedy in soccer's history. After blame was apportioned, English clubs were suspended from European-wide competition for five years and Liverpool for seven. Juventus and its fans were exonerated.

Madness?

Of all the forms of football, only soccer has generated hooliganism in the sense we now understand it: a collective, violent activity conducted principally at football stadia, but often in the surrounding areas, between rival fans. Soccer is not only the most popular game in Britain, but also in the world and, while the specific form of hooliganism originated in Britain in the 1960s, it quickly spread all over Europe and South America. The title of Janet Lever's book on the South American game captures the almost crazed enthusiasm of fans, *Soccer Madness*.

All manner of explanation has been offered as to the causes of football violence: sports writers, historians, psychologists, sociologists and ethologists have all advanced theories as to why only soccer fans are driven to destructive behavior. Or is it destructive? Perhaps not from the hooligan's perspective. Let's summarize the main positions.

Observation. The first slew of arguments came primarily from sports journalists, whose observations of the games and the crowd disorders led them to believe there was a connection between the two. As more money began to circulate in soccer, so the competition hotted up: cash incentives for winning games, trophies or climbing the league standings introduced a rawer, more ruthless and often physically brutal form of play. The violence among the crowds was a reflection of the violence on the field of play, fans mimicking the aggression of the players in a kind of crude role-playing. Robert Arms *et al.* replicated several earlier studies into this phenomenon and concluded that "the observation of aggression on the field of play leads to an increase in hostility on the part of spectators" (1987: 261). Dismissed as simplistic and mechanical by many academics, a version of the theory was to return over thirty years later, as we will soon see.

Marxist approach. 1970s-style Marxists, like Ian Taylor, argued that the behavior was a working-class reflex: as British soccer became more commercialized and removed from the old communities where it had originated, it left behind a corpus of fans who felt the clubs were somehow theirs. The violence was seen as a symbolic attempt to confirm their control over the clubs. Not only hooliganism, but industrial sabotage, vandalism, gangs and a variety of subcultural exotica were explained with reference to the breakup of the traditional working class in the post-war period. The argument may have appeared reasonable in the 1970s, but has not worn well and is clearly inadequate to explain the continuing violence and its virtual universality.

Ethological account. Alternatives, influenced by ethological perspectives, focused on the ritualistic elements of the violence, viewing it as part of a huge dramatic performance in which youths acted out their parts without risking life and limb. Examining the sometimes quite elaborate hierarchies around which clubs' fans were organized (into troops, divisions, etc.), Peter Marsh and his associates concluded that, while the belligerent behavior witnessed at football grounds appeared to be chaotic and unplanned, there were, on closer inspection, what he called *The Rules of Disorder.* Anybody who has been to a big game at a British stadium and witnessed first hand, or worse been on the receiving end, of crowd violence will be aware of the limitations of Marsh's approach. Nice idea when you're sitting in your ivory tower in the quiet university town of Oxford, where Marsh *et al.* did their research; ridiculous when you're in the thick of a brawl in London or Glasgow.

Figurational perspective. Norbert Elias's theories have influences far and wide. It was almost inevitable that his colleagues at Leicester University in the English Midlands would apply his concepts to the study of hooliganism. Eric Dunning and a team of researchers undertook a detailed historical and contemporary analysis of football violence in Britain and elsewhere in Europe and produced the most sophisticated and plausible account available. Far from being a recent phenomenon, violence related to soccer has a history as long as the game itself.

The origins of violent behavior lay in the neighborhoods, where status was often the reward for being the hardest, toughest and meanest – the baddest – character around. Not having the money to acquire prestige through conventional resources, like cars, clothes and other material possessions, inhabitants of the 'hood would fight their way to the top of the pecking order. Inspired by Gerald Suttles' American analysis of *The Social Order of the Slum,* Dunning and his colleagues discerned a status hierarchy and fighting was the way to climb it. Habituated to fighting, the slum dwellers, or the "rough" working class as they called them, were the same people likely to go to watch a soccer game.

Risk displacement theory. While he didn't cite the Leicester research,

Simon Jenkins, a writer for the London *Times*, complemented it with his own version of "risk displacement theory" (*Times*, 18 February 1995). "This states that most people need a certain amount of 'risk' and will find it where they can," wrote Jenkins. "Every visit to a soccer game embraces an element of risk, including the danger of crowd trouble." English soccer's authorities thought they had virtually eliminated the possibility of violence in the early 1990s when they ordered all Premiership and Football League clubs to improve their stadia by installing seats instead of the old-style terraces on which fans used to stand. This worked to an extent: but the violence transferred from the grounds to the streets and the pubs, creating what one writer called "landscapes of fear." The risk element is present in a number of sports and its complete elimination would probably detract from the enduring fascination we seem to have with danger and uncertainty. We will revisit this idea in the conclusion, but for the moment, let's take note of Jenkins' point that spectators at British soccer matches are clearly aware of the risks they take and, presumably, make a kind of cost–benefit analysis, concluding that the thrill is worth the risk. Jenkins goes as far as saying that it is part of the appeal of attending the stadium.

Reversal theory. In a way psychologist John Kerr has combined elements of the figurational and risk displacement theories in his attempt to understand "the pleasure of being destructive" (1994). "Understand" is the key word here because Kerr's theory is based on the individual's interpretation of the meaning or purpose of his or her own action. Basically, he argues that young people who get involved in fan violence are satisfying their need for stimulation through forms of behavior that involve risk and novel or varied situations. One of the attempts behind this approach is to get away from theories that offer the impression that we are consistent. Kerr believes that human behavior is completely inconsistent. "This means that a soccer hooligan who on one occasion smashes a shop window may on another occasion do something completely different." This depends on our "metamotivational state": we can "reverse" between them as easily as a traffic light changes from red to green; it all depends on the situation, or contingent circumstances.

Landscapes of fear

Surprisingly, the term comes not from a tabloid newspaper but from John Bale's study *Sport, Space and the City*: "A surprisingly large proportion of fans feel frightened when visiting certain football stadiums . . . it is still *the* most popular spectator sport in Britain and for most of those involved the sport is relatively benign. Yet for some residents (a 'silent majority' in some cases) football can frequently constitute a nuisance and sometimes generate real fear" (1993: 95)

"The soccer environment provides a rich source of varied pleasure for those who wish to pursue and enjoy the feelings of pleasant high arousal," writes Kerr (1994: 47). Most regular fans reach a satisfactory level of arousal; others do not and develop their own extreme variation in their quest for excitement. Ergo destructive behavior, which can, given the right motivational state and a conducive situation, be as gratifying as watching a good movie or poring over a work of art. Kerr detects that one way of achieving a high arousal is through "empathy with the team" and this particular method was seized by a number of writers in the immediate aftermath of the Dublin episode in 1995.

Copycat effect. The copycat effect has been invoked to account for a number of violent episodes over the years. Riots have been a stock favorite. The uprisings in English cities in the early 1980s and the Rodney King incidents of 1992 were thought to have been perpetuated by the mass media which, in transmitting images of rioters, virtually invited people to duplicate them. Two murders in Britain in the early 1990s were blamed on the movie/video *Child's Play 3*, which was watched by the culprits shortly before the crimes.

The theory holds that once the mass media get hold of a newsworthy topic their tendency is to amplify or exaggerate it, presenting the impression that the event, or events, are larger, more important, more serious or more widespread than they actually are. But here the self-fulfilling prophecy kicks in: in creating distorted images, the media are actually establishing precisely the kind of conditions under which those images are likely to become a reality. Let's say a minor event at, for example, Joe Robbie Stadium, Miami, is reported by a local tv station in a dramatic way that misrepresents what goes on. "Serious crowd disturbances at the Dolphins' game," announces the newsreader under images of a minor fight between two groups of fans whose inhibitions have been lowered by several cases of Budweiser. But the images have been dramatically edited as if they had been picked off the cutting room floor after the *Natural Born Killers* team had left for the day. (*NBK* was itself blamed for an outbreak of violence that coincided with its release in 1994 and delayed its opening in Britain.)

Determined not to be outdone, local newspapers join in the misrepresentation and soon the nationals get interested. "Is this the first evidence that the violence that's afflicted soccer for decades is creeping into American football?" they ask. The tempting and thoroughly exploitable possibility has scholars rushing out of their offices, journalists calling frantically for soundbites, church leaders tut-tutting about the collapse of morality, politicians scrambling for the highest moral plateau and, of course, the police chiefs promising that every football game will be subject to more stringent controls than ever.

All this is very exciting for at least a segment of the football-following population who could use a little more action off-field and would welcome the chance to experience the same kind of thrill their European cousins have been enjoying for years. Next Sunday they go to their games ready for action, prepared for the kind of behavior the mass media have been focusing on for the past seven days. And, sure enough, the violence breaks out. The "prophecy," as sagely foretold by the media and an assembly of others, has duly been fulfilled.

An unlikely scenario perhaps; but one that illustrates the self-fulfilling potential held by the media. Events can be created as well as shaped or influenced by the way the media covers them. Those who swear the media is behind all the hooliganism in Europe and Central and South America have a tall order. They would also be hard-pressed to explain why the first events occurred – unless, of course, they were phantoms of an over-keen journalist's imagination. Critics of this type of explanation complain that it reduces the actual incident to an almost motiveless reaction to an image or sound. It heaps blame on a movie or the media for initially showing the image and, in so doing, deters investigation into the more complex issues surrounding the incident. But we should acknowledge that the mass media and the copycat effect that it triggers are certainly parts of a complicated jigsaw.

Theories are like flared pants: they come into fashion, go out and, just when you think they are gone for good, back they come. Mimickry was thought to be at the back of the first outbreaks of hooliganism in Britain in the 1960s, but it was dispatched when the more scholarly analyses of the subject urged a wider scope than the playing field. History, culture, the economy, the mind of the hooligan: these were all factors that needed to be brought into the picture. But, in the 1990s, after a relatively tranquil period, back came the violence and a new version of the observation approach to explain it.

Two weeks before the Ireland–England game, Eric Cantona had leapt at a fan in a manner befitting a card-carrying hooligan. Within a week, a game between two London clubs, Chelsea and Millwall, ended with mounted police on the field to forestall a pitch invasion as fans stormed at each other. It was the first serious disturbance in Britain for years and presaged the more serious Dublin outbreak a week later. Sports writers understandably linked the episodes, citing the increasingly boorish and disorderly conduct of players both on and off the field as poor examples for fans.

Despite being suspended, Cantona drew a certain amount of sympathy from many quarters, including the chair of the Football Association, who defended him after a television journalist found himself on the wrong end of Cantona's boots and ended up in a hospital with cracked ribs.

Around the same time, another football player, Vinny Jones, bit the nose of a radio reporter, drawing blood, threw a jug of orange juice over another journalist and, generally, made a pain of himself. Dennis Wise, a Chelsea player, found himself in court after an attack in a London nightclub. "Fans do have a way of aping their heroes," wrote soccer journalist, Joe Lovejoy," who reported the affair for his newspaper the *Sunday Times* (15 February 1995, sect. 2, p. 20). But, this is by no means automatic: we might also ask why every fan exposed to violence by players doesn't behave in the same way? Why didn't viewers of the scrap between Deion Sanders and Andre Rison, in the 49ers–Falcons 1994 game, rush out and start whaling at each other in emulation of the stars?

There is a relationship between the violent behavior of players and that of fans, but probably not a direct one. Both groups operate in an atmosphere charged with competitive intensity in which rationality is rendered vulnerable to emotion and self-control is put to the most stringent physical tests. Attachments in soccer are unlike any other sporting ties: they often have a lineage dating back to the nineteenth century; affiliations are inherited like family wealth, except in this case the families, being mostly working class, have no wealth to speak of.

Soccer fandom was once about rank, domain, a collective way of marking one's territory. And, while those features might have been modified over the decades, their essence remains: British fans call themselves supporters; they see themselves as representatives of their clubs, defenders of their names, bearers of their traditions. It's revealing that, even in the 1990s when Premiership clubs' bank balances were healthily in the black, most official supporters' clubs insist on contributing a modest amount to their teams' finances. No matter how insignificant the amount, the value of the contribution was as a token of fans' assistance.

Feeling part of a unit capable of winning national and perhaps international honors, or at least challenging for them, has acted in a compensatory way for millions of soccer fans the world over. Once drawn from the industrial poor and deprived, the sport has never lost its base of support and continues to attract its most passionate following from working-class people whose occupations – if they are employed – are comparatively dull and unrewarding and offer little or no personal or professional gratification. By contrast, soccer does. Supporters don't just watch a game of soccer: they vicariously participate in it; they are part of the overall culture of which the actual 90 minutes of play is but one part. And, as activities on the field of play have become more overtly violent, the responses of many sections of supporters in the crowd have become so. In other words, there is a relationship between the two, but it is mediated by a cultural change that has affected the context in which the link between players and fans exists. This change has encouraged, or at the very least permitted, violence in sport – not just soccer but all sports. In turn, this has prompted attempts to control it. We will consider this next.

Fandom

From fan, or fanatic, and "dom," meaning a collectivity or the ways of (e.g. kingdom, officialdom), this refers to the condition in which whole congregations of people devote parts of their life to following, supporting or just admiring an individual or sports team. Devotees of Madonna, for instance, have been seen as a fandom of "wannabes," trying to emulate or mimic the rock star. Sports fans exhibit traces of this, though their orientation typically lacks envy and is based more on devotion. Gunther Parche, a devotee of Steffi Graf, in 1993 knifed Graf's rival Monica Seles in the back so that his idol could be no. 1 in the world. Often fandom revolves around loyalty to a club. In recent years, there have been two ball clubs that have generated fandoms far greater in quantity and quality than any others: Manchester United and the Oakland Los Angeles Raiders.

Manchester United. In terms of actual achievements, United has little to boast when compared to continental European clubs: United has won the European club championship once, as against Real Madrid's five, Liverpool's four and AC Milan's four. Yet the United fandom far oustrips these. Its fans travel from all over Europe to Manchester, and there are branches of its official supporters' clubs in virtually every Commonwealth and European country, as well as Japan, Malaysia, South Africa and the USA. There is even a branch on the Indian Ocean island of Mauritius.

The source of the club's special status probably lies in 1958 when a plane carrying members of its playing and coaching staff from Belgrade where the team had just clinched a place in the European Cup semi-final, crashed on take-off after a refueling stop at Munich. Nineteen died, including eight players, three staff and eight journalists. Sympathy for the club went far beyond the conventional limits of soccer or even sport itself. People who ordinarily had no interest in sports were touched by the scale of the disaster. The sympathy translated into a passive support, which in turn converted into a more active allegiance when passed on to a new generation. A warrantable third generation of United fans now follow the team around Europe; the team's success in the English league in the 1990s guaranteed it entry into prestigious European-wide competitions, which sustained the fandom. Added to this was an aggressive approach to marketing United merchandise.

Oakland Raiders. It is almost impossible to visit a country anywhere in the world without seeing someone wearing the black and silver and the Jolly Roger-style insignia of the Raiders. Officially licensed

Raiders merchandise regularly accounts for 40 percent of all NFL gear sales. Yet the team hasn't won a Super Bowl since 1984 and has detached itself from its original fans by moving the franchise from Oakland, California. The suspicion arises that its roots in Oakland may hold the key to understanding the world-wide popularity of the club. This was the birthplace of the Black Panther movement which began operations in 1965 after the riot in the Watts district of Los Angeles. The movement was radical and militant, committed to the ideology of Black Power, which proposed that the steady progress of the civil rights movement was misguided and that violent means should be used where necessary to break down racism.

The Panthers unwittingly acquired a radical chic: the signature black gloves were worn by Smith and Carlos in the 1968 Olympic gesture; cars were soon adorned with bumper stickers signifying allegiance. In fact, a 1971 study involved 15 participants, all of whom had clean driver's licenses, driving about with said stickers on their cars for 17 days, during which they picked up a total of 33 traffic violation tickets. Raiders had the same kind of chic; like the Panthers they had what we now call attitude, playing no-frills, smash-mouth football. For Raiders' opponents, football was a form of torture. This was the type of football perfectly suited to the radical late1960s/early 1970s when to be "bad" was a positive attribute; and a generation of fans across the USA warmed to it. Subsequent generations have attached themselves to the same Raiders image, dressing in black and silver to express a different type of radicalism, one that owes more to style than politics and is no doubt enhanced by the number of California-based musicians who wear the colors.

By fair means or foul

Given the amount of money at stake in professional sports it's hardly surprising that many competitors are prepared to do what it takes by fair means or foul to get the desired result. A win can mean an awful lot to players: many players have bonus agreements actually built into their contracts. Winning a major championship makes a big impression on your bank statement should you have a clause like Ricky Jackson's: he was on a $800,000 (£500,000) bonus if his team went all the way to the Super Bowl in 1995. It did.

The exponential growth of commercialism brought about by television, as we have seen, introduced to sports more money than could have been

EXPLANATION		ORIGINS	DYNAMIC	PURPOSE	RESULT
OBSERVATION		ONFIELD BEHAVIOR	MODELLING	SELF-ENHANCEMENT	VIOLENT UPWARD SPIRAL
MARXIST		CLASS INEQUALITY	UPRISING	SOLIDARITY BUILDER	SYMBOLIC STRIKE AGAINST SYSTEM
ETHOLOGICAL		NATURAL IMPULSE	RITUAL AGGRESSION	ENERGY RELEASE	SAFETY VALVE
FIGURATIONAL		HISTORICAL CHANGE	PURSUIT OF EXCITEMENT	REMAINDER OF THRESHOLDS	HISTORICAL CONTINUITY
RISK		PSYCHO-LOGICAL NEED	DANGER-SEEKING AROUSAL	RESTORES RISK PLEASURE	BALANCED LIFE
REVERSAL		PSYCHO-LOGICAL STATES	LOSS OF RESTRAINT	EXCITEMENT	SATISFYING AROUSAL
COPYCAT		MEDIA IMAGE	EMULATION	CONGRUENCE OF BEHAVIOR	FEELINGS OF FELLOWSHIP

dreamt of 20 years ago. In Chapter 8, I argued that the increase in the use of performance-enhancing drugs by performers is one result of this. Coaches over the years have driven competitors as hard as they could, pushing and prodding them to their peak performances. But the carrot is mightier than the stick. There's no better way to get the ultimate effort out of a performer than to offer irresistible incentives.

The results of this are obvious: perfectly conditioned, highly motivated, tunnel-visioned, win-oriented performers, who continually frustrate critics and sometimes governing authorities with the excellence of their play. One product of the high-stakes culture is Pete Sampras, an athlete so well-trained and charged with the desire to win that he achieved virgin levels of excellence untouched by others. Tennis authorities have considered changing the rules of the game or using different balls to reduce the advantage the power-hitting Sampras enjoys. Less visible, but similar, is Geet Sethi, who, in the 1990s, occupied a position of supremacy in billiards to that of Sampras in tennis. He held the world-record break of 1,276,000 and billiard's rule-makers implemented changes to blunt his skills. In both cases, the brilliant efficiency of the players made their games repetitive and tedious.

Tennis and billiards are sports in which the competitors are physically separated. Although they are opposed, their prowess is exhibited in relative isolation. They don't, for example, break tackles, knock opponents out or dribble a puck around defending players. In sports where contact or collision is inevitable, either by design or default, the effort to win by any means necessary takes on a different complexion. Physical encounters are less restrained than they might have been where only pride was at stake. Serious injuries are accepted as part-and-parcel of today's sports. Illegal play is seen as permissible as long as it goes unnoticed by officials. When the price of failure is measured in terms of what might have been gained, success is pursued with a fury unimaginable in early periods of sports history.

Objectors will scoff at this suggestion, reminding us of former sports stars, like Jack Tatum, Jake LaMotta or Nat Lofthouse, none of whom were known for their pat-a-cake styles of play. These individuals stand out for their ferocity, single-mindedness and callous disregard for others. My point is: they *do* stand out. Nowadays, there are so many sports performers with the same approaches that we don't regard them as extraordinary. The qualities that distinguished Tatum and the others are now the norm.

This is most evident in contact sports, of course, where players' bodies clash and clatter as a normal part of the flow, such as in hockey and basketball. The success of the National Hockey League from the 1970s, it could be argued, has been based on the frequent eruptions of violence during any game. Watch the hockey played at Olympics Games, where there is a high degree of technical competence but none of the almost theatrical fighting that punctuates an NHL game: the experience is quite different and, I dare say, not as entertaining for an NHL fan.

At the start of the 1980s, basketball lagged way behind hockey in terms of popularity in the USA. It now vies with baseball as the most-watched sport around. Much of its success has been based on marketing strategies that have worked like a charm and a format that suits television perfectly. But, again, compare your experiences: watch a game of basketball from any Olympics before 1992, when an all-professional American "dream team" dominated. The action is fast, nimble and precise; yet there is something lacking; and I don't mean the climactic slam-dunks. The physical contact is almost polite alongside the bumps and shoves we are used to seeing.

Players don't get sent splaying after running into a colossus like Shaq O'Neal. None of the players has the mien of a pro boxer, as does Charles Barkley. The NBA purveys a different game from the basketball played by the rest of the world ten years ago. It is harsher, more physical and brings with it an undertow of violence that has made it commercially attractive. Small wonder that tv networks have clamored to throw money at the NBA, which has in turn plowed it through the clubs which have been able to pay players salaries to rival those of the best-paid boxers and baseball players. This has pumped up the stakes even higher, reinforcing the intensity of competition that characterizes the NBA.

The phrase "only in America" springs to mind when we come to comparing this trend with sports elsewhere in the world. Or, perhaps, only North America, because efforts south of the Rio Grande and throughout Europe have been aimed at eliminating the violence that has been allegedly escalating in soccer. The sport has always been tough, of course; but the world's governing organization FIFA, in the 1980s, became concerned that the pre-eminent teams were those that employed particularly physical players, whose specialty was intimidation. This had commercial implications, though they were never spelled out: if the finesse players were succumbing to the "cloggers" as they were known (*clog* meaning to impede or hamper), then the shape of the sport would change fundamentally, skill being replaced by a more robust style of play in which only the strong would survive. Soccer was once described as a game of pianists and those who carry the pianos for them. At a time when FIFA was expanding into Africa and Asia to make the sport genuinely universal and needed television monies to fund its mission, it could ill-afford to lose its virtuosos.

Over a period of years, FIFA issued a series of directives to soccer referees to control not only violent play, but disagreements with referees' calls (classed as "dissent"), time-wasting (the clock runs continuously apart from half-time in soccer) and "professional fouls." The penalties for these and other violations were severe: without the hockey-style sin bins, soccer players were ejected from games for the duration and faced further suspensions as a result. Despite attempts to contain aggressive behavior in many sports there remains a paradox. For many sports to be effective as competitive spectacles, some element of aggression has to be present. One only needs to see coaches before a game; they are never caught gazing reflectively out of a locker room window, whispering gently to their players, "Relax, we'll win if it's meant to be." More likely, they'll be roaring with passion, using every device they know to bring their players to an aggressive peak.

Seen like this, sports create a milieu that sometimes sanctions or encourages physical violence or at least creates conditions under which the possibility of violence is heightened. It then covers that milieu with a sheltering canopy as if to prevent outsiders interfering with internal affairs. The cases of Paul Smithers and Dennis Wise make the point. Smithers was a hockey player convicted of manslaughter in 1973 after beating an opposing player to death in a parking-lot fight after a game; Wise a Chelsea soccer player who was convicted of assaulting a cab driver and sentenced to three months' imprisonment. Change the context and the results would be completely different. While neither players' behavior would have been condoned on the playing area, it's likely that long suspensions and heavy fines would have been the limit of the penalties.

Occasionally, the violence has reached a pitch where redress on the field of play has not been sufficient. Players have claimed that the context of sports affords a protection to other professionals whose conduct would otherwise be punishable by law and that this protection is artificial. Dissatisfied with the penalties imposed by the sport itself, they have taken their complaint elsewhere and with interesting results.

All part of the game

As anyone who has watched the NHL knows, hockey is a perilous sport: sticks are wielded like axes, fists fly furiously and players are bundled about the ice. In their *Hockey Night in Canada*, Richard Gruneau and David Whitson write "hockey actually seems to celebrate fighting outside the rules as a normal part of the game" (1993: 189). Not so, said Ted Green, of Boston Bruins, who almost died as a result of a stick blow to the head that fractured his skull. The game in which it happened took place in 1969. In the following year, both Green and his attacker, Wayne Maki, of St Louis, appeared in separate trials in Ottawa, charged with assault causing bodily harm. It was alleged that Green provoked Maki. Both were acquitted on grounds of self-defense.

Within months of the Green–Maki case, a Canada-wide poll conducted by *Maclean's* magazine indicated that almost 40 percent of the respondents, male and female, liked to see physical violence in hockey. They were not disappointed over the next several years as the amount and intensity of what Michael Smith calls "quasi-criminal violence" increased – as, incidentally, did the popularity of hockey.

Violence in sports is not a phenomenon to which Canadians are unaccustomed. "The belief that violence sells and that eliminating fighting would undercut the game's appeal as spectacle has been the official thinking among the NHL's most influential governors and officers," detect Gruneau and Whitson (1993: 185). Yet, in 1976, the Attorney-General of Ontario ordered a crackdown on violence in sports after a year that had seen 67 assault charges relating to hockey. In the same year, a particularly wild brawl occurred during a World Hockey Association playoff game between Quebec Nordiques and Calgary Cowboys, whose player Rick Jodzio was eventually fined C$3,000 (US$2,200, or £1,360) after pleading guilty to a lesser charge than the original causing bodily harm with intent to wound. There were also convictions arising from a Philadelphia–Toronto game in 1976: the interesting aspect of this one was that, in legal terms, a hockey stick was designated a dangerous weapon

Professional foul

This phrase was objected to by many in soccer for dignifying what many thought a gross, inexcusable violation of rules. It involves three players: the goalkeeper(G), the player in possession of the ball (A) and the defensive player (D). A is in an attacking position heading for goal and has only G to beat; D chases from behind. Sensing he is unable to catch him and not wishing to allow him a free strike on goal, he either grabs A around the upper body to drag him back, or, more usually, slide-tackles him from behind, aiming at his ankles rather than the ball. Either way, A loses control of the ball and misses the chance of a shot. There is no obvious equivalent in American football, but pass interference in or approaching the endzone is a comparable violation. The penalties are very different: in soccer, the player is "sent off" for the rest of the game; in American football, the defense loses yardage and the player incurs no specific punishment.

Not all the sports-related court cases in this period were from hockey. The first case in recent history was the 1965 Giants–Dodgers game in which the San Francisco hitter Juan Marichal whacked LA catcher John Roseborough with his bat. Marichal was fined by the league and suspended, but Roseborough sought the retribution through a civil suit that was eventually settled out of court. In basketball, a huge case in 1979 involved not only the fining and suspension of the Lakers' Kermit Washington, but an accusation leveled against his club for failing to train and supervise the player adequately. He was ordered to pay damages in excess of $3 million (£1,800). The player whom he attacked, Rudy Tomjanovich, was effectively forced into premature retirement as a result of his injuries.

Quasi-criminal violence

This is defined by Michael Smith as "that which violates not only the formal rules of a given sport (and the law of the land), but to a significant degree the informal norms of player conduct" (in *Violence and Sport*, 1983: 14). Typically, it will result in some form of injury that brings it to the attention of officials and, later, tends to generate public outrage when the mass media report it. Sometimes, civil legal proceeding follows, though, according to Smith, who it must be remembered was writing in 1983, "less often than thought." In the 1990s, court cases are more prevalent.

Perhaps the most memorable case of its kind occurred in an NFL game during the 1975 season. The plaintiff, Dale Hackbart of the Denver Broncos, suffered a career-ending fracture of the spine following a big hit from Charles Clark of the Cincinnati Bengals. Taking his case to the District Court, Hackbart was told that, by the very fact of playing an NFL game, he was taking an implied risk and that anything happening to him between the side-lines was part of that risk. An appeals court disagreed and ruled that, while Clark may not have specifically *intended* to injure his opponent, he had engaged in "reckless misconduct." This paved the way for his employer, the Bengals, to be held accountable. This case was to have echoes almost two decades later in England, when a Chelsea soccer player, Paul Elliott, pursued a case against Dean Saunders, then playing for Liverpool. Following a tackle from Saunders, Elliott sustained injuries that prevented him from playing again. The court found that the context of soccer mitigated the offense and that Saunders was not guilty of reckless or dangerous play. Elliott's case was weakened by the fact that the play was not penalized by the referee during the game and so the judge was effectively asked to use a video and other evidence to overturn the referee's decision.

John Fashanu was taken to court twice for play that seriously injured fellow soccer players: one was settled out of court and he was cleared of the other, underscoring the point that guilt in a law court and guilt on the playing field are two different things. It could be argued that a player who directs his or her aggression against another in a wild and reckless way is doing so out of a desire to win rather than malice. The relevant principle was originally stated in English law in the *Condon* v. *Basi* case of 1985, when it was decided that, even in a competitive sport whose rules indicate that physical contact will occur, a person owes a duty to an opponent to exercise a reasonable degree of care. In Condon, the court accepted the evidence of the referee in an amateur football game that the defendant had broken the plaintiff's leg by a reckless and dangerous tackle and damages were awarded. In Elliott's case it was decided that Saunders attempted to play the ball and accidentally injured Elliott, which was how the game officials called it. This might suggest that officials' decisions are respected, though there are exceptions, the most remarkable coming in the aftermath of the European middleweight title fight between Alan Minter and Angelo Jacopucci in 1978.

A few hours after being knocked out, Jacopucci collapsed and ultimately died. In 1983, after a protracted and complicated series of legal actions, a court in Bologna, Italy, acquitted the referee and Jacopucci's manager of second degree manslaughter on the basis that they should have stopped the fight before the twelfth and last round. The ringside doctor, however, was con-victed, ordered to pay Jacopucci's widow the equivalent of $15,000 (£10,000) damages and given a suspended eight-month prison sentence.

The courts have been wary of intervening in Britain, though the incident involving Duncan Ferguson, Eric Cantona and Paul Ince were exceptions that may prove to be the rule in future. Before examining this, let's retreat to 1975 and the case of Henry Boucha who played for the Minnesota North Stars of the NHL. During a home game against the Boston Bruins, Boucha got into a fight with Dave Forbes, for which they were both sent off for a period in the penalty box. On their way back to the game, Forbes lashed out with his stick, dropping Boucha to the ice. Concussed and bleeding, Boucha was helpless as Forbes leapt on him and, grabbing his hair, slammed his head onto the ice repeatedly.

Forbes escaped with a relatively light suspension of ten games from the NHL, but a Minnesota grand jury charged him with the crime of aggravated assault by use of a dangerous weapon. Forbes pleaded not guilty and the jury was unable to reach a unanimous verdict after 18 hours of deliberations. The court declared a mistrial and the case was dismissed. Boucha meanwhile needed surgery and never played again. Remember: *State* v. *Forbes* was a criminal case and its lack of a definite verdict left several pertinent questions unresolved. Smith believes the main ones revolve around whether Forbes was culpable or whether the club for which he played and the league in which he performed were in some way responsible for establishing a context for his action (1983: 20).

It's also relevant that the actual violent event took place as the players were re-entering the playing area rather than in the flow of the game itself, which is why it bears resemblance to the Cantona affair. At first Cantona committed a foul during his team's game with Crystal Palace; for this, his second serious offense, he was dismissed from play. While walking from the field he was provoked verbally by a fan who had made his way to the edge of the playing area. Cantona turned toward the fan, lurched at him feet first and started to fire punches. Seeing the commotion, Cantona's team-mate Paul Ince ran to the scene and engaged with another fan.

While only Cantona was singled out for punishment by his club and the FA, both players were charged with common assault, Cantona being sentenced to two weeks' imprisonment. More severe was the three-month prison sentence imposed on Ferguson for head-butting a fellow professional soccer player in a game between his club, Rangers and Raith Rovers in Glasgow in 1994. One of the usual protections afforded sports performers in similar circumstances is the context: players frequently behave in ways that would be alien to them outside of the sporting arena; they forge rivalries that have no meaning apart from in their sport; they consciously psych themselves to an aggressive level in order to maximize their effectiveness. In other words, their disposition toward violent action is specific to the sport itself.

It is quite possible that the person might have violent tendencies that are only activated by competition. Or it could be that the player's "normal" character is at odds with the violent persona he or she feels bound to assume during a game. The player could just be aggressive in and out of sports. In a sense, none of this is relevant because the behavior itself is meshed into the context of the sport. Forbes, we presume, held nothing personal against Boucha and, if they met at, say, a party, they may well have got along together. Cantona would almost certainly have never met the man he assaulted had they not been player and fan respectively. If sport has provided a sheltering canopy, we can only conclude that it is wearing threadbare.

Sports are violent, but, as Michael Smith in his study *Violence and Sport* points out: "The fact is, sports violence has never been viewed as 'real' violence" and the public "give standing ovations to performers for acts that in other contexts would be instantly condemned as criminal" (1983: 9). Yet, in the years since the publication of Smith's book, many of those acts *are* being condemned as criminal and the impression is that governing bodies of sport have lost their ability to police themselves. Lawyers are already moving into areas that were once taboo. We will return to this issue in the concluding chapter. For now, let us stay mindful of the fact that sport can't be regarded as the sealed-in unit it has tried to be. It is so much an integral part of our culture that it would be unreasonable to expect it to remain aloof from the conflict and turbulence that occurs elsewhere. Equally, we can't expect it not to be affected by the same kinds of legal controls that operate everywhere else.

In the next chapter we will find further evidence of sport's inability to lock itself away from events that swirl around it when we consider the impact of politics on sport and vice versa.

FURTHER READING

Sport, Physical Activity and the Law by Neil Dougherty, David Auxter, Alan Goldberger and Gregg Heinzmann (Human Kinetics, 1994) is a source book and has obvious utility for those practically involved in sports. Its value for students lies in its interesting use of case-studies to illustrate its arguments.

The Social Significance of Sport by Barry McPherson, James Curtis and John Loy (Human Kinetics, 1989) is a general textbook, but has a strong chapter on "Sport, law and politics," in which it is argued: "If sports leagues will not police themselves, criminal and civil action will be needed to bring about order."

Football, Violence and Social Identity edited by Richard Giulianotti, Norman Bonney and Mike Hepworth (Routledge, 1994) collects essays from around the world to show the narrowness of theories that attempt to reduce fan violence to a single type of analysis.

Understanding Soccer Hooliganism by John Kerr (Open University Press, 1994) is a somewhat technical social psychological account based on reversal theory which purports to explain the changeable and inconsistent nature of human behavior by reference to "metamotivational states" which may be oppositional and antagonistic. We can switch or "reverse" between one and another according to situations and contingent events.

ASSIGNMENT

A bitter rivalry between two NHL teams has been given an extra edge by a facial injury suffered by Crawley, a player for the Saskatchewan Scorpions after an aggressive encounter with Gaea of the Tacoma Titans. The injured Crawley vows revenge and is reprimanded by his club for inflammatory remarks made to the media. The buildup to the next meeting of the teams is marked by the media's attention to the two players concerned and the "revenge" comments. In the game itself, Crawley is sent cartwheeling by a hard tackle from Gaea. His flailing skate catches Gaea across the throat. Gaea bleeds to death on his way to hospital. While it is a freak incident, there are strong reactions. Examine the fall-out from the point of view of (1) the two clubs; (2) the NHL; (3) the mass media; and (4) the criminal justice system. (The players and clubs in this example are fictitious, though the incident is based on the death of Sweden's Bengt Åkerblöm who died after an accidental collision with a fellow hockey player in a 1995 practice game.)

Chapter twelve

Same rules, different game
How sports have been used as political footballs

Propaganda and boycott

This is the reason why sport and politics mix so well – because people think they shouldn't. So when political factions, or even whole nations, consciously manipulate events to make their points decisively and dramatically, they often opt for sport, knowing that the rest of the world will be so outraged that they'll take immediate notice. Hold a press conference in New York to announce that civil rights in the USA have amounted to nothing and that the majority of blacks are still struggling in poverty and the response of the media will be "so what?" Announce the same message, this time silently and symbolically, with just two black people disdaining the US national anthem, and listen to the electronic click-whirrs of the press cameras. You have a political event on a near-epic scale. The difference? In the latter example the two people in focus are Olympic medalists and the moment they choose to make their gesture is after being awarded their medals on the victory rostrum. In the event – at the 1968 summer Olympic games in Mexico City – sport worked as an instantly effective vehicle

for what was obviously a political statement. Sport *is* political if only because of its undoubted utility; it draws attention to particular issues, disseminates messages internationally and, occasionally, eases or exacerbates diplomatic relations.

In this chapter we will see the diverse – and, to some, perverse – ways in which the development of sport has been and will continue to be influenced by political considerations and at certain points in history. We will also see how sport is just too useful a tool not to be used politically. Denials of this come freely from the lips of those who have interests in presenting sport as an independent, transcendent force, one of the few jewels decorating a tarnished crown. "Sport is completely free of politics," declared Avery Brundage in his capacity as president of the International Olympic Committee in 1956. Ironically, he was responding to an event that actually undermined his central point – the withdrawal of six Olympic member countries from the Melbourne games in protest at the military conflicts in Hungary and Suez. The protests were part of a general pattern established before 1956 and which continue to the present day. Countries absenting themselves from Olympic games, either as a gesture of protest, or because of exclusion, have been a feature of Olympic history this century. They usually make headlines and attract the rhetoric of interested parties, who talk regretfully about how unfortunate the whole business of sport and politics has turned out to be.

The summer Olympics have bristled with political issues. They have been manipulated, often quite expertly, to spread messages to a mass audience; sometimes the messages have been quite doctrinal. Propaganda is the word used to describe the message and its dissemination. Sport has been a serviceable machine for propaganda because of the naïveté surrounding it. Comments like Brundage's give substance to the view that sport is politically neutral. So messages that do slip through are virtually subliminal, influencing opinion without being consciously perceived as such (hence sport's general appeal to advertisers, as we saw in Chapter 10).

If, though, a political message is given potency by dispensing it in the package of a major sporting event, it has just as much effect when administered in the form of *avoiding* an event. Instead of using sport actively, it is deliberately avoided when a boycott goes into motion. This isn't a passive withdrawal; it's the systematic refusal of a faction, or nation, to participate in an event or a series of events. It issues a political snub, the boycotters effectively saying, "We're not opposed to sport. We just object to engaging in competition with people representing a regime we find politically and morally repugnant."

The objects of scorn may themselves be part, or representative, of a political regime involved domestically in repression (South Africa being an outstanding case), or involved internationally in hostility (the Soviets'

Propaganda
This describes a body of political, religious, or even scientific information that is dogmatically taught; or it is the apparatus – "the propaganda machine" – through which the information is disseminated to a large population. An agent responsible for the dissemination is known as a *propagandist*.

---

advance on Afghanistan being an example), or, the group may only have maintained contacts with such a regime (as New Zealand did with South Africa). Those instigating the boycott wish to minimize their contacts either to escape stigmatizing themselves, if only by association, or to isolate that regime. Either way, the message recorded is a resonant one: the boycotters are opposed to the political regime in question and want to place political distance between themselves and that regime.

In the course of this chapter we will examine the various ways in which political messages have been stamped onto sport. Tensions are frequently catalyzed when major events, such as the Olympic games, are the focus and we will chronicle the political sub-plot of the games since the 1930s. As the games offer host nations the opportunity for some high profile media coverage and, thus, the chance to demonstrate how well their political systems must be working to stage such an extravagant event, propaganda of some degree is embodied in all Olympic games. But many of the controversies of the games, especially in recent decades, have centered on the use of the boycott to shame or embarrass nations and raise questions about their political operations.

Boycotts of Olympic games are often blows struck against particular nations because of their involvement in a specific event. Yet one boycott went on continuously so that it achieved the status of a permanent fixture in sport. It concerned South Africa and its relevance extended far beyond the Olympics. So much so, in fact, that the South African issue deserves attention in its own right – which it gets in a later section.

Talk of sport and politics invariably leads to discussion of propaganda and boycott, but the chief area in which the two elements fuse is in state. Sport has been used by states, ancient and modern, for a variety of purposes. Soviet systems are often seen as the ultimate expression of state involvement in sport: an extensive program of centralized control and direction ensured a persistently high level of excellence in Soviet countries and in many systems following their example. Westerners may admire the achievements but often deplore the bureaucratic system that facilitated them and the ideology that underpinned them. Yet, the state has tended to penetrate sports in the West too. There is nothing novel in this; even in the heartland of modern sports, England, where the amateur gentleman was an ideal to be revered, the state has for long been a force in the development of sport. The final section of this chapter will compare the state's involvement in sports in the two systems, with a view to assessing the overall "politicization" of sport in the contemporary world.

The Olympic weapon

"Sport is a latently political issue in any society, since the cultural themes which inhere in a sport culture are potentially ideological in a political sense." So writes John Hoberman in *Sport and Political Ideology* (1984: 20). If anyone doubts the point, they need look no further into history than 1936, the year of the "Nazi Olympics." The Berlin games were an occasion for Nazis to flex their Ayrian muscles and demonstrate the physical supremacy of the master race. Hitler had expressed his doctrine of the racial supremacy of the Ayrians and sought an international stage on which to reveal tangible evidence of this. The neutral arena of sport was such a stage.

Coubertin, in his original conception, saw the Olympics as having bridge-building potential. He wanted to bring nations of various political hues together in a spirit of healthy competition, always stressing that participation was to be considered before winning. Hitler's visions were as ambitious, but less noble. The political ideology he sought to propagate at the Berlin games concerned the superiority of one nation over all others and the essential disunity, rather than oneness, of humanity. While the blatant use of sport as a propagandist tool at Berlin was roundly denounced, subsequent hosts were to sense the potential and turn the games into jingoistic extravaganzas. This was illustrated at the Los Angeles Olympics of 1984, an event popularly regarded as the crudest and most shamelessly nationalistic Olympics in the post-war period, but, as Rick Gruneau argues, "in no way a significant departure from practices established in earlier Olympics" (1984: 2). Still, it seems fair to suggest that the particular utility Nazism found in sport warrants special attention, if only as a benchmark against which to gauge later expressions of nationalism.

Friedrich Jahn's gymnastics Turner movement of the nineteenth century was partly designed to prepare German youth to wage war against Napoleon. Jahn was a significant figure in fostering the "volkish" thought, which eventually gained political expression in Nazism, with its *leitmotif* of an overarching German essence. This was to be made visible through displays of physical control and strength, "a spectacle of masculine power." Hitler had no interest in sport other than this: to express national superiority and internal unity. His ally Mussolini, by contrast, was greatly enthusiastic about sport and promoted

> **Turner movement**
> This was the name of exponents of a system of gymnastics and physical exercises devised by Friedrich Jahn (1778–1852). During the 1870s and 1880s, the Turner movement staged regular exhibitions in Germany. The concept behind the movement was to use physical performance to enhance political unity, and as such it avoided what it regarded as "vulgar" competitive elements.

its pursuit at all levels from the 1920s. The Weimar Republic had assisted the growth of sport in Germany as part of the general morale restoration after the First World War. But, under Hitler's National Socialism, it came to mean much more. "Fitness was declared a patriotic obligation," writes historian Richard Mandell, author of *The Nazi Olympics* (1971).

The anti-Semitism that characterized Nazism affected sport; in 1933, when the boycott of Jewish businesses came into effect, the organizing bodies of sport excluded Jewish performers and officials. Two years later there was complete segregation in German sport, something that clearly contradicted Olympic ideals. In the USA, an abortive boycott campaign targeting the proposed 1936 Olympics failed to command support. Avery Brundage, the then president of the American Olympic Committee, warned that: "Certain Jews must now understand that they cannot use these Games as a weapon in their boycott against the Nazis" (quoted in Hain 1982: 233). Germany reassured the world that the extent of anti-Semitism and segregation had been exaggerated and, to underline this, included the fencer, Helene Mayer, who was "half-Jewish", in the national team.

Reservations went beyond the Olympic movement. In December 1935, a soccer international between England and Germany in London was opposed by Jewish organizations supported by the Trades Union Congress and the Communist Party. In the event, the match went ahead. In a subsequent international in 1938, this time in Germany, the England team was instructed to give the Nazi salute as the German national anthem was played before the match. Thanks to newsreel, the moment will live on as one of English sport's most mortifying moments, coming as it did so close to the outbreak of the Second World War.

Newsreel also depicts the Berlin games as a *faux pas* for Hitler, showing him leaving the stadium in apparent disgust as black American athlete Jesse Owens shook the ramparts of the Nazi's ideological platform by winning four gold medals. Doctrines of racial supremacy looked oddly out of place. Yet Hitler's departure was but one uncomfortable moment in what was in other respects a satisfactory and rewarding Nazi spectacle. Not only did Germans lead the medal table, they "demonstrated to the whole world that the new Germans were administratively capable, generous, respectable, and peace loving," as Mandell puts it (1984: 244). "Hitler, particularly, was greatly emboldened by the generally acknowledged, domestically and internationally, triumph of this festival grounded on the pagan (though very new) rituals of modern sport" (1984: 245). In terms of propaganda, the entire Olympic essay was of value to the Nazis: as the world exulted, Germany stepped up its rearmament program and stamped down on Jews.

Only in retrospect was the full resonance of the "Nazi Olympics" realized. No single games since has approached it in terms of ideological pitch. Its sheer scale deserved the posterity afforded it by the openly propagandist film directed by Leni Riefenstahl, *Olympia*, which idealized German sportsmen as *ubermenschen*, or supermen.

Yet equally, no summer Olympics meeting since has escaped political incident. The defeated nations of Germany, Italy, and Japan were excluded from the first games after the war in London in 1948. Holland, Egypt, Iraq, and Spain boycotted the 1956 games in protest at the British and French invasion of Suez. In 1964, South Africa was suspended and subsequently expelled from the Olympic movement (in 1970). Zimbabwe, then Rhodesia, a country which adopted a similar system of stratification to apartheid, was barred in 1972, having made a Unilateral Declaration of Independence from the Commonwealth. New Zealand maintained sporting links with South Africa in the face of world opinion and the fact that it too wasn't expelled from the Olympics spurred 20 African nations to boycott the 1976 games in Montreal. Boycotts have since proliferated. Taiwan also withdrew after it was refused permission to compete as "China."

The USA team pulled out of the Moscow games in 1980 after the Soviet invasion of Afghanistan. British Prime Minister Margaret Thatcher exhorted British athletes not to go, but the British Olympic Association went ahead. Soviet bloc countries (except Romania) and their allies replied by steering clear of Los Angeles in 1984, though China sent a limited delegation of 200 athletes. And, in 1988, Cuba stayed away from Seoul after the South Korean government refused to share events with North Korea (which itself pulled out). In 1992, the political tensions were primarily internal, Barcelona, the host, being a municipality with a strong conservative tendency and nationalist Catalonian feelings. Its problem was in maintaining its autonomy while seeking the assistance of Spain's central government in Madrid. As Christopher Hill comments in his *Olympic Politics*: "The political affinity one might expect it [Madrid] to have with Barcelona seems often to be strained by the rivalry between the two cities, as well as by the different traditions from which the national and local socialist parties spring" (1992: 219–20). Every Olympics has been associated with some form of political issue, which has often prompted boycotts.

Incidents internal to the games sometimes led commentators to suggest that the Olympics themselves were hemorrhaging so badly that they would have to be either stopped, or scaled-down drastically. If any single event can be said to have provoked this, it was that at Munich in 1972 when eight Palestinians occupied the Israeli team's quarters and demanded the release of 200 Palestinian prisoners in Israel. Negotiations proved fruitless and gunfire opened up. Ten athletes were killed. There followed a day's mourning before the competition resumed. Avery Brundage, by this stage notorious for his blundering efforts to separate sport and politics, drew parallels between the politically charged incident with the equally political but quite different attempt to force the IOC into squeezing out racist Rhodesia.

The games immediately preceding this, in Mexico in 1968, had underscored the point made so strongly by Berlin's "Nazi Olympics": that sport, given its world prominence, can be an effective stage on which to make a political point. The point in question was made by two black US track athletes, Tommie Smith and John Carlos. As occupants of the first and third places in the 200 meters, they stood on the victory rostrum to receive their medals. After receiving them, they bowed their heads and extended their black-gloved hands into the air to symbolize their detachment from America and American ideals. Throughout the victory ceremony, Smith and Carlos wore black berets, *de rigueur* headgear of members of the black power movement, which was at that stage sweeping across the United States. Frustrated at the lack of material improvement in the lives of blacks, despite the alleged progress of liberal civil rights movements, black power followers formulated a radical alternative to careful negotiation. They took violently to the streets, issuing messages of "burn, baby, burn!" and arguing for a radical type of separation. The gestures on the rostrum were not spontaneous responses; they were planned parts of a much wider campaign to bring to the attention of the world the specific grievances of blacks in the USA. And the strategy worked wonderfully. Not only did the demonstration supersede the 200-meter race itself but the runners were martyred by the US athletic bodies and barred from future competition. Take any sports writer, ask him or her to list the ten most evocative sports images of the century and they will almost certainly include that of Smith and Carlos, their fists clenched as if punching a hole in the American dream.

The Olympic games have the kind of generic relevance that makes them a perfect theater in which to play out political dramas. Ostensibly sporting occasions, the games have continually managed grandly to capture tensions, protests, and sometimes atrocities that circle the world. By celebrating the alleged unity, at least in spirit, of the world's population, Olympic games have sought temporarily to suspend terrorism, racism, imperialism, and other "worldly" matters that are the bane of our age. Instead, they have been hijacked by them. The setting and imagery of the games have been used to dramatize events seemingly unconnected with sports. We opened this section with the observation that many of the themes inherent in sports have political and ideological potential: nationalism, competition, the pursuit of supremacy, the heroism of victory; all have a wider application. Differences between the contrived competition of the track and field events and the real conflict in the streets have often melted in the spectacle of the Olympics.

An Olympic games attended by all member nations is unlikely in the future. Issues that cleave loyalties are sure to precipitate boycotts of some order. These will be, as in the past, boycotts over specific issues rather than a more general anathematization in which a political regime or its doctrine is denounced. The outstanding example of this process is South Africa and we move to this next.

South Africa's short delivery

In 1968, Basil D'Oliveira, a black cricketer from South Africa's Cape who had settled in England in 1960, reached the peak of his form. Selected for the English national representative team, he scored a triumphal century against Australia at London's Oval and was, almost without question, the most effective batsman in the country at the time. Yet when the national team for the winter tour of South Africa was announced, D'Oliveira's name was missing. The events that unfolded after the announcement presaged one of the longest-standing political controversies in the history of sports.

David Sheppard, a former England captain, later to become Bishop of Liverpool, led a protest, accusing selectors of submitting to the requirements of apartheid, which included the strict separation of those deemed to belong to different "races." D'Oliveira, having relatively pale brown skin, was officially classed by South Africans as "colored" and so had no legal right to share facilities with whites. Needless to say, the South African team comprised only white players. Several England team members threatened to resign as the protest gathered momentum, prompting the selectors to slip D'Oliveira into the squad as a replacement for an injured bowler, Tom Cartwright. It was an act of unheard-of nerve as far as South Africa's premier John Vorster was concerned: he smartly denounced the squad as "not the team of the MCC but the team of the Anti-Apartheid Movement, the team of SANROC [the South African Non-Racial Olympic Committee]."

Wounded by the accusation, the English team's governing organization, the MCC, called off the tour. Vorster's intransigence and the MCC's pull-out

Apartheid

This word is Afrikaans – the South African language derived from Dutch – and means "apartness." It was first used by the ascendant National Party as an election slogan. But in the preceding 300 years, South Africa had developed a pattern of segregation of "races" that was spasmodically enforced by law. This type of segregation was common to many imperial situations. What's peculiar about apartheid is that it was brought forward at a time when imperial rule was receding and the enforcement of segregation was being relaxed. South Africa went against the world trend by strengthening barriers between blacks and whites and attempting to rationalize this by reference to ideas about racial purity.

were crucial: the former in hardening South Africa's policy in the face of suspicions that Vorster himself was beginning to soften; the latter in showing the rest of the world's sports governing bodies how they might in future react to South African policies.

The effects weren't immediate and in the following January the MCC actually countenanced a projected tour by the South African cricket team in 1970. This was met with a "Stop the Seventy Tour" campaign and a series of disruptions of the Springbok's rugby tour of the UK, which served as a reminder of what would happen to any attempted cricket tour by the South Africans. The cricket tour did not take place. Progressively, more sports minimized or cut contacts with South Africa, effectively ostracizing that country's sport and creating a problem that has resisted a decisive resolution in the decades since the D'Oliveira affair.

The episode itself was by no means the first to surface: it simply captured the elements more dramatically with a victim-cum-hero, *ex cathedra* statements from South Africa, and the refusal of the MCC to be dictated to by a regime that had been widely condemned. By grabbing the attention of the world's media, the D'Oliveira case made the sport–South Africa link a significant political as well as sporting topic and one which would press governments into action.

The political significance of South Africa in sports had been realized for at least ten years before D'Oliveira forced it into the open. South Africa had, in 1956, made a formal declaration of its sports policy program, which, it insisted, should stay within the boundaries of its general policy of apartheid. The physical segregation embodied in apartheid was instituted in 1948 and encouraged by pass laws, police brutality, and a repressive state that dealt unsympathetically with any attempt to challenge its authority – as the slayings at Sharpeville in 1960 illustrated. Sports performers and teams visiting South Africa were, said the statement, expected to "respect South Africa's customs as she respected theirs" (quoted in Horrell 1968: 9).

Justifications, unnecessary as they were in a country utterly controlled and dominated by the numerically small white population, included the arguments that blacks had no "aptitude" for sport and the alleged potential for conflict in "mixed" teams and crowds of spectators. On the second point: blacks, who constitute over 70 percent of South Africa's total population, were barred from a new rugby stadium in Bloemfontein in 1955. In the following year, Bishop Trevor Huddleston, who was to become a prominent member of the anti-apartheid movement, observed that sport may be South Africa's Achilles' heel, in the sense that its national teams were so obviously good in certain sports, particularly Rugby Union. To deny South Africa the opportunity to demonstrate its excellence would, as Huddleston put it in his *Naught for Your Comfort*, "shake its self-assurance very severely" (1956: 202).

Sharpeville

A black township in South Africa that, in March 1960, was the scene of a conflict that ended in 69 deaths (all black) and 180 wounded. It signalled the first organized black resistance to white political rule in South Africa. The Pan-African Congress (PAC) had asked blacks to leave their pass books at home and go to police stations to be arrested. They did so voluntarily, but refused to be dispersed by the police who, eventually, opened fire. Sharpeville triggered nation-wide demonstrations. The reaction of the government was to arrest leaders of PAC and the other main black organization, the African National Congress (ANC), and ban both movements.

Another world power in rugby, New Zealand, had traditionally selected Maoris in its national team, but capitulated to South Africa by picking only white players to tour. This opened up a national controversy in 1960, especially when a New Zealand tour went ahead despite the atrocities at Sharpeville. This event crystallized many fears about South Africa, and a cricket tour in Britain in its aftermath prompted demonstrations. Cries that "sport and politics should be kept separate" sounded pathetically weak in the context of 1960 and, in fact, the whole decade that followed was to be filled with examples of the inseparability of the two.

Sporadic protests continued, both at street level and at official levels. The integration-oriented South African Non-Racial Olympic Committee (SANROC) was launched in 1962 with the intention that it should apply for recognition from the International Olympic Committee and officially replace the whites-only Olympic and National Games Association. The government pre-empted matters by banning SANROC. As the 1964 games drew near, the IOC, whose charter forbids racial discrimination, demanded large concessions from South Africa before its entry could be approved. Some concessions were made in the trials, but the South African government maintained its insistence that sport comply with "custom" so South Africa was denied entry to the Tokyo games.

New Zealand continued to send touring rugby sides to South Africa amidst negotiations aimed at allowing the entry of Maoris. But, in a key speech in 1965, the then premier Hendrik F. Verwoerd reaffirmed that no Maori players would be allowed to enter South Africa. Coming from the country's leader, the message was filled with political significance. In 1966, New Zealand finally declined an invitation to tour, but accepted another extended in 1968 under a new South African premier, John Vorster. In the interim, newly independent African states had begun to recognize South Africa's vulnerability to sporting boycotts and were strenuously trying to convince the rest of the world's sports organizations to expel South Africa. The Supreme Council for Sport in Africa, as the alliance was called, reminded the world that, while sport may conventionally have been regarded as trivial or unrelated to politics, "South Africans do not consider it minor" (quoted in Guelke 1986: 128). Outbursts from Verwoerd and Vorster confirmed this. They left no doubt that what was at first glance a sports issue was also one on which premiers were obliged to dispense judgements.

At a different time in history Vorster's conclusion that the MCC's selection of D'Oliveira was designed, as he expressed it, "to gain certain political objectives," may have passed virtually unnoticed by all those cricket devotees and anti-apartheid campaigners. In 1968, an *annus mirabilis* in which conflicting forces of protest gathered and collided all over the world, its effects were more far-reaching. The year had seen student demonstrations and protests from young people from all over Europe and the United States. Vietnam provided a focal point for the protests, though there was a more generic unrest underlying this. It was a time in history when people began to sense that collective efforts by "the people" could change world events. It was thought that not even apartheid was immune from "people power."

The IOC had already withdrawn its invitation to South Africa to attend the Mexico Olympics. A threat of boycott from about fifty member countries and protests from the black members of the American team were factors in the decision. British Rugby Union, a sport reluctant to dissolve its relationship with South Africa, entertained a Springbok touring team in the 1969–70 season and every match was seriously disrupted by mass demonstrations. The message from the tour was that any future visit by South Africans was likely to be met with a show of force. In May 1970, a planned cricket tour of South Africans to the UK was aborted quickly after the threat of uproar on the 1969–70 scale in the lead-up to a General Election. The same year saw the severance of more links with South Africa: expulsion from the IOC; elimination from the Davis Cup tennis competition; suspension from athletics; and a bar from gymnastics.

Isolation stirred Vorster into action and, in 1971, he announced what he called a "multinational" sports program in which "whites," "Africans," "coloreds," and "Asians" could compete against each other as "nations," but only in international competitions. This rather devious move effectively allowed black sports performers to compete, provided they were affiliated to one of the government's "national" federations. As such it served to divide blacks: some wishing to compete felt compelled to affiliate; others rejected the racist premise of the divisions and refused to affiliate. With international links receding, the government permitted domestic contests between "nations," and later club-level competitions between "nations."

Rugby Union resisted the international trend and, in particular, New Zealand set itself against world opinion by wilfully maintaining contacts. During a tour of South Africa in 1976, the near-cataclysmic Soweto uprising (official figures: 575 dead, 2,389 wounded) prompted evermore searching questions. As New Zealand seemed intent on prosecuting links regardless of the upheavals, should it too be isolated? The answer from the black African Olympic member countries was affirmative and New Zealand's admission to the Montreal Olympics in 1976 caused a mass boycott. Thus the crisis deepened.

Commonwealth heads of governments met at Gleneagles in Scotland in 1977 to formulate a now-famous agreement "vigorously to combat the evil of apartheid by withholding any form of support for, and by taking every practical step to discourage contact or competition by their nationals with sporting organizations, teams or sportsmen from South Africa." The agreement was between governments not sports organizing bodies and, as subsequent events were to show, the ability of governments to overrule individual organizations was often tested. Rugby's robust stance against governments gave rise to several anomalies. In 1979, Britain entertained a "mixed" Barbarians side (eight whites, eight "coloreds," and eight blacks). Critics dismissed the team, which was said to reflect the tripartite structure of South African society, as window-dressing. The British Lions' subsequent tours in which they competed with similarly composed teams, met with much the same skepticism. It was, so the argument went, a case of South Africa using sport to project a distortedly

Soweto

On 16 June 1976, South African police opened fire on protesting students in Soweto, a large African township near Johannesburg, killing two and injuring many. The students retaliated by attacking government property and officials. Police countered and soon violence spread to every part of the republic except Natal. For months, schools were closed. Students forced workers to stay away from their factories and offices in a series of one-day strikes. Some migrant workers refused and a battle between workers and students resulted in 70 deaths. The total number killed as a result of the conflict which began in Soweto was officially reported as 575 with 2,389 wounded – almost certainly an underestimate.

liberal image of itself while preserving its essential tyranny and oppression. The majority of black players belonged to the South African Rugby Union (SARU), which remained outside the aegis of the organization from which sides selected for international competition were drawn. Hence the sides were hardly representative.

Gleneagles Agreement

The issue of sporting links with South Africa prompted government involvement at high levels and, in 1977, at Gleneagles, Scotland, Commonwealth heads of government unanimously accepted to over-ride the autonomy of sporting bodies and "take every practical step to discourage contact or competition by their nationals with sporting organizations, teams or sportsmen from South Africa or from any other country where sports are organized on the basis of race, colour and ethnic origin." Sanctions were to be applied to those ignoring the agreement. The full agreement was published by the Commonwealth Secretariat, London.

It was a period of public relations initiated by Pretorian officials bent on convincing the world that every measure was being taken to desegregate sport – though not education, employment, and housing. For all its promises, South Africa fell short on delivery. Invitations went out to individual players of international repute who were drawn by moolah to South Africa to engage in what were known as rebel tours. Cricketers, buoyant after the triumph of the individual over governing bodies, courtesy of Kerry Packer, went to South Africa in their scores, both to play and to coach, usually in contexts that were notionally "multiracial." British soccer players took short-term contracts to coach, some, like Stanley Matthews, working exclusively with blacks. American boxing champions, like Bob Foster and Mike Weaver, both black, defended their titles in South Africa against whites. South Africa made no secret of the fact that it had an embarrassment of riches with which to lure top sports performers.

There were prices to pay, however. In 1981, the United Nations special committee against apartheid published its first "blacklist" (an embarrassing misnomer) of sports performers who had worked in South Africa. This served as an effective prohibition and ostracized South Africa further. Starved of decent-quality opposition, promising South Africans, like Sidney Maree, a black athlete, and Zola Budd, who was white, left to campaign abroad. Maree took US citizenship, while Budd was rapidly granted British citizenship, a move that caused the anti-apartheid campaigners to roll up their sleeves and unfurl their banners once more. On this occasion, the campaigners may have missed one point – that is, that the isolation of South Africa was working so well that individuals with potential were forcibly leaving their country in order to realize it. The counterpoint was that, regardless of the citizenry, the performers were still, if only by accident of birth, South African, and their success would inevitably reflect on that country.

Controversies followed both those leaving South Africa and those who continued to flout the prohibition by going there. British cricketer Robin Jackman, who had played in South Africa, was deported from Guyana in 1981 just as a test match against the West Indies was about to begin. The match was abandoned. Others, like Geoff Boycott and Graham Gooch, were banned for a number of years from test cricket as punishment for their "sins."

It wasn't until 1989 that the International Cricket Conference (ICC) passed a resolution, in defiance of a crucial summons obtained by the right-wing Freedom Association, to formalize sanctions against players, coaches, or administrators who worked in South Africa. Automatic suspensions from test cricket were the penalty. It was the most unambiguous pronouncement on sport and apartheid since the Gleneagles agreement. The decision was reached after the cancellation of England's scheduled winter tour of India, when Indians refused to play a team that included players with South African connections. "A victory for sport over racism," was how the resolution was greeted by Sam Ramsamy of SANROC. Norris McWhirter, the leader of the Freedom Association, described it as "a crushing blow against cricketers' freedom to trade" and exhorted individual players to take out civil injunctions to prevent ICC carrying out its ban. It could be argued against this that the freedom of over 21 million black South Africans to trade – and not just in cricket – was of far greater significance than that of a relatively small number of cricketers.

The election of Nelson Mandela to South Africa's Premiership in 1993, and the collapse of apartheid which preceded it, effectively ended the isolation of South Africa in all senses and sporting relations were resumed. South Africa was readmitted in the Olympic movement, its rugby teams were allowed to tour and its cricket teams was permitted to play test series against the world's other major cricket powers. The West Indies cricket team was the first to tour South Africa after the announcement of apartheid's dissolution in 1991. Black representation in the country's national teams was still scant, though not because of any deliberate exclusion. Generations of segregation means that black performers have been denied access to resources, including coaching and facilities; the only sports in which they are decent are those that need little equipment; namely, track, soccer and boxing. "Deracializing" sport, as the process is called, is underway in South Africa, though the imprint of years past will take time to erase.

The intrusion of the state

The traumas of the Olympic games and the issue of apartheid raised big un-answered questions about sport and politics, the biggest being, "how do we separate them?" There is no effective answer to this. What's more, we might add that sport is nowadays more political than ever in the sense that it's supported, assisted and, very occasionally, obstructed by political groups. The Soviet system and societies within its sphere of influence are held up as models of state-controlled sport; yet it could be argued that the state has had a deep penetration in sport in the West – and not just in recent years.

The Soviet Union, in particular, encouraged a vigorous role for the state in directing sport; it integrated sport into its more general political program. There are a number of reasons for this, one being the strategic military value of having a sports-oriented population, the other being the international prestige drawn from success in sports. Neither idea is new. A glance back into history tells us that activities that might now resemble competitive sport were once training maneuvers for the military. Chapter 4 suggested that ancient versions of sport were retained as much for their strategic worth as their autotelic value. Sports have frequently had an instrumental element to them: geared to attaining military-level physical standards and the discipline that is important in combat. The physical well-being of individuals is a foundation for the nation's vitality: this is an abiding idea. For all his fine ideals, Pierre de

Coubertin also had pragmatic goals when he revived the Olympic games in 1896. Distressed by France's poor military efforts, especially against Germany, Coubertin felt his country was in need of a reminder of the importance of physical endeavor.

The Soviet Union Communist Party's 1925 resolution influenced the entire Soviet approach to sport, in which "physical culture must be an inseparable part of overall political and cultural education." This passage is quoted by James Riordan in one of his publications on sport in communist societies (1982: 219). In his book *Soviet Sport*, Riordan wrote that in Soviet society where it had been decided that sport "should be as free and natural as the air people breath, there has to be government intervention on a wide scale" (1980: 19). This makes sport political because, "in a centrally planned state in which health and education and much else are administered centrally, it would seem natural to run physical culture on the same lines" (1980: 19).

Initial suspicions about the competitive element of sport being a reflection and relic of capitalism disappeared completely by the 1930s – a fact probably not unrelated to the military potential of sport training glimpsed in the First World War. By the early 1950s, competition and record-breaking excellence had been given priority by Stalin's regime. After that, sport was used to fulfill a number of functions, none of them strikingly new, though the way in which the Soviet state co-ordinated them made them seem that way. For example, there's nothing unusual in a nation using sport as a means of obtaining the kind of physically fit and co-operative workforce that complements economic efficiency and military strength. The very origins of sport lie in this complementarity. In recent times, this function hasn't been fanfared in the West, although Stephen Jones, writing on British state intervention in sport, notices how, "for wartime policy-makers, leisure was directly related to military aims and objectives" (1987: 164).

The Soviet system consciously employed sports as a way of improving general standards of health and hygiene, by educating people about the benefits of exercise and nutrition. A healthy working population is more effective than a sick one. Similar uses of sport have been made by many industrial societies: sometimes the initiative has come from management, as in Japan where exercise sessions are integrated in the working day; and sometimes from workers' organizations, as in the endorsement of Britain's Trades Union Council of a National Fitness campaign in the 1930s.

Any society that is industrialized has had to negotiate the bumps and jolts that accompany a mass movement of population from rural areas into the cities. The transitions were accompanied by the growth of organized sport in Western Europe and the USA. Team sport in particular helped smooth the passage, gathering people together and unifying them with the *esprit de corps* that competitive sport elicits. Team sports were made focal points during the

USSR's industrialization; they encouraged the communal identification with representative teams that was ultimately crucial to internal stability. One further function of sport in the longer term was a buffing up of the image of the Soviet system abroad. Tony Mason sums up, stating that, by the 1950s, "sport in the Soviet Union had come to have a similar function to that which it had in the capitalist West: to improve physical fitness, provide mass entertainment, gain support for the regime and build international prestige" (1988: 101).

In employing sport to fulfill these three basic functions, the Soviet system did not deviate from Western patterns, though the depth of state penetration meant that the functions were much more centrally controlled and promoted. This was manifest in state-initiated policies and active programs, like GTO, or *Gotov k trudu i oborne* (ready for labor and defense) which began in the 1930s and which was aimed at involving young people and, later, children in some form of disciplined sport. Sport, or physical culture was integrated in educational curricula and institutes of physical education were established for those showing aptitude and needing to specialize in order to develop it. A whole structure of establishments was built to accommodate a range of interests and capabilities. Institutes of physical culture laid special emphasis not only on practical elements but also on the theoretical foundations of sport and the scientific analysis of sport, and sporting performance became an accepted scholarly pursuit some years before its acceptance in the West. Institutes of higher learning, while not specializing in sport, demanded of their students some mastery of a sport, in the same way as they would demand a qualification in chemistry and languages. This suggests the significance attached to sports, which, according to Riordan, "has been regarded as too important to be left to the whim of private clubs with restricted entrance, commercial promoters, circus entrepreneurs and foreigners" (1982: 226). His observation is a general one. States have decided that sport is of strategic value and deserving of political attention, assistance, and planning.

One almost inevitable consequence of this has been a bureaucratization of sport. There is no chance of some penniless youngster making his or her way to the local park, borrowing a pair of training shoes and turning on a display that has a scout reaching for professional contracts. One-off "discoveries" never just happened in the Soviet system: sporting prowess was cultivated through an ever-specializing series of academic and vocational establishments, each stage being carefully controlled and monitored by state agencies that had the latest developments in sports science and technology at their fingertips. The reason they had it at their fingertips was that sport-related research was continually funded and highly concentrated. Physical and psychological profiles were matched with apposite events at an early age. And the fruits of all this were obvious.

The athletic pre-eminence of the USSR for a 30-year period ending in 1991 is unquestioned, but the German Democratic Republic's progress in international terms has also been impressive, especially so in the light of its lack of natural resources and small population compared to its former Soviet partner. Basically, the reasons for sport's importance in the USSR hold good for the GDR. Although lacking in military strength, the GDR opted for a mighty sport's program as an *alternative* way of commanding international respect rather than as an adjunct. As we have seen, a vigorous sporting tradition was already well-established in Germany thanks to the Weimar government and, before this, the nineteenth-century Turner movement. From the 1950s, sport was incorporated into education up to university level, where participation in some events was made compulsory. But education was only one area: trade unions, the police, and the military were all made to develop sports divisions, again not as adjuncts but as integral parts of their structures.

The flagship of the GDR program was the University of Physical Culture, opened in Leipzig in 1950. By 1975 it had attracted 2,000 students. Some measure of the effect, of this was gauged one year later at the Montreal Olympics of 1976, when the GDR's medal haul suggested its arrival as an international power to compare to the USA and USSR. A study around the same time attempted to quantify this: it divided countries according to size of population and measured the per capita output of world-class sports performers. The GDR had 17 million people in its total population; about the same as California. John Bale, the study's author, concluded that Finland edged the GDR out of first place with the USSR way down in fifteenth place, one spot above Britain (1982). Tempering this is the fact that excellence achieved by the GDR was in a relatively narrow range of sports: world-class competitors tended to specialize in gymnastics, soccer, track and field events, and particularly swimming. The military emphasis of sport is reflected in the GDR's redoubtable record in shooting and riding.

Some critics have argued that children were tramlined into very narrow and specific areas and given little chance to develop imaginative skills and capacities in other aspects of sport. Related to this is the problem – if, indeed, it *is* a problem – of compulsion. This is applicable not only to the GDR but to all former and present communist countries, Cuba included, that place onerous pressures on children to reach proficiency in sport. Inevitably, many will fail and fall by the wayside; those who succeed will train more intensely. Westerners might find the high level of participation in sport artificial because it is compulsory. Those brought up to accept a more voluntary conception of sport, in which the individual freely chooses whether or not to participate, find the Soviet method unacceptable as sport – at least in the Corinthian sense of the word.

But the historical ideal referenced in Chapter 4 is not applicable in the Soviet context: sport did not have connotations of free will, individual expression, and conscious choice. It was approached very much as Westerners might approach physics or geography; as an integral part of the curriculum which children were made to study. If children showed aptitude, then they would be favored to attend specialist establishments where potential could be developed and exploited. Their position in society would be as sports performers: not people who were good at certain sports, but people who were state-financed as specialists in a valued occupation and whose successes would reflect favorably on the entire system.

Soviet sport had no need to wrestle with the problem of amateurism, or shamateurism. Physical culture had not been conceived as a ludic pursuit distinct from work or education. As a central part of social and political life, it was approached with a seriousness that would have been abhorrent to Westerners until quite recently. Contrasts with Western sport, which is ostensibly meant to be enjoyed rather than assiduously worked-at or even bred-for, have given rise to pejorative stereotypes. David Triesman captures one typical image of Soviet female athletes: "Drug-soaked, electrically-stimulated, manly women, who've been whiteslaved into sport from the cradle" (1984: 26–7). This is a ludicrous exaggeration, but one with perhaps some truth concealed in it. Athletes haven't been "slaved" into sport; but they have been selected at an early age and ushered toward specialist training on the basis of formative physiological and psychological analyses.

Valery Borzov, the Ukrainian sprinter who reigned supreme for a period in the 1970s, is usually cited as the computerized athlete par excellence because he was screened as a child and given the benefit of every scientific training facility in his progress. His entire career was supported by continuous state assistance; as was that of any top Soviet sports performer. Such programs have been criticized as dehumanizing and tyrannical; a state-centralized control of sport meant no room for individual choice or freedom of expression. The fact that there has been little dissent from Borzov *et al.* is dismissed as the product of fear.

The voluntary conception seems to be isolated by the Soviet methods of selection and planning. There's no evidence one way or the other to indicate whether the child or youth had much autonomous choice within the parameters set by the state. But how realistic is it to view the typical Western youth as unrestricted in choice, given the kind of social and historical constraints considered elsewhere in this book? Questions of loyalty, commitment, and obligation enter into the equation when we try to identify factors in the typical Soviet performer's motivation. The prospect of status or prestige may have loomed larger than material rewards. For many Western youths the prospect of material and status success in sport is often the only one they have.

They certainly exercise choice, but often within very limited frameworks of opportunities.

This in itself is ultimately a political issue of sports, but of more immediate relevance is the intrusion of the state. Those who oppose the large-scale assistance of athletes by the state usually lapse into a *laissez-faire* idealism in which state interference is minimized. They would cite the collapse of the USSR as an example of the monstrous consequences of *dirigisme*, a policy in which the state plans and directs all social and economic matters – a total politicization of sport.

But, even in the birthplace of organized sport, the idea of state involvement is not so odd. Stephen Jones's study traces the origins of state involvement to the nineteenth century. By the early twentieth century, the principle was well-established in Britain. Jones argues that "state intervention took two forms: first, covert legislative control; and second, overt governmental manipulation for political purposes" (1987: 176).

He gives details of the national and local-level legislation covering sport and the more general area of leisure from the 1920s onwards, adding that "such an official framework necessitated state intervention." The "most direct piece of interventionist legislation was the Physical Training and Recreation Act of 1937." This was by no means the first legislation aimed at achieving "a better standard of physical development in adults," but it was certainly the most ambitious to date, providing more facilities and offering more opportunities. Recent memories of the war would not have taken much reawakening and the fear of repetition was clearly a motivating factor behind the Act. Money was spent encouraging the population to exercise more, especially in the swimming pool: between 1937 and 1939, the government approved local authority plans to spend £3 million on public pools. Tennis courts, football pitches, and bowling greens were also subject to government initiatives. The central state was involved not only in funding, but in elevating the position of physical education in schools' curricula. PE, which later became synonymous with sport, was established as part of a proper, balanced educational program.

The most significant development in modern times has been the Sports Council which was granted its Royal Charter in 1971 with the remit to build bridges between the various voluntary organizations handling particular sports and the more general bodies like the British Olympic Association and the Central Council of Physical Recreation, the bureaucracy of which was eventually taken over by the Sports Council. Financed by the Department of the Environment, the Sports Council was a quasi-governmental organization ("quango"), with sufficient autonomy to make strategic decisions affecting both commercial and public sectors. It continues to formulate policy, nationally and regionally, and gives advice and financial support to all manner of organizations whether amateur or professional. Its original wide focus, which included promoting sport as a family activity, narrowed after the urban disorders of the early 1980s and, in recent years, its cardinal concern has been with working-class inner city youths.

As well as targeting groups and involving them in sport, the British Sports Council is charged with responsibility for centers of excellence geared to the needs of top-flight sports performers who require specialist coaching and training. It also gives assistance to specific governing bodies in sport to create and support national representative teams, an arrangement which has enhanced its own power and reduced that of individual sports organizations. Many sports are virtually dependent on continuous aid from the Sports Council. It has become the state's main vehicle for financing and affecting the overall development of sport in Britain. The USA has no need for such an organization, of course: its role is superfluous in a country where colleges and universities are conveyor belts leading directly to professional clubs. State-funded institutions typically have grand athletics programs geared to the provision of facilities and coaching for the stars of tomorrow.

Returning to Jones, whose interest is specific to the interwar years, we find other forms of state intervention, "political manipulation," in a number of areas. Earlier in this chapter, we identified some issues in which governments were prepared to become involved, sometimes quite deeply. The English soccer team's matches against Germany in the mid-1930s were alive with political interest. Slightly earlier, in 1933, England's returning cricketers were summoned to the prime minister after their notorious "bodyline" tour of Australia. Their punishing tactics had bruised not only Australian batsmen, but also politicians, who ventured to call diplomatic relations into question. In the 1980s, the government's attempt to abort Britain's entry to the Moscow Olympics was a major political interference set against a background of diplomatic strains. The South Africa affair has been covered in detail.

Yet the main form of manipulation has come about not so much as a result of international tension, but of domestic disorder – or, more precisely, the prospect of it. There has been no hesitation by governments to overrule sporting bodies and make pronouncements, such as in 1922 when a heavyweight boxing contest between the white Joe Beckett and black Battling Siki was prohibited because of the dangers of the "color issue." Soccer games were forbidden for periods on the ground that they threatened public order, though the imprisonment of seven boys who were playing street football in Glasgow in 1933 seemed an over-reaction. Successive governments to the present day have directly intervened in sports affairs, often in defiance of the governing organizations in sport and public opinion; the implementation of an identity card system for English soccer in 1989 presents a modern illustration.

Control and manipulation: these two terms describe the methods of state intervention and reflect the political nature of sport, certainly in the UK and most probably in the Western world generally. Critics of the Soviet system of state-planning control and co-ordination of activities too often ignore the true extent of political involvement in sport in the West in the futile effort to establish its autonomy, an autonomy that is, as we have seen, largely mythical. The Western world still can't see a mirror image of itself when it faces the Cubans or North Koreans. What it can see are trends, tendencies, and instances that might appear to contradict traditional notions of sport, but which have been incorporated with requisite changes into Western systems.

It is too glib a generalization to say that the conception of sport adopted by the former Soviet societies is something of a model which Western systems will emulate. But both systems have accommodated the idea of sports performers training and competing on a full-time basis with a reimbursement for their time and effort. Whereas the state was once wholly responsible for making this possible in the Soviet system, a combination of public funding and private sponsorship operates in the West.

All the other features that make the old Soviet system appear distinct and, to some, a type of "white slavery" including its integration of sport into formal education curricula, have counterparts in the West. The USA has prestigious sports scholarships which attract specialist sports performers. In Britain, sports academies are being established for that elite group of pupils who warrant the label sporting prodigy. The Football Association's National School and the International Sports College are two examples. The West might have taken a while to cotton on to the idea that plucking raw talent and shaping it isn't necessarily as harsh and pitiless as some might have supposed after viewing the emaciated Olga Korbut in her early twenties, only a few years after her Olympic triumphs. But in the 1980s, the system of early selection was adopted by many Western nations.

This leads directly to questions about the future of sport. Is the convergence between the Soviet and Western systems set to continue? The final part of this chapter has shown that the development of sport in the East and West has not had widely dissimilar trajectories, despite fundamentally different ideologies, which have been reflected in the organization of sport. Sport has been afforded importance and has been addressed by the state accordingly. But will state involvement in the West intensify and with what consequences?

These are the kinds of questions that discussions of sport and politics inevitably throw up. Questions about whether or not they can be kept separate are non-starters when we consider the intertwining of politics and sport. The big issues like South Africa and boycotts have managed to seize the headlines, but political influence in sport is pervasive and usually not worthy of sustained media coverage which is presumably the reason why many assume that sport, for the most part, remains unaffected by politics when the opposite is true.

Sport and International Politics by Barrie Houlihan (Harvester Wheatsheaf, 1994) is an excellent analysis of the interconnections between sport and politics and an argument that situates sport in the wider political terrain; it is complemented by the selection of extracts collected in part 8, "Sport and Politics: The international dimensions" of *Sport in Contemporary Society: An anthology*, 4th edn, edited by Stanley Eitzen (St Martin's, 1993).

Olympic Politics by Christopher Hill (Manchester University Press, 1992) is a history of the underside of the Olympic games, including the boycotts, bans, political controversies and the machinations behind the bids for the games. Hill also examines the commercialism that has swept through the games, particularly since 1976.

Power and Ideology in American Sport by George Sage (Human Kinetics, 1990) has a chapter "Sport and the state," in which the author reminds us: "American expenditures of an estimated $1 billion [£625 million] per year for promoting national unity through sport raises the specter of distorted priorities. It is possible that national unity could be more appropriately promoted by raising the standard of living of the downtrodden."

The Revolt of the Black Athlete by Harry Edwards (Free Press, 1970) documents the build-up to the Smith–Carlos gesture at Mexico. What might have seemed to be a piece of rash judgement was actually a carefully prepared and executed operation against a background of civil unrest in the USA. As a case-study of the political uses of politics, this stands the test of time better than any other.

ASSIGNMENT

You are a national volleyball manager-coach in the final stages of your squad's preparation for a major international tournament to be attended by the world's volleyball powers. In a newspaper feature profiling one of the squad's outstanding attacking players, he/she reveals that he/she is a member of the *Order*, a group opposed to what it calls ZOG (Zionist Occupation Government) and which, as the newspaper journalist uncovers, has links or sympathies with the Ku Klux Klan, the Posse Comitatus, the Nazi Parties of Britain and the USA, and other anti-Semitic and racist groups. What is the likely fall-out and how will you, as manager-coach, deal with it?

Chapter thirteen

Things to come
The future of sports

We began this book with the question "Why?" We finish with "What happens next?" One of the conclusions of this book is that sports have mutated into products. Whatever they once were, they are now packaged and distributed in a manner not dissimilar to any other commodity that can be bought and sold. So, like other products, sport is subject to marginal differentiation and renewal. Sport is not a uniform practice: it has evolved into hybrid forms: skiing, for instance, has several variations. A whole palette of activities is being produced, each slightly different from the others. Some, like the American *Gladiators*, owe far more to showbusiness than they do to traditional sports, but the suspicion grows that this type of event is leading rather than following sports.

This type of show, manufactured specifically for television viewers, is actually quite an instructive case-study. It wouldn't have been possible without a culture in which (a) television is all-pervasive and (b) physical fitness is a popular ideal. It seems only yesterday that we were talking of the cult of the body: a preoccupation with health, good looks and the general well-being that comes through physical fitness. It doesn't matter where you are reading this book: chances are there is a gym, health club or similar within two miles. But, the latest effort is not simply to be fit and healthy, but to exhibit this. The tv show trades off the willingness of ordinary

consumers to pit themselves against fully trained professional gladiators in full view of millions of viewers.

You might be tempted into assuming that a culture that relies so heavily on television to replenish itself would encourage passivity and possibly inertia as more and more people sit vegetating in front of the tube. But that same culture places a high value on health and so coaxes its viewers off their couches and into the gyms or onto the streets. Interest in sports shows no signs of abating.

As for the changes we can anticipate, I group them into two sections, the first dealing with the people who we will be watching and following in the future, the second dealing with how we will be watching and how they will be playing.

Patterns of participation

In Chapters 6 and 7 we identified two groups, one of which (blacks) has been severely overrepresented in sport, the other of which (women) has been underrepresented. One doesn't need to be a blithe and blind optimist to imagine a gradual tailing off of the enormous participation of blacks in sport. It's a virtual equation of our times that fewer blacks in sports equals less racism in society at large. So, if you're going to predict a decline in racism, then you're going to have to take account of a few less Patrick Ewings and Emmitt Smiths. But is this strictly true? Racism and equal opportunities are related but not invariably correlated in the sense that a decrease in one always implies an increase in the other. It's possible to see the erection of equal opportunity (eo) apparatuses and a proliferation of eo policies – as we have in both Europe and the USA – without necessarily seeing an end to racism. As I disclosed in my book *The Logic of Racism* (1987), the same poison comes in assorted shaped bottles. In other words, people can harbor racist views and values but may not allow these to affect their day-to-day lives, nor the routines of the organizations in which they operate.

I don't necessarily foresee racism being ground down by eo policies, though I do see an opening up of choices for ethnic minorities. The obstacles to progress in education, and especially work, will come clattering down as if hit by an inept hurdler. As more blacks find their way into careers and climb to senior positions, one of the necessary conditions for their entry into sport will go: that of blocked opportunities. Debate over the merits and demerits of sports scholarships will go on. Serious questions have already been raised about the desirability of using educational benefits to draw young blacks out of one ghetto into what may be another. One of the many consequences of this will be a loss in the mesmeric power of sport. It will cease to attract black youths seeking a stable career simply because it isn't stable and, for the overwhelming majority, it isn't a career either. To use Jack Olsen again, it's a meaningless dream. Over the next several years it will be recognized as precisely that.

The position of women is almost the reverse in that they have been forcibly prevented from competing in sport at the highest level. Now we're firmly in the postfeminist era, the archaic images of gentle femininity which were essential to women's subordination have been well and truly eroded, though not destroyed – they've demonstrated a tough resilience. Still, women in sports have contributed appreciably to the onslaught, clocking great times on track and field events, posting significant victories in many individual sports, and showing impressive form in team games like rugby and basketball, which were once utterly dominated by men. Chances are they won't achieve the same standards as men without the stimulus of open competition, but their progress will be accelerated by the greater number of women entering competitive sport on a serious basis.

Again, one doesn't have to draw any conclusions about society at large from this. Women are chipping away at myths about their biological status and are proving the equals of their male counterparts in significant areas of employment as well as sport. This won't translate automatically into a drop in sexism or sexual discrimination, but it will open a few more doors for what was once regarded as the "gentle sex."

Women still haven't achieved parity in terms of salaries and wages. But they're getting there slowly. Equally slowly, they're pushing their way into hallowed areas. One of the most prominent bastions of male supremacy in British sport, namely the MCC, may yet be overhauled. Marylebone Cricket Club, whose doors were closed to women throughout its 200-odd-year existence, in 1989 circulated its 18,000 members with a newsletter suggesting, albeit gently, that, as women now had voting rights and equal opportunities, they might also be allowed access to the club's venerated Long Room. England's "ladies' team" was allowed in for two one-day internationals. Besides Lords, only Manchester's Old Trafford continued to bar women. With one-half of the old guard considering the change, it could mean a very significant breakthrough for women.

Quite apart from the crumbling of male institutions, there is the cash incentive for women. Currently, not many sports offer women the chance of riches, nor perhaps even bread-and-butter. Successful careers in golf, tennis, or track athletics are exceptions. Yet, as women's sport gains in popularity, as it surely will, the money will become available and this will enhance the attractiveness of sport. Equal opportunity policies will diminish the chances of young blacks going into sport, but in an entirely different manner it will pave the way for more young females, of all ethnic backgrounds, to sink their efforts into a sports career.

> **Sport for the disabled**
>
> In its original conception competitive sport for the disabled was intended as an unconventional form of rehabilitation. Its inspirer Sir Ludwig Guttman, who set up the spinal injuries unit at Stoke Mandeville Hospital in England in 1944, set up the first organized meeting involving patients from different rehabilitation centers in 1948. At first the meets were informal, but international teams were soon attracted by the idea and regular competition led to more organization. The British Sports Association for the Disabled (BSAD) was formed in 1961 and began co-ordinating with what became known as the Paralympic movement. Olympiads specifically for the disabled were held to coincide with Olympic meetings and, on all but two occasions after 1960 (Mexico 1966; Moscow 1980) countries hosting Olympic games also hosted an international event for the disabled. The 1976 games in Canada included events for the blind and partially sighted, paraplegics, tetraplegics and amputees. Later, they were joined by those with cerebral palsy and les autres. From its original idea sport for the disabled turned into genuine competition rather than a method of rehabilitation.

We can barely mention eo without considering the senior citizenry. Once seen as a young person's turf, sport has never discriminated on the basis of age, though there were murmurings in the early 1990s that pro boxing should impose an upper age limit on its license holders for their own safety. Thank goodness it didn't, or we would have been deprived of the almost unbelievable sight of George Foreman recapturing the world heavyweight title at the age of 45, a full 20 years after he had lost it to Muhammad Ali. Admittedly, Foreman's achievement was made possible by a dismally poor champion and nondescript contenders, but it was still a triumph of historic importance. Becoming a world champion in any sport at an age when many are studying seed catalogs and wheezing as they reach the top of their stairs is accomplishment enough; but to do so in boxing is startling.

Foreman was a wrinkly icon of the 1990s, but a lesser-known athlete equalled his performance in her own way: 42-year-old Yekaterina Podkopayeva of Russia was the world's number one ranked female 1,500 meters runner of 1994 and one of only two to break four minutes. In head-to-heads over the season, she finished 3–2 against Sonia O'Sullivan, 26, the Irish world silver medal winner, and 2–1 against Hassiba Boulmerka, 26, the Algerian Olympic champion. She was rejected by her agent Jos Hermens as too old when she first approached him at the age of 38. Hermens realized his error and signed her only after she had demonstrated her worth.

Foreman and Podkopayeva have shattered the received wisdom that there is an aging process that begins to affect sports competitors at about 30 and sets into a steep decline at 35. Most contemporary sports scientists reject the concept of an attrition that occurs independently of cultural definitions. But cultural definitions are extremely powerful: in the West we're accustomed to expecting the peak years of a top-class sports performer to be between the ages of 24 and 28, with maybe three years latitude either way. Performers themselves have their perceptions and expectations structured by the culture of which they are part: they, as much as anyone else, do not expect to scale the heights after the age of 30 at max. Their response is to limit their horizons.

A corresponding drop in motivation yields irregular quality training and less determination to succeed in competition. When those cultural conventions are absent, the horizons are less apparent. Miruts Yifter, for instance, came from Ethiopia: he won two gold medals at the 1980 summer Olympics at an uncertain age, but thought to be as high as 43. Marathon runners are conventionally thought to mature late; Carlos Lopes must have had this in mind when he set a world's best time for the distance at the age of 32. Physiologically, there is a decline in muscular power and flexibility; but this typically occurs in the late 40s. The bell-curve-shaped career parabola of most sports performers is a product of our thinking rather than our aging.

Sheer demographic changes have forced us to rethink our ideas about age: advances in health care and medicine, a better understanding of nutrition and an elimination of the harshest aspects of poverty have produced a growing population of over-60s, many of whom are vibrant and alive to the widening possibilities of later life. Changing ideas about age have their counterpart in sports. No one doubts that Foreman and Podkopayeva are exceptional, but the effect of their triumphs is that we might not regard a world boxing champion or an Olympic track gold medalist of, say, 36, as extraordinary.

Joe Montana may have been past his best when he traded to Kansas City Chiefs in 1993; he was also returning from serious injury. Yet there was never any doubt that he would make a valuable contribution to the Chiefs over the next few years. The traditional roadsign reading "Retirement – 2 years" that most competitors are meant to see when they hit 30 may still be there. The difference is that, nowadays, more and more are just ignoring it and this means that the distinction between veterans and all others is becoming less obvious.

The unseen malefactor called Aids is no respecter of distinctions at all: blacks, whites; women, men; young, old – all are targets. In the 1980s, the HIV virus spread and mutated at a rate that simply left medical science stranded. No cure and only limited and expensive treatments were discovered. The only way to handle the prospect of Aids was to change lifestyles; forget the heady days of the 1960s and 1970s, when promiscuity was all but commended. In the late 1980s, the call was for "safe sex" – stable, monogamous relationships or (possibly, and) condoms. Showbusiness has already had a number of Aids victims, but the world of sport has so far escaped relatively lightly. Magic Johnson's stunning revelation ushered in more, including former tennis player Arthur Ashe.

Sports themselves have to develop procedures for ensuring that the pandemic cannot spread through the physical contact that many events entail. In Britain, a professional Colombian boxer Ruben Palacios was prevented from fighting after he tested positive for HIV prior to a scheduled match. This is a sport in which facial cuts are frequent and close exchanges make it possible to ingest one's opponent's blood via the mouth, or possibly the eyes. Hence infection is very possible.

Other sports don't carry such risks, but many involve personal contact and others, like swimming, involve the chance of absorbing others' body fluids. And, while the chances of contracting Aids in the pool are remote, one wonders how many of Greg Louganis's rivals at the 1988 summer Olympics would have followed him had they known that the double gold medalist, who cut his head and spilled blood attempting a reverse two-and-half pike during a preliminary round, had been diagnosed HIV positive six months before. In 1995, Louganis disclosed in his autobiography, *Breaking the Surface*, how he had kept his secret from fans and the governing bodies in sports. The doctor who treated Louganis's wound did not wear protective gloves, though latex or polyurethane materials through which particles as small as HIV viruses can't pass are now used in a variety of ways in sports. Mandatory Aids-testing procedures are bound to become as commonplace as drug testing in a great many sports.

The shape of sports

And so to changes in the shape of sport itself, its content, administration and rules. A key point to bear in mind is that the sources of such changes are most likely to lie outside the formal structure of sports itself. Television, as we have seen, has upped its influence, particularly over the past 25 years. It now virtually governs some sports. Many changes will surely come about as the result of television's insistence. The ones that don't will still have a pronounced commercial inflexion.

Contractual changes

One of the conventions in sport has been broken by the steady but inexorable commercialization process: that is, that sport is a unique industry and should not be bound or evaluated by standards applicable to other areas of commercial activity. Everything covered in this book points to the opposite. And, as if further proof was needed, we can point to the rise of free agency as the vindication of sports as a market. Many professional sports performers now have the same kind of freedom to select employers and negotiate conditions of service as other employees. In the USA, most major sports have recognized the antitrust implications of signing players to lifelong contracts with no "get-out" clauses; and players out-of-contract are now free agents. The proliferation of football trades in the early 1990s indicated that the NFL was like a well-shaken can of soda: once the ring was ripped off, the contents gushed out all over the place. Moon to Minnesota, Sanders to Dallas, Montana to Kansas and so on.

The introduction of free agency to sports has brought sports performers into line with other paid employees. Major League Baseball is rather anomalous in this respect: it enjoys a unique monopoly status, partly the result of history and partly the result of its refusal to disperse power. A committee of club owners makes decisions on practically everything, including salary caps and franchise distribution. To minimize the risk of bidding wars pushing up players' salaries (which average $1 million, or £625,000 p.a.), young players have been indentured for many years to minor league teams owned by the major teams. When the owners were finally forced to agree to a limited free agent system in the 1980s, they continued to conspire among themselves to hold down salaries and were fined $280 million (£175 million) in 1990 for their collusion. Baseball's exemption from antitrust laws and from government regulation is either at or somewhere very near the center of the labor problems, including the $600 million (£375 million) loss-making strike of 1994/5.

Baseball is not the only sport that will come under pressure to organize itself in a way that reflects other industries. Soccer has, for years, operated an indentureship system in which players are tied to a club even when out of contract. Unlike in the States, where a player may be traded without a fee being charged by the club from which the player leaves, a soccer club will typically offer a lump sum, a series of phased payments or a player plus money in exchange for the services of the player it wants. Technically, the transfer fee, as it is called, is compensation for the unexpired portion of a player's contract, but effectively the player is not free to move even when his contract is completed.

Sometimes, players profit hugely from this. A transfer fee of £8 million ($12.8 million) is not uncommon for a top-class player, who – if he has not requested the transfer himself – will be entitled to a 10 percent slice of the gross, £800,000 ($1.28 million). Other times, the player who seeks to move to a club offering him more attractive salary and conditions may be stuck because the buying and selling club can't agree on a fee. The latter case scenario will prove troublesome for European soccer in particular over the coming years. The legality of doubly locking a player to a ball club through contract and transfer fee restrictions was tested by Jean-Marc Bosman, a player for the Belgian club RC Liegeois, who argued that this was in violation of the Treaty of Rome, which allowed freedom of employment, and was prepared to take this to the European Court.

Whether soccer will remain an exception to other European-wide rules that affect labor and industry is in doubt. Should the transfer fee be abolished, three developments are possible. First, clubs will seal players into contracts that cover the prime years of their playing careers, possibly of ten years or more, and at very high salary rates. Second, a tiny clique of clubs will consolidate their already strong position in soccer's elite. Transfer fees are a valuable source of revenue for smaller clubs who face being stripped of their best players with nothing in return, unless they align themselves as "feeder clubs" or nurseries for richer clubs, as is the case in the NHL and MLB. The third is that soccer will try to temper this elitism by imposing caps on the gross salaries they are allowed to pay out collectively to players and on the number of players registered at any one time. The NFL model is the obvious one to follow.

Sleaze

As we saw in Chapters 9 and 10, sport is not just like business it *is* business. Business, of course, has its sleazier aspects. It would be unusual if they were absent from sports. Corruption in sport is not new: the 1919 baseball World Series was marred by the most famous "fix" in history when eight Chicago White Sox players were indicted for allegedly having agreed to lose the series to the Cincinatti Reds in return for money. Gamblers had used a go-between to contact the players and laid out serious money on the Reds. The eight were ultimately acquitted after the confessions of three players went "missing." The episode is the subject of John Sayles's movie *Eight Men Out*.

In 1965, ten professional soccer players in Britain were jailed for trying to fix games on which they had bet. Three prominent players, including England international representatives Peter Swan and Tony Kay, were imprisoned for four months for conspiracy to defraud. Bookmakers stopped taking bets on individual games. The 1976 summer Olympics at Montreal were bedevilled by accusations of kickbacks before even the opening ceremony. Three years later, the Italian soccer star Paulo Rossi was at the center of a game-rigging scandal. Interestingly, Rossi was permitted to play for the Italian team that won the World Cup in 1982. British soccer club Arsenal's general manager, George Graham, was fired in 1995 after becoming embroiled in a complex and recondite case in which payments known as "bungs" were received not for rigging games but for facilitating the transfer (trading) of players. In 1995, three England-based soccer pros were arrested by detectives investigating allegations of bribery and game fixing by East Asian gambling syndicates.

Perhaps the seediest case in soccer's history involved the French club Olympique Marseilles, which was accused of attempting to bribe members of the Valenciennes club against whom it played in a French championship game in 1993. For the club's owner, Bernard Tapie, it was the latest in a line of legal difficulties that left him bankrupt and ineligible for public office. The case even involved a French politician, who admitted that he perjured himself to cover up for Tapie. Even the hallowed sport of gentlemen and players could not escape the punishing penalties of commerce: the Pakistani team was accused of easing up in a game of cricket in 1995.

Rossi's "slap-on-the-wrist" punishment was a virtual condonation, the verdict being effectively that fraud in sports is not the same as real fraud. It seemed as unsatisfactory in the 1970s as it does today. The difference is that now we are accustomed to it. Sport is big business and it would be unwise to expect it to remain above change; in a relatively short period of time sport's previously recognized distinctness has gone. It is now seen as an area where deals are done, fixes go in and money corrupts just as effectively as any other sphere of commercial activity. Perhaps it has been a feature of contemporary professional sports for decades and we have only recently started to recognize its scale; hence our alarm. What we can be sure of is that there is more to come. All major sports, and maybe some minor ones, will have their sleaze unearthed as journalists and investigators become more vigilant. Sport has long since lost its innocence; now its worldly aspect will be opened up for general inspection.

Law

It's almost logical that, if sports expose their dirty linen, launderers from the outside are going to step in. Already in this book we have referred to the cases of Reynolds, Cantona and Bosman among others who have been at the center of legal disputes of one kind or another. Try as sports may to contain their deviance, there are now legal specialists in sport who are poised to deepen their involvement in areas once governed by sports organizations. Lawyers are already key personnel in sports. In the USA, baseball, basketball, hockey and football all have qualified lawyers as their commissioners. British administrators have resisted this, but such are the legal complexities of contemporary sports that they will not be able to do so for much longer.

Television

Broadcast tv in the United States and Britain has been under some pressure from the cable/satellite networks, whose subscriptions enable them to stage sports events on the grandest of scales. I use "stage" because tv has become a prime mover in many events, approaching sports promoters and making money available to them. Many sports events would be inconceivable without the active interest of television companies and the cables have pursued their interest aggressively. Home Box Office (HBO) has landed many coups often to the chagrin of the big broadcast networks – and the non-cabled viewing population. In addition to its table d'hôte fare at a fixed price it offers its subscribers à la carte choices of sumptuous events – not only major sports contests, but new films. In return it asks the viewers to pay extra money for the particular event. If you watch the latest title fight, you order it and have $40 (£25) or so painlessly extracted from your monthly subscription account. There are grounds for believing that more of the big sports events could be annexed from the terrestrial networks' possession over the next few years; which will lead to a pay-per-view delivery of events to the screens of subscribers only.

This is a more specific subtrend in what is already a major movement: tv taking control of sport. The trend has been discussed in previous chapters and speculation on the future can only project more of the same. Money from the media is no longer a welcome supplement to most sports coffers: it is the main source of revenue. It requires little analysis to conclude that the arrangement will lead to a greater asymmetry of power in which "he who pays the piper ... ".

There is nothing too evil or corrosive about this; some people will pay to watch sport and other people will make money from it. The important indeterminacy of sport will always prevent it from becoming just another branch of showbusiness, even if the methods of its marketing suggest very close similarities. Some traditional sports, wrestling being the obvious example, have been transformed into sheer theater. But there the theatrical element has replaced the indeterminacy and modern wrestling has long ceased to be a legitimate competitive sport, despite the protestations of some of its followers. Competitive Graeco-Roman wrestling still exists, but as a very minor Olympic event; Sumo has begun to enjoy cult status outside its native Japan.

Other pursuits, which aren't certifiable sports, are worried by the possibility of the opposite process once television takes an interest. Mountaineering, a practice that pitches co-operative teamwork and intricate human craft against obdurate natural forces, is presently being reminted for the screen. The painstakingly long and studious negotiation of rock faces do not make for dramatic watching, so a more febrile competitive event is promised with individuals or small teams asked to race each other to given destinations. Archery, one of the most ancient of sports, is one of the most recent recipients of television's attentions. What was once an all-day event with direct lines of descent from the medieval tournaments is being squeezed into a more tv-friendly format. These are illustrative cases, as they will compress slow and exacting processes into relatively short competitive bursts. One-day cricket, 12-round boxing, and international rules squash *sans* the server-only-scores rule are instances of how television has tampered with rules so as to make events shorter and more exciting. The enlargement of soccer's goal frames by a couple of feet to encourage more goals and boost viewers' interest has already been discussed by FIFA and, though it was shot down, it may yet resurface.

For reasons to do with sovereignty one of television's potentially genuine contributions to the enrichment of "live" sports is likely to be stymied by governing bodies which are willing to protect the discretionary power of their referees in matters of fine judgement. The replay experiment in football was officially a failure and it's unlikely to be restored in the foreseeable future. The rule entitled teams to question a referee's call in certain situations; a panel of replay judges would then review a slo-mo of the incident and either endorse or overrule the referee. It eliminated dubious decisions, but added to the length of the game, which was the official reason for its failure. One suspects that another reason was that the authority of game officials was seriously undermined every time a judgement was reversed and, as replay judges became more adept and sped up the process, officials would be further compromised. In the mid-1990s, British soccer was faced with a similar dilemma: whether to enhance fair play or stay loyal to game officials and allow referees to maintain their sovereignty over the whole field of play. Television "requested" soccer to consider equipping game officials with radio transmitters. Ultimately, its next "request" will determine how the dilemma will be resolved.

Other sports, including tennis and cricket, employ supervisory referees to oversee umpires and players and they observe games on tv monitors to gain variety of perspective. Tennis has embraced new technology with the Cyclops machine that aids line calls. The resistance of referees in sports where this is not established practice is understandable, though not always justifiable. Boxing, for example, is riven with concerns for safety and referees are increasingly asked to make decisions that are clearly outside their sphere of expertise. They may solicit the advice of a qualified medical officer on matters of cuts and other injuries; the medical officer may also intervene between rounds. But, essentially, the referee has full control of the proceedings and, in Britain, the ref is also the sole judge of domestic title and nontitle fights. Boxing has been slow to harness science and technology to its regulatory framework. At some point in the future, a medical overseer seated at ringside, with access to a tv monitor and power to overrule referees will be considered. And, as surely as night follows day, referees will issue declamations.

Professionalism

As water washes against stone, one expected television to take its time in affecting the hardiest of amateur sports. The British, as we saw, invented the concept of the amateur, exported it to other parts of the globe and, in the case of Rugby Union, hung on to it as long as possible. But, in 1995, with Rupert Murdoch-owned News Corporation's £370 million ($590 million) deal with Australia, New Zealand and South Africa completed, rugby brought to an end the age of amateurism.

As we have seen, amateurism was less a principle – that of competing for sheer love and enjoyment – more of a form of class distinction: a way of separating upper-middle-class gentlemen and working-class players. Gentlemen could afford more leisure time while players would receive compensation for missing time from work. It was always a distinction bound to spawn anomalies; especially as spectator sports rose to prominence. The introduction of television money made it impossible. Rugby Union (as opposed to the frowned-upon Rugby League, which has always been professional) prided itself on being above money: it took delight in emphasizing that the game was for the player; the crowd was incidental. So, when it succumbed to the temptation of media money, it was a significant event.

The instrument that finally destroyed the amateur sport was rugby's World Cup, which brought together the powers of (Australia, England, France, Ireland, Scotland, South Africa, New Zealand and Wales) with other nations, such as Argentina, Tonga and Japan. It placed rugby on a broader stage than it had ever occupied and stimulated international interest. At the same time, such competitive levels made demands on players and coaches which could not be sustained against the amateur principles. When Murdoch's package was followed by Australian media mogul Kerry Packer's proposals, the road toward professionalism was plain.

Revolution this was not: it was an acknowledgement in its final years that the twentieth century had finally arrived. While other major sports had accepted the inevitable and restructured themselves to accommodate the pervasive influence of television and its demand for a commercial product, rugby alone had stuck its head in the sand. When we reflect back on the century, Sunday, 27 August 1995 will be recorded as the day when sport's amateur hour ended. After this, it is impossible to envisage that any sport with potential to attract crowds – and much more significantly, television viewers – will be able to cling to any vestige of amateur status.

Violent tendencies

There will also be quite specific changes of accent in sports. In the 1960s, many people hit upon the idea that sporting action would grow more violent. They mistakenly looked to a tv "sport" called roller derby, which was really a contrived piece of mayhem more akin to tv wrestling than competitive sport and which was violent enough to make ice hockey look like a game of croquet. The thrilling blur of roller derby sped to the big screen in the form of the movie *Rollerball* in which the majority of the players left the rink on stretchers (some in bodybags). "I've seen the future of sport and it looks like this!" crowed critics leaving the movie theaters.

One of the subtexts of the movie was the message that sport functions as a substitute for war by providing a relatively safe outlet for aggression. A sustained spell of relative world peace meant more violence in sport. Implicitly, the thesis tied in with that of ethologists, like Desmond Morris (whom we considered in Chapter 5) and his mentor Konrad Lorenz who believed all humans are innately aggressive creatures. Sport serves as a safety valve – it is better that people discharge their aggression on the sports field than in the street or on the battlefields.

But if Norbert Elias, whom we also met in Chapter 5, is to be believed, violence isn't such a permanent and finite quality. In fact, violence in sport decreases as the level of acceptable violence in society generally declines. The civilizing process involves an appropriation of the legitimate use of violence by the state and this process is mirrored in sport. As we saw, gouging, maiming, and a miscellany of physical brutality were acceptable in folk sports of the eighteenth and nineteenth centuries. But as the "thresholds of repugnance" descended, so we stopped enjoying and grew disgusted at the sight of excessive damage being inflicted on humans and animals.

Despite this taking place within what Elias calls a "civilizing spurt," the actual changes appear gradual to those who live through them and only when we draw back and look at history do we realize the extent to which violence has been reduced in sport. This realization gives no real foundation for the view that it will suddenly increase. Since the release of *Rollerball* in the mid-1970s there has been a continuation of the civilizing trend in sport; referees in soccer and American football vigorously enforce rules to protect players' physical safety, jockeys have been sternly warned against "whip abuse" – lashing the racehorse too much in the final stretch – and another kind of abuse, that of the tennis racket, has been an official offence and players prone to tantrums are deducted points and fined.

These are but small modifications, yet they reflect a refusal to tolerate overt and gratuitous violence in sport. As we saw in Chapter 11, the law has dragged performers out of the arena and into the courts when governing bodies appear weak in policing their sports. Having recognized this, we should also acknowledge that many sports, probably the majority, entail an aggressive approach and a violent disposition on behalf of the competitors. Aggression is talked of in a very positive sense in most sports: defense may be admirable on occasion, but too much of it is downright boring. Even outright violence is encouraged in some combat sports, though always in a controlled setting – witness the admonishments of boxing authorities at the first hint of extracurricular fisticuffs.

Traditionalists sometimes share misty-eyed reminiscences about the time when sports were hard but there was no ballyhoo about it. They may be right, but even a cursory comparison of major contact sports reveals a callousness that was not evident 20 years ago. The arrival of big money is not coincidental: my argument as outlined in previous chapters is that competition has become more ruthless in proportion to the money available for success. Many sports *are* violent, but, as Michael Smith in his study *Violence and Sport* points out: "The fact is, sports violence has never been viewed as 'real' violence" and the public "give standing ovations to performers for acts that in other contexts would be instantly condemned as criminal" (1983: 9). Despite this, audiences are getting very slightly queasier; we just don't notice it.

In the first edition of this book, I wrote: "Two hundred years ago, people would give standing ovations to executioners; now they'd find it repulsive." Since then, the rising support for capital punishment in both the USA and Britain has forced me to reconsider. Elias, in his theory, allows for regressive spurts; perhaps we're in the midst of one as we approach the end of the millennium. Public taste for violence may not be disappearing as quickly as sports authorities would like, at least officially.

My remarks in the introduction about the reasons for sports are relevant here: we all have a propensity to take risks and we probably displace this onto others when it comes to sports. How many times have we heard a football crowd urge its team to "go for it!" on fourth down? We want others to take risks and enjoy watching them do so, even if it means – or possibly *especially* if it means – their risking their own well-being. Organizing bodies can add as many "filters" as Adams calls them, as they like, but, to reduce the risk thermostat of a sport to zero will finish it as a spectacle (1995).

Aggression–performance

The effect aggression has on sporting performance has led many psychologists to conduct experiments, though their results are rather contradictory. Many favor a positive link; competitors who exhibit an aggressive behavioral state and hold positive attitudes toward committing violent acts are generally more successful than those who don't, in individual and team sports. Another research finding is that there is a curvilinear relationship; successful performers were either highly aggressive, or extremely non-aggressive; and moderately aggressive performers were usually mediocre. Another interesting finding is that aggression is effective when used early in a contest, but not later. An article by W. Neil Widmeyer (1984) provides a valuable summary of the research.

Enhancing performance

The sophistication of drug-testing and the rapidity with which tests can provide results will prove a major disincentive to sports performers inclined toward performance-enhancing dope, particularly steroids. Yet, I suggested in Chapter 8 that drugs would continue to be used and their design or combination of use would proceed apace with improvements in testing procedures. There will also be a resort to drug-free performance enhancement. Neuromuscular electrical stimulation is one possibility: coupled with intense anaerobic exercise, the muscular gains from this technique are comparable with those from anabolic steroid use. At the moment, there are no manifest risks to health, nor known methods of detection.

This is another illustration of how medicine and sport have become joined over the past several decades. The initial collaboration over the treatment of sports-related injuries branched into several different areas. Soviet societies were quick to appreciate the potential contribution of medicine, not only for the treatment of injuries but for the maximization of performance. Medicine has made an immense input in terms of treatment, diet, monitoring, and, of course, specific training techniques.

> **Neuromuscular electrical stimulation (NMES)**
> This technique was developed by a medical research team headed by
> Anthony Delitto at Washington University. Small amounts of electrical
> power were initially used to improve the recovery of knee surgery
> patients. The problem was to increase the power and stimulate the
> major muscle development without causing unbearable pain. Over a
> period of eight years before the 1988 Olympics, the research team
> became aware of the potential application to sport and chose as a
> subject Derrick Crass, a weightlifter, whose lifts improved by 45 lbs in
> the first two weeks of treatment and, eventually, by 85 lbs. Delitto
> claimed treatment with anabolic steroids over a similar period would
> lead to an improvement of only 20 lbs. NMES was effective only when
> coupled with exercise. Delitto suspects Soviet sport scientists have used
> NMES for some time. Crass was troubled by a shoulder injury in the
> games and managed only eleventh place.

Ironically, the best-known medical practitioner in sports is notorious rather
than famous. Dr Jamie Astaphan's reputation grew with the revelations
about the Ben Johnson case. It was he who played the role of the evil
alchemist in the drugs melodrama. Retained by members of the Canadian
national athletics team, Astaphan designed anabolic steroid programs to
enhance performances. The hearings of the case, in 1989, revealed that
Johnson himself was by no means in a minority. It also added substance
to beliefs that sport was rapidly reaching the stage where the performers
themselves were bit-part players and the major roles were filled by the near-
anonymous medics who prescribed their training as well as their dope.
"Scientist vs scientist" was how the future of sport was imagined; like clashing
Svengalis, medics wielded almost total control over their subjects.

The image is deliciously amusing rather than sinister. Medics will
continue to assist sports performers; in fact, they will probably be absolutely
indispensable. But they will not produce performances, rather they will be one
factor in an ever-elaborating production line. I'm not romantic and ingenuous
enough to say the performer is the most important factor, if only because the
whole of this book is filled with analyses of factors lying outside the individual
which have crucial effects on the end-product – the performance. The
performer is but one element amid countless others.

Progress as reflected in improvements in performances isn't the result
of new breeds of supersportsmen and women. They come about because of
better nutrition, more sophisticated training, effective recuperative and recovery

treatment, and, of course, intense competition. Athletics and swimming have had demonstrable improvements which can be accurately measured. There's no reason to suppose that other sports haven't progressed in a similar fashion.

Bar room arguments about "who was best?" invite false comparisons. "The 1960s Pittsburgh Steelers would have beaten today's 49ers." "The Wolverhampton Wanderers of the 1950s would have seen off the Manchester United of the 1990s." "Margaret Court, who dominated women's tennis in the 1960s, would have run rings around Arantxa Sanchez Vicario." "The heavyweights of today would be no match for those of the 1930s." None of these can be proven. No one says, "Roger Bannister would have burnt off Venuste Niyongabo," probably because it can be so easily disproved. Niyangabo consistently clocks times about 15 seconds faster than Bannister's best for 1,500 meters or a mile. By the same reasoning, we should have accepted that all other sports, including those that rely more on technique and strategy than sheer fitness, improve their standards at roughly the same pace. The old Steelers team probably wouldn't even have survived in the World League. Sanchez Vicario would dispose of Court, most likely without dropping a game. Few of the relatively small (Joe Louis weighed just over 200 lbs, or about 14 stone) and immobile heavies would last the distance with today's 230-pound behemoths.

If the actual performers of previous eras enjoyed the benefits of better diet, training, and strategy as well as better social conditions, then the story might be different. Conditions change and these yield improvements. There will continue to be improvements, though at a slowing pace. Sebastian Coe's father and coach, Peter, once captured the logic of this when responding to the question of how fast the mile could be run. I paraphrase him: "It's like taking a straight line, dividing it in two, splitting it again, then again and again and again and so on *ad infinitum*. The lines get smaller and smaller, but you're always left with something." This means that, every time an improvement of standard in any sport is made, the relative size of the next improvement is likely to be smaller.

Quantitatively big improvements, such as Bob Beamon's long jump, Coe's 800-meter and Jarmila Kratochvilova's 800-meter records are aberrant performances explicable only in terms of freak atmospheric conditions or exceptionally fierce competition or some undisclosed form of assistance. Beamon's world record was set at the 1968 summer Olympics where the rarified air of Mexico City was conducive to an extraordinary distance that wasn't bettered for 23 years, when Mike Powell jumped 8.95 meters in Tokyo. (Powell actually eclipsed this in 1992, when he jumped 8.99 through the thin air of Sestriere, Italy, but assisted by a following wind blowing at nearly twice the legal limit.)

Some sports have seen performances progress to the point where

> ## Progress
>
> Progress in sport is a uniquely human phenomenon, based more on intellectual abilities than physical ones. For example, over 1,500 meters, Noureddine Morceli is about 40 seconds faster than his counterpart of 130 years ago. Yet if we compare the Kentucky Derby or Grand National winners over a similar period, modern horses run only about 10 seconds faster. The reason for the difference is that a trained racehorse will maintain between 85–95 percent of its maximum speed, metabolizing anaerobic energy, which is, as we have seen, counterproductive in the long term as it produces lactic acid and retards muscle contraction. Humans have improved their performances through advances in techniques and training, including muscle-building. They will run at between 65–70 percent of maximum speed for most of a middle distance race, kicking over the final phase. This requires timing, anticipation, and a tactical awareness as well as improved capacities to assimilate stress and discomfort – features that are built into today's training. There is also incentive: a horse has only a whipped flank to motivate it in the final stretch, whereas a human has plentiful rewards and for these he or she may be prepared to suffer. Apart from intellectual stimulus, we should note that humans are physically inefficient at running compared to horses, whose capacity for running is an evolutionary adaptation, probably resulting from their relative defencelessness. Humans' desire to run fast over distances is more a product of self-induced challenge; the machine itself has only modest locomotion capacities.

they have become dangerous. Motor cars go faster and endanger the lives of drivers; javelins can be thrown far enough to hit members of the crowd. In both cases, interventions have been made by authorities in the interests of safety. Tennis players now hit the ball so hard that the spectacle of the sport itself is under threat. Tennis authorities curbed the big hitters by reducing the pressure of tennis balls by 5 percent. In all these cases, modifications have reversed the direction of progress: cars were once built to travel as fast as possible; javelins were meant to be thrown as far as possible; tennis players strove to hit the ball with maximum velocity.

Talk of "progress" in sports or of any kind is all but prohibited in many quarters today. As we approach the century's end, it seems almost inhuman to describe as progress a 100-year period that has seen the genocidal murder of the second World War, the Hiroshima devastation that effectively ended that war, and the horrors of Cambodia. We are living through a phase in history when modernity is seen to have exhausted itself; in its place we have a postmodernity that fights shy of grand theories that purport to explain the world in terms of one totalizing framework that ends with "ian," whether Freudian, Marxian or whatever. Equally it is suspicious of political ideologies that claim a true and perfect society is within our reach. The demise of communism put paid to all that. Instead, we are offered a vision of a plural world that meshes uneasily with a much more developed global unity than ever existed. It is not unrealistic to anticipate a truly global order; it is to anticipate a global uniformity. What we are looking to here is a global cosmopolitanism in which recognition of difference goes hand-in-hand with a collective human effort.

Sports, it could be argued, is ahead of the field in this respect. Its fissiparious tendencies have ensured an almost continuous growth of new sports, either products of existing sports – (World League football) or pastimes reorganized as competitions (skateboarding, for instance). These were once created for one audience. Not so at century's end: sport is a product and the product has a universal market, thanks to television. The outrageous rugby super league venture mentioned in Chapter 10 is one of a number of genuinely transnational leagues, in this case integrating Australian, French, British and New Zealand clubs into a single competition and screened throughout two continents – Asia and Europe.

One possible change in sport that we should finally mention is that it will be taken even more seriously as a proper subject for academic and scientific study. A book such as this would not have been written ten years ago; maybe not even eight years ago. But recently we have seen a proliferation of sports science, sports studies, and many related degrees and programs of studies, all based on the view that sports deserve considered attention – that is, the kind of attention normally reserved for "obvious relevant" phenomena such as crime, education, technology, employment, and any number of other subjects that have been the topic of textbooks. Sport hasn't achieved a comparable status, but there is certainly a greater recognition that it is a key area in society and one that has been too neglected in the past. Its association with frivolity, recreation, and play is virtually over. If there is one abiding theme spread through these pages it is that sport is now a serious business. No one doubted that it was business; more and more are realizing that it's serious enough to merit scholarly study.

There are still areas of bewilderment over the apparent irrationality of some aspects of sport, the near-manic following it commands, the almost suicidal tendencies of some of its participants, and the inexplicable political controversies it occasionally provokes. But, after 13 chapters, we are hopefully in a better position to comprehend these. For all their supposed lack of reason, we have at least been making sense of sports.

ASSIGNMENT

Describe what role, if any, sports would play in the world as depicted in two of the following futuristic (and, in some cases, fantastic) movies/videos: Terry Gilliam's *Brazil*, in which the world has become a vast bureaucratic labyrinth; Ridley Scott's *Blade Runner*, where androids coexist with human beings; Rachel Talalay's *Tank Girl* set in 2003 after an ecological cataclysm has devastated the land and left water the scarcest resource; Danny Cannon's *Judge Dredd*, in which the criminal justice system is upheld and administered by a series of mobile "judges" who are constantly battling anarchic forces; Steven Spielberg's *Jurassic Park*, in which a prehistoric theme park filled with dinosaurs has been created via DNA cloning techniques; or Marco Brambilla's *Demolition Man*, in which cryogenics is an everyday reality, Taco Bell runs every restaurant and the only sex available is "virtual."

Bibliography

Adams, J. (1995) *Risk*, London: UCL Press.

Alexander, R. M. (1975) *Biomechanics*, New York: Chapman and Hall.

Allison, L. (ed.) (1986) *The Politics of Sport*, Manchester: Manchester University Press.

Arms, R., Russell, G. and Sandilands, M. (1987), "Effects on the hostility of spectators of viewing aggressive sports," in A. Yiannakis, T. McIntyre, M. Melnick and D. Hart *Sport Sociology*, 3rd edn, Dubuque: Kendall/Hunt.

Ashe, A. (1988) *A Hard Road to Glory: A history of the African-American athlete since 1946*, New York: Amistad, Warner Books.

Bale, J. (1982) *Sport and Place*, London: C. Hurst.

Bale, J. (1993) *Sport, Space and the City*, London: Routledge.

Barnett, S. (1990) *Games and Sets: The changing face of sport on television*, London: British Film Institute.

Baudrillard, J. (1983) *Simulations*, New York: Semiotext(e).

Bauman, Z. (1979) "The phenomenon of Norbert Elias," *Sociology* 13: 117–35.

Becker, H. (1953) "Becoming a marijuana user," *American Journal of Sociology* 59: 235–42.

Beecher, H. K. (1955) "The powerful placebo," *Journal of the American Medical Association* 159: 1602–6.

Birke, L. and Vines, G. (1987) "A sporting chance," *Women's International Studies Forum* 10(4): 337–47.

Birrell, S. and Cole, C. (eds) (1994) *Women, Sport and Culture*, Champaign, Illinois: Human Kinetics.

Birtley, J. (1976) *The Tragedy of Randolph Turpin*, London: NEL.

Blue, A. (1987) *Grace Under Pressure*, London: Sidgwick & Jackson.

Brill, A. A. (1929) "The why of a fan," *North American Review*, pt 228: 429–34.

Brohm, J.-M. (1978) *Sport: a Prison of Measured Time*, London: Ink Links.

Brower, J. (1976) "Professional sports team ownership," *Journal of Sport Sociology* 1(1): 15–51.

Canter, D., Comber, M. and Uzzell, D. (1989) *Football in its Place: An environmental psychology of football grounds,* London: Routledge.

Cashmore, E. (1982) *Black Sportsmen*, London: Routledge & Kegan Paul.

Cashmore, E. (1987) *The Logic of Racism*, London: Allen & Unwin.

Chandler, J. (1988) *Television and National Sport: The United States and Britain*, Urbana: University of Illinois Press.

Coakley, J. J. (1978) *Sport in Society*, St Louis, Mississippi: Mosby.

Cohen, G. L. (ed.) (1993) *Women in Sport*, Newbury Park, Calif.: Sage.

Costa, M. and Guthrie, S. (eds) (1994) *Women and Sport: Interdisciplinary perspectives*, Champaign, Illinois: Human Kinetics.

Cunningham, H. (1980) *Leisure in the Industrial Revolution*, London: Croom Helm.

Curtis, J. and Loy, J. (1978) "Race/ethnicity and relative centrality of playing positions in team sport," *Exercise and Sport Sciences Review* 6: 285–313.

David, R. (1989) *Lester Piggott: Downfall of a Legend*, London: Heinemann Kingwood.

Davis, P. W. and Solomon, E. P. (1974) *The World of Biology*, 2nd edn, New York: McGraw-Hill.

Dougherty, N., Auxter, D., Goldberger, A. and Heinzmann, G. (1994) *Sport, Physical Activity and the Law*, Champaign, Illinois: Human Kinetics.

Dunning, E. and Sheard, K. (1979) *Barbarians, Gentlemen and Players*, Oxford: Martin Robertson.

Dunning, E., Murphy, P. and Williams, J. (1988) *The Roots of Football Hooliganism*, London: Routledge & Kegan Paul.

Dunning, E., Maguire, J. and Pearton, R. (1993) *The Sports Process: A comparative and developmental approach*, Champaign, Illinois: Human Kinetics.

Dunning, E. and Rojek, C. (1992) (eds) *Sport and Leisure in the Civilizing Process*, Basingstoke: Macmillan.

Eco, U. (1986) *Faith in Fakes*, London: Secker & Warburg.

Edwards, H. (1970) *The Revolt of the Black Athlete*, New York: Free Press.

Edwards, H. (1973) *Sociology of Sport*, Homewood, Illinois: Dorsey Press.

Eitzen, D. S. (ed.) (1993) *Sport in Contemporary Society: An anthology*, 4th edn, New York: St Martin's Press.

Eitzen, D. S. and Sanford, D. (1975) "The segregation of blacks by playing position in football," *Social Science Quarterly* 5(4): 948–59.

Eitzen, D. S. and Yetman, N. (1977) "Immune from racism?," *Civil Rights Digest* 9(2): 3–13.

Eitzen, D. S. and Sage, G. H. (1993) *Sociology of North American Sport*, 5th edn, Dubuque: Brown & Benchmark.

Elias. N. (1982) *The Civilizing Process*, 2 vols, New York: Pantheon.

Elias, N. (1986a) "Introduction," in N. Elias and E. Dunning (eds) *Quest for Excitement*, Oxford: Blackwell.

Elias, N. (1986b) "An essay on sport and violence," in N. Elias and E. Dunning (eds) *Quest for Excitement*, Oxford: Blackwell.

Elias, N. and Dunning, E. (eds) (1986) *Quest for Excitement*, Oxford: Blackwell.

Fasting, K. (1987) "Sports and women's culture," *Women's Studies International Forum* 10(4): 361–8.

Gibson, K. and Ingold, T. (eds) (1993) *Tools, Language and Cognition in Human Evolution*, Cambrige: Cambridge University Press.

Giulianotti, R., Bonney, N. and Hepworth, M. (eds) (1994) *Football, Violence and Social Identity*, London: Routledge.

Glossop, M. (1982) *Living with Drugs*, London: Temple Smith.

Goldlust, J. (1988) *Playing for Keeps*, Melbourne: Longman Cheshire.

Gorman, J. and Calhoun, K. (1994) *The Name of the Game: The business of sports*, New York: John Wiley.

Gorn, E. J. (1986) *The Manly Art: Bare-knuckle prize fighting in America*, Ithaca: Cornell University Press.

Gruneau, R. (1983) *Class, Sports and Social Development*, Amherst, Massachusetts: University of Massachusetts Press.

Gruneau, R. (1984) "Commercialism and the modern Olympics," in A. Tomlinson and G. Whannel (eds) *Five Ring Circus*, London: Pluto Press.

Gruneau, R. and Whitson, D. (1993) *Hockey Night in Canada*, Toronto: Garamond.

Guelke, A. (1986) "The politicisation of South African sport," in L. Allison (ed.) *The Politics of Sport*, Manchester: University of Manchester Press.

Guttmann, A. (1978) *From Ritual to Record*, New York: Columbia University Press.

Guttmann, A. (1986) *Sports Spectators*, New York: Columbia University Press.

Hain, P. (1982) "The politics of sport and apartheid," in J. Hargreaves (ed.) *Sport, Culture and Ideology*, London: Routledge & Kegan Paul.

Hardin, G. and Bejema, C. (1978) *Biology: its Principles and Implications*, 3rd edn, San Francisco: W. H. Freeman.

Hare, N. (1973) "The occupational culture of the black fighter," in J. Talamini and C. Page (eds) *Sport and Society*, Boston, Massachusetts: Little, Brown.

Hargreaves J. (ed.) (1982) *Sport, Culture and Ideology*, London: Routledge & Kegan Paul.

Hargreaves, J. (1986) *Sport, Power and Culture*, Oxford: Polity Press.

Hargreaves, J. (1987) "The body, sport and power relations," in J. Horne, D. Jary and A. Tomlinson (eds) *Sport, Leisure and Social Relations*, London: Routledge & Kegan Paul.

Hargreaves, J. (1994) *Sporting Females: Critical issues in the history and sociology of women's sports*, London: Routledge.

Harris, M. (1993) *Culture, People, Nature*, 6th edn, New York: HarperCollins.

Hart, M. and Birrell, S. (eds) (1981) *Sport in the Sociocultural Process*, 3rd edn, Dubuque, Iowa: Brown.

Henderson, E. (1949) *The Negro in Sports*, Washington, DC: Associated Publishers.

Hill, C. (1992) *Olympic Politics*, Manchester: Manchester University Press.

Hoberman, J. (1984) *Sport and Political Ideology*, Austin, Texas: University of Texas Press.

Hoberman, J (1992) *Mortal Engines: Human engineering and the transformation of sport*, New York: Free Press.

Hoberman, J. and Yesalis, C. (1995) "The history of synthetic testosterone," *Scientific American*, 272(2).

Hoch, P. (1972) *Rip Off the Big Game*, New York: Anchor Doubleday.

Hoffman, S. (ed.) (1992) *Sport and Religion*, Champaign, Illinois: Human Kinetics.

Hoggett, P. (1986) "The taming of violence," *New Society* (17 October): 36.

Holt, R. (1989) *Sport and the British*, Oxford: Oxford University Press.

Holt, R. (1990) *Sport and the Working Class in Modern Britain*, Manchester: Manchester University Press.

Horne, J., Jary, D. and Tomlinson, A. (eds) (1987) Sport, Leisure and Social Relations, London: Routledge & Kegan Paul.

Horrell, M. (1968) *South Africa and the Olympic Games*, Johannesburg: Institute of Race Relations.

Houlihan, B. (1991) *The Government and Politics of Sport*, London: Routledge.

Houlihan, B. (1994) *Sport and International Politics*, New York: Harvester Wheatsheaf.

Huddleston, T. (1956) *Naught for Your Comfort*, London: Collins.

James, C. L. R. (1963) *Beyond a Boundary*, London: Hutchinson.

Jarvie, G. and Maguire, J. (1995) *Sport and Leisure in Social Thought*, London: Routledge.

Jhally, S. (1989) "Cultural studies and the sports/media complex," in A. A. Wenner, (ed.) *Media, Sports and Society*, Newbury Park: Sage.

Jiobu, R. (1988) "Racial inequality in a public arena," *Social Forces* 67(2): 524–34.

Jones, S. J. (1987) "State intervention in sport and leisure in Britain between the wars," *Journal of Contemporary History* 22: 163–82.

Jones, S. J. (1989) *Sport, Politics and the Working Class*, Manchester: Manchester University Press.

Kane, M. (1971) "An assessment of black is best," *Sports Illustrated* 34(3): 76–83.

Kerr, J. (1994) *Understanding Soccer Hooliganism*, Philadelphia: Open University Press.

Klatell, D. and Marcus, N. (1988) *Sports for Sale: Television, money and the fans*, New York: Oxford University Press.

Lapchick, R. (1984) *Broken Promises*, New York: St Martin's Press/Marek.

Lapchick, R. (1986) *Fractured Focus*, Lexington, Massachusetts: Heath.

Lapchick, R. (1991) *Five Minutes to Midnight*, Lanham, Maryland: Madison Books.

Leonard, W. (1988) *A Sociological Perspective of Sport*, 3rd edn, New York: Macmillan.

Lever, J. (1983) *Soccer Madness*, Chicago: University of Chicago Press.

Levine, L. (1977) *Black Culture and Black Consciousness*, New York: Oxford University Press.

Levins, R. and Lewontin, R. (1985) *The Dialectical Biologist*, Cambridge, Massachusetts: Harvard University Press.

Levy, H. (1967) *Chinese Footbinding: The history of a curious erotic custom*, New York: Bell.

Lindsey, L. (1990) *Gender Roles: A sociological perspective*, Englewood Cliffs, New Jersey: Prentice-Hall.

Lorenz, K. (1966) *On Aggression*, New York: Harcourt, Brace and World.

Louganis, G. (1995) *Breaking the Surface: A life*, New York: Random House.

Loy, J. and McElvogue, J. (1970) "Racial segregation in American sport," *International Review of Sport Sociology* 5: 5–23.

Lucking, M. (1982) "Sport and drugs,", in J. Hargreaves (ed.) *Sport, Culture and Ideology*, London: Routledge & Kegan Paul.

Lukas, G. (1969) *Die Körperkultur in frühen Epochen der Menschenentwicklung*, East Berlin: Sportverlag.

Lüschen, G. (1976) "Cheating," in D. Landers (ed.) *Social Problems in Athletics*, Illinois: University of Illinois Press.

McCrone, K. (1988) *Sport and the Physical Emancipation of English Women, 1870–1914*, London: Routledge.

McIntosh, P. (1980) *Fair Play*, London: Heinemann Educational.

McPherson, B., Curtis, J. and Loy, J. (1989) *The Social Significance of Sport*, Champaign, Illinois: Human Kinetics.

Mandell, R. (1971) *The Nazi Olympics*, New York: Macmillan.

Mandell, R. (1984) *Sport: a Cultural History*, New York: Columbia University Press.

Mansfield, A. and McGinn, B. (1993) "Pumping irony," in S. Scott and D. Morgan (eds), *Body Matters*, London: Falmer

Marsh, P. (1979) *Aggro: The illusion of violence*, London: Dent.

Marsh, P., Rosser, E. and Harre, R. (1978) *The Rules of Disorder*, London: Routledge & Kegan Paul.

Mason, T. (1988) *Sport in Britain*, London: Faber & Faber.

Mason W. H. and Marshall, N. L. (1983) *The Human Side of Biology*, New York: Harper & Row.

Matza, D. (1969) *Becoming Deviant*, Englewood Cliffs, New Jersey: Prentice-Hall.

Messner, M. (1992) *Power at Play: Sports and the problem of masculinity*, Boston, Massachusetts: Beacon Press

Messner, M. and Sabo, D. (eds) (1990), *Sport, Men and the Gender Order: Critical feminist perspectives*, Champaign, Illinois: Human Kinetics.

Michener, J. (1976) *Sports in America*, New York: Random House.

Midgley, M. (1979) *Beast and Man: the Roots of Human Nature*, London: Methuen.

Morgan, W. and Meier, K. (eds) (1988) *Philosophic Inquiry in Sport*, Champaign, Illinois: Human Kinetics.

Morris, D. (1981) *The Soccer Tribe*, London: Cape.

Mottram, D. (ed.) (1988) *Drugs in Sport*, London: E. & F. N. Spon.

Naison, M. (1972) "Sport and the American empire," *Radical America* 6(4), July/August.

Niednagel, J. (1994) *Your Key to Sports Success*, Nashville, Tennessee: Nelson

Novak, M. (1976) *The Joy of Sport*, New York: Basic Books.

Olsen, J. (1968) *The Black Athlete*, New York: Time Life.

Parry, J. (1988) *Participation by Blacks and Ethnic Minorities in Sport and Recreation: A review of the literature*, London: London Research Centre.

Paulsen, G. (1994) *Winterdance: The fine madness of Alaskan dog-racing*, London: Gollancz.

Perry, C. (1983) "Blood doping and athletic competition," *International Journal of Applied Philosophy*, 1(3): 39–45.

Phillips, J. C. (1993) *Sociology of Sport*, Boston: Allyn & Bacon.

Poliakoff, M. (1987) *Combat Sports in the Ancient World*, New Haven: Yale University Press.

Rader, B. (1984) *In its Own Image: How television has transformed sports*, New York: Collier-Macmillan.

Ramsamy, S. (1984) "Apartheid, boycotts and the games," in A. Tomlinson and G. Whannel (eds) *Five Ring Circus*, London: Pluto Press.

Regen, R. (1990) "Neither does King," *Interview*, p 20 (10 October), pp. 104–15.

Richards, G. (1987) *Human Evolution*, London: Routledge & Kegan Paul.

Rigauer, B. (1981) *Sport and Work*, New York: Columbia University Press.

Riordan, J. (1980) *Soviet Sport*, Oxford: Blackwell.

Riordan, J. (1982) "Sport and communism – on the example of the USSR," in J. Hargreaves (ed.) *Sport, Culture and Ideology*, London: Routledge.

Ritzer, G. (1993) *The McDonaldization of Society*, Newbury Park, Calif.: Pine Forge Press.

Robins, D. (1982) "Sport and youth culture," in J. Hargreaves (ed.) *Sport, Culture and Ideology*, London: Routledge & Kegan Paul.

Roman, L. and Ellsworth, E. (eds) (1988) *Becoming Feminine: The politics of popular culture*, Philadelphia: Falmer.

Sage, G. H. (1990) *Power and Ideology in American Sport*, Champaign, Illinois: Human Kinetics.

Sammons, J. (1988) *Beyond the Ring*, Camden, New Jersey: University of Illinois.

Scott, J. (1971) *The Athletic Revolution*, New York: Free Press.

Silva, J. and Weinberg, R. (eds) (1984) *Psychological Foundations of Sport*, Champaign, Illinois: Human Kinetics.

Smith, M. D. (1983) *Violence and Sport*, Toronto: Butterworth.

Snyder, E. and Spreitzer, E. (1983) *Social Aspects of Sport*, 2nd edn, Englewood Cliffs, New Jersey: Prentice-Hall.

Solomon, E., Berg, L., Martin, D. and Villee, C. (1993) *Biology*, 3rd edn, New York: Saunders College Press.

Sowell, T. (1994) *Race and Culture: A world view*, New York: Basic Books.

Spears, B. and Swanson, R. (1995) *History of Sport and Physical Activity in the United States*, 4th edn, Dubuque, Iowa: Brown & Benchmark.

Stoddart, B. (1988) "Sport, cultural imperialism and colonial response in the British empire," *Comparative Studies in Society and History*, pt 30 (October): 649–73.

Suttles, G. (1968) *The Social Order of the Slum: Ethnicity and territory in the inner city*, Chicago: University of Chicago Press.

Taylor, I. (1971) "Soccer consciousness and soccer hooliganism," in S. Cohen (ed.) *Images of Deviance*, Harmondsworth: Penguin

Thompson, R. and Sherman, R. (1993) *Helping Athletes with Eating Disorders*, Champaign: Human Kinetics.

Torto, G. (1992) *Principles of Human Anatomy*, 6th edn, New York: HarperCollins.

Triesman, D. (1984) "The Olympic games as a political forum," in A. Tomlinson and G. Whannel (eds) *Five Ring Circus*, London: Pluto Press.

Vamplew, W. (1989) *Pay Up and Play the Game*, London: Cambridge University Press.

Verma, G. and Darby, D. (1994) *Winner and Losers: Ethnic minorities in sport and recreation*, London: Falmer.

Villee, C. A. (1977) *Biology*, 7th edn, London: W. B. Saunders.

Vinnai, G. (1973) *Football Mania*, London: Ocean Books.

Vogler, C. C. and Schwarz, S. (1993) *The Sociology of Sport: An introduction*, Englewood Cliffs, New Jersey: Prentice-Hall.

Voy, R. (1991) *Drugs, Sport and Politics*, Champaign, Illinois: Human Kinetics.

Wankel, L. (1982) "Audience effects in sport," in J. Silva and R. Weinberg (eds) *Psychological Foundations in Sport*, Champaign, Illinois: Human Kinetics.

Weir, J. and Abrahams, P. (1992) *An Imaging Atlas of Human Anatomy*, St Louis: Mosby-Wolfe.

Weisman, J. (1993) "Big-buck basketball: Acolytes in the temple of Nike," in D. S. Eitzen, (ed.) *Sport in Contemporary Society: An anthology*, New York: St Martin's Press.

Wenner, L. (ed.) (1989) *Media, Sports and Society*, Newbury Park, Calif.: Sage.

Whannel, G. (1983) *Blowing the Whistle: The politics of sport*, London: Pluto Press.

Whannel, G. (1992) *Fields in Vision*, London: Routledge.

Widmeyer, W. N. (1984) "Aggression-performance relationships in sport," in J. Silva and R. Weinberg (eds) *Psychological Foundations of Sport*, Champaign, Illinois: Human Kinetics.

Wiggins, D. (ed.) (1995) *Sport in America: From wicked amusement to national obsession*, Champaign, Illinois: Human Kinetics.

Wilson, E. O. *(1975) Sociobiology: The New Synthesis*, Cambridge, Massachusetts: Harvard University Press.

Wilmore, J. and Costill, D. (1994) *Physiology of Sport and Exercise*, Champaign, Illinois: Human Kinetics.

Wilson, N. (1988) *The Sports Business*, London: Piatkus.

Wolf. N. (1991) *The Beauty Myth: How images of beauty are used against women*, New York: Morrow.

Yesalis, C. (ed.) *Anabolic Steroids in Sport and Exercise*, Champaign, Illinois: Human Kinetics.

Zajonc, R. (1965) "Social facilitation," *Science* 149: 269–74.

Zimbalist, A. (1992) *Baseball and Billions*, New York: Basic Books.

Zolberg, V. (1987) "Elias and Dunning's theory of sport and excitement," *Theory, Culture and Society* 4: 571–5.

Name and subject index

Title index